THE *Golden Hands* COMPLETE BOOK OF **roidery**

The greater part of the material published in this
book was first published by Marshall Cavendish Ltd.
in "Golden Hands." The British edition entitled
Golden Hands Encyclopedia of Embroidery was
published by William Collins & Co. Ltd.

Library of Congress Card Catalog Number 73-5011
ISBN 0-394-48568-8

Manufactured in the United States of America

CONTENTS

Embroidery

Needlepoint

CONTENTS (continued)

Collector's Pieces

ACKNOWLEDGEMENTS

Text:
Margaret Beautement, Eileen Lowcock

Photographers:
Malcolm Aird, Adèle Baker, John Carter, Victoria Carter, Bob Croxford, Richard Dormer, Anne Dyer, Guy Gibbard, Su Gooders, Martin Harrison, Chris Lewis, Eileen Lowcock, Graham Murrell, Tony Moussoulides, Paul Redman, Bruce Scott, David Swann, Chris Thomson, Peter Watkins

Illustrators:
Janet Ahlberg, Barbara Firth, Isobel Hollowood, Anna Kostal, Francis Newell, Josephine Rankin, Julian and Renée Robinson, Frances Ross Duncan, Joy Simpson, Jill Smyth, Paul Williams, Arka Graphics

Designers:
Kate Bailey, Margaret Beautement, Esta Cairnes, Victoria Carter, J. & P. Coats U.K. Ltd, Valerie Cock, Frances Coleman, Mrs Cowie, Mrs Cutbush, Dorothy Darch, DMC, Dr P. Doplyn, Frances Duncan, Anne Dyer, Emmy Elphick, Louis Gartner, Joan Gilbert, Louise Grosse, Patty Knox, Wendy Lees, Elizabeth Manley, M. McNeill, Frances Newell, Joan Nicholson, Mrs Pemberton, Patricia Phillpott, Angela Salmon, Marjorie Self, Jo Springer, Mrs J. M. Stuart, Martyn Thomas, A. Thompson, Valerie Tullock, H. G. Twilley Ltd, Janice Williams, May Williams, Gill Wing, D. Wooding

Credits:
Camera Press, London: GMN, Lars Larsson, Kalle Nordin, Kjell Nilsson, Fuer Sie

We would like to thank the following for their help and co-operation:
The American Museum, Bath; The Bodleian Library, Oxford; J. & P. Coats U.K. Ltd, The County Borough of Hastings, The Embroiderers' Guild, London; The Needlewoman Shop, London; Patons and Baldwins Ltd, Victoria and Albert Museum, London; The White House, London

Introduction

This embroidery encyclopedia is designed to appeal to both the beginner and the expert. We lead you step by step through the various stages of embroidery and needlepoint, from the basic running stitch to the luxurious technique of metal thread embroidery, from cross-stitch to the flame inspired patterns of Florentine.

Learn how to enlarge and reduce designs, set up embroidery frames and work from a chart. You can explore the many varieties of thread available in our Yarn Chart, where each one is described according to its texture and the different techniques to which it can be applied.

Each method and stitch is explained in diagrams, Stitch Libraries and photographs, while beautiful examples of the work introduce, illustrate and conclude each technique. These Collector's Pieces have been selected to encourage experimentation and design.

Consider the arts of embroidery and needlepoint as a method of self expression. You can take your favorite pattern from the book and simply by choosing your own color scheme, using alternative stitches to vary the texture of the work and interlacing different colored threads into the canvas, or hanging a bead here and there, you have created your own design and left the imprint of your personality on the work.

Apart from describing the methods associated with embroidery and needlepoint, our encyclopedia gives you a wider range of different patterns and designs. Make an appliqué panel for your children's bedroom, a tablecloth in drawn threadwork for that special dinner party or a fashionable tote bag in double cross-stitch to add a splash of color to your wardrobe.

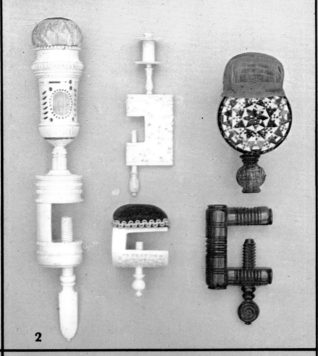

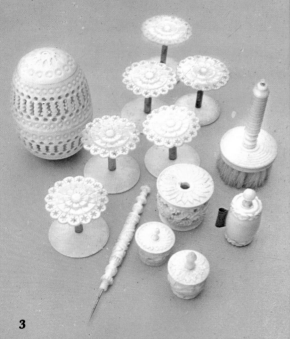

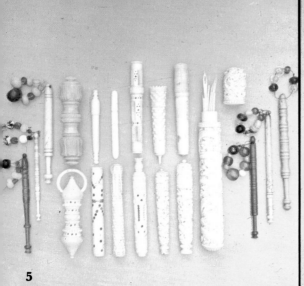

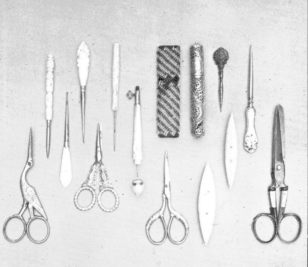

Collector's Piece

Tools of embroidery

Genteel young ladies of the 19th century were trained to excel in the gentle arts, and needlecraft was considered a most necessary and elegant accomplishment. Needlework accessories were appropriate gifts for a bride-to-be, and beautifully turned spools of ivory and mother-of-pearl, silver filigree needle cases, engraved scissors and carved boxes and tools were presented by friends and relatives. These exquisitely made accessories had a practical value too. Materials for needlework were expensive and therefore precious, and great care was taken of them. Silk thread, for instance, was purchased in a skein, carefully re-wound onto a spool which was inserted into a protective barrel-shaped cover, the thread being withdrawn through a hole in the cover.

1. *Chatelaines, such as this, were attached to a belt worn around the waist. This one carries a needlecase, a pincushion, a tape measure, a thimble bucket and scissors.*
2. *Clamps, used in lacemaking and for securing material to the table while the seamstress sewed long seams.*
3. *Mother-of-pearl thread spools and ivory thread barrels. On the right, a wax container, a tape measure, and a brush and pricker for marking out designs.*
4. *Several kinds of tape measures, thimbles and pincushions.*
5. *Bobbins for making pillow lace, an assortment of needle cases and a case of netting tools.*
6. *Stilettos of ivory, mother-of-pearl, silver and ormolu, used for pricking embroidery eyelet holes. Also, mother-of-pearl crochet hook, bead and filigree needle cases, tatting shuttles and scissors.*
Right: Pincushions made of ebony, cedar, pewter and Tunbridge ware, usually filled with emery powder.

Chapter 1

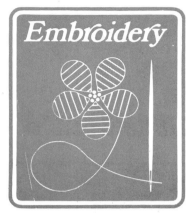

Introduction to embroidery

Embroidery is at last being recognized as an art form and is finding its way into the museums of modern art. If you are bent on adding decorative touches to your wardrobe and home, or want to design a beautiful panel, it's worth looking through our collection of stitches and designs, both modern and historical, to find inspiration and clear instructions on how to work the stitches.

Nowadays you can create exciting textures and three-dimensional effects by using strong designs and color schemes and a fascinating variety of stitches and yarns. But remember, if you are embroidering things which need to be laundered, make sure that all the materials have fast dyes and are washable, and avoid using stitches which are too long, or they may catch and spoil the look of the article.

Designs

Ready-made embroidery designs are usually sold in three ways:
(a) as transfers ready to iron onto your own choice of fabric
(b) already printed on cloth, often in a kit complete with yarns
(c) with charts for counted threadwork (for example, cross-stitch).
In later chapters you will discover how to make your own designs, and how to enlarge and adapt.

An embroidery hoop clamped onto a table.

Know your needles

Sharps needle	medium length, with small eye —for sewing with cotton or a single strand of 6-strand floss.
Crewel (or Embroidery) needle sizes 6-8 size 5	medium length, sharp, long eye —for 6-strand floss, Coton à broder, pearl cotton No. 8. Larger eye—for tapestry wool, and pearl cotton No. 5.
Chenille needle No. 18	short and sharp, with large eye —for thick threads, tapestry wool, soft embroidery cotton.
Tapestry needle	blunt end—for whipped and laced stitches, needlepoint, drawn fabric and drawn threadwork.
Beading needle	fine—for sewing on beads.
Tambour hook	today, substitute a very fine steel crochet hook—used for attaching beads and tambour embroidery.

Which fabric to work on

You can work embroidery on almost any fabric unless you are following a charted design for counted thread embroidery or drawn threadwork. For both these you need an even-weave cloth. This fabric has an even number of vertical and horizontal threads per square inch, and comes in a variety of colors. It is the best type to use for a beginner, as it helps to keep stitches even.

Well-stocked needlework shops and departments may have even-weave fabrics. You will also find that some linens, cottons and rayons in dress and upholstery fabric departments are also evenly woven, and are equally suitable.

Hoops and frames

Although some embroidery can be worked in the hand, it is usually better for the background fabric to be stretched on either an embroidery hoop or frame. The frame is like a wooden picture frame over which the work is stretched: this will be dealt with in Embroidery Chapter 18. There are four types of embroidery hoop all basically used in the same way. The simplest is the hand-held hoop—a wooden (not a metal) one with a thumbscrew is recommended. The other types are the hoop which clamps onto a table, the hoop on a stand for table or lap, and the hoop on a floor stand.

Setting up a hoop

Adjust the screw so that the rings fit together well. Separate the two rings and place the fabric over the inside ring, centering the design. Press the outside ring over the inside ring until one is inside the other. Gently ease the fabric down until it is taut and smooth, being careful not to pull the fabric on the bias. Tighten the screw if necessary and you are ready to begin. It is important to remove the hoop each time the work is put away.

If you are working with a delicate fabric, cover it with a layer of protective tissue before pressing down the outside ring. This tissue must be cut to within half an inch of the ring before starting.

*An embroidery frame: the piece of needlepoint
is entitled "Young Girl Reading"*

Yarn Chart

Threads for you to choose from

Some techniques require a particular thread, but in many stitches you can experiment with several kinds of yarn.

Yarn/description/uses

1. Knit-Cro-Sheen/knitting and crochet cotton/basic stitches
2. Clark's Big Ball Crochet Cotton/fine knitting and crochet cotton/basic stitches, drawn threadwork
3/4/5/6. Pearl Cotton/twisted, shiny cotton, ranging from very thick to thin/basic stitches, blackwork, counted threadwork, drawn threadwork, Hardanger embroidery, smocking
7. Transparent thread/nylon filament/invisible multi-purpose sewing thread, couching
8. J. & P. Coats Dual Duty Plus/mercerized cotton-covered polyester/multi-purpose sewing thread
9. Coats & Clark's Pure Silk Twist/basic sewing
10. Dual Duty Plus Extra Strong Button and Carpet Thread/mercerized cotton-covered polyester/basic stitches
11. Coats Super Sheen/mercerized cotton thread/multi-purpose sewing thread

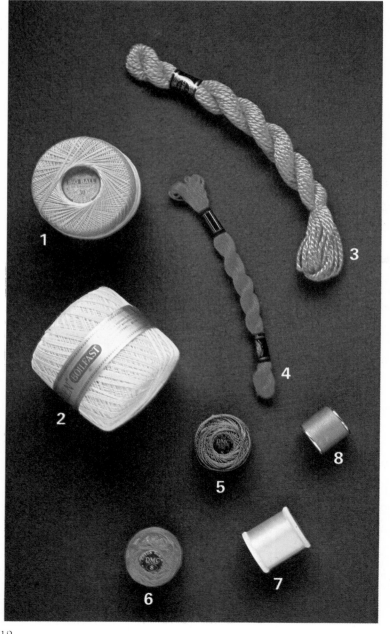

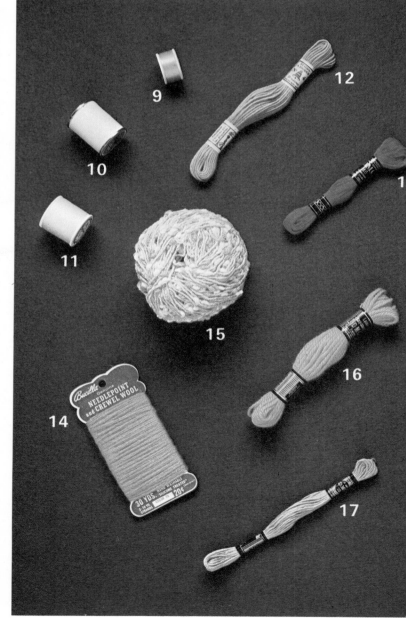

12. Matte Embroidery Cotton/twisted, matte cotton/basic stitches, couching, Hardanger embroidery, smocking

13. Coton à Broder/twisted, shiny cotton/basic stitches, cut work, drawn threadwork, Hardanger embroidery, smocking

14. Crewel Yarn/twisted, matte wool strands, separable/basic stitches, couching, needlepoint, crewel embroidery

15. Slub Yarn/knitting wool, uneven surface/couching

16. Tapestry Yarn/twisted, matte wool/basic stitches, couching, pattern darning, needlepoint

17. Six-strand Floss/twisted, separable, shiny cotton/basic stitches, counted threadwork, drawn threadwork, Hardanger embroidery

18. Filo-Floss/six-strand embroidery silk/basic stitches

19. Mohair/fluffy knitting yarn/basic stitches (limited use), couching

20. Hi-Straw/rayon raffia/basic stitches, couching, needlepoint (limited use)

21. Knitting Worsted/basic wool knitting and crochet yarn, separable/basic stitches, needlepoint

22. Craftsman's Yarn/heavy acrilic, separable/basic stitches, needlepoint

23/24. Metallic Cord/fine, untarnishable twist/basic stitches, drawn threadwork, blackwork, metal thread embroidery

25. Lurex/flat, metal thread/metal thread embroidery

26/27. Penelope Lurex/fine, nylon braid/basic stitches, metal thread embroidery

28/29/30. Smooth Purl, Pearl Purl, Rough Purl/three different weights of spiral metal thread/metal thread embroidery

31. Metallic Yarn/washable, untarnishable, coarse thread/basic stitches, metal thread embroidery

32. Maltese Silk/fine sewing thread/couching

33. Japanese Gold/pure gold thread wound on a silk core/metal thread embroidery

34. Passing Gold/metal thread wound on a silk core/metal thread embroidery

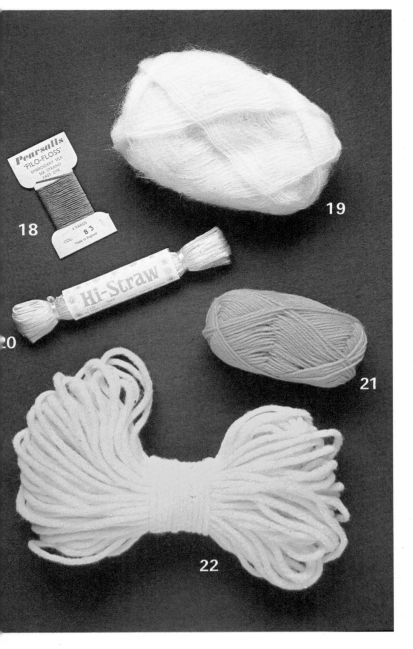

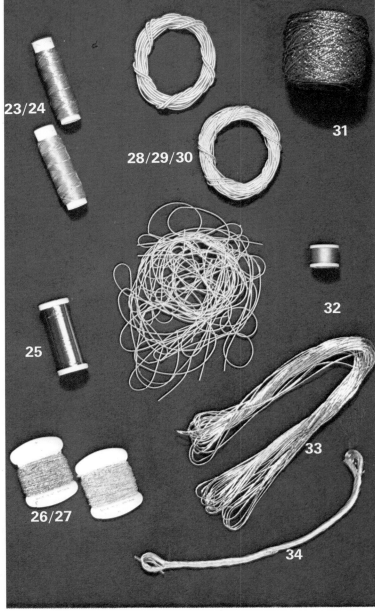

Chapter 2

How to plan a color scheme

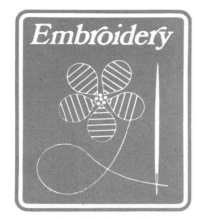

A well chosen color scheme can make all the difference between a good piece of embroidery and a really beautiful one. This chapter gives some general principles to follow, but there is plenty of scope for individual taste within them. The colors you choose can be based on natural objects like flowers, stones, shells, or even a transient moment of beauty like the soft blue-grays, pinks and oranges of a sunset. You could take the colors from a dress fabric, or use the colors from a Renaissance painting. The sources of inspiration are endless—just keep your eyes open.

It is very easy to get confused when talking about color, so here are the key terms to make it easier to understand.

Primary colors—red, blue and yellow, at the three points of the central triangle.

Secondary colors—any mixture of two primary colors.

Tone is the light to dark range of a color.

Shade is the darker tones of a color, i.e. mixed with black.

Tint is the lighter tones of a color, i.e. a color mixed with white.

Planning a color scheme

The easiest way to plan a color scheme is to iron the transfer (if it is a multiprint) onto a sheet of paper, and try out colors with crayons, or by laying on pieces of colored paper or thread (see Embroidery Chapter 4).

Color schemes are most successful if you use an odd number of colors. Look at a flower, and you will find that it usually has an odd number of colors (3, 5, or 7)—one dominant, one in very small amounts, and any others in fairly equal quantities.

One-color schemes depend upon stitch and texture for effect.

Two-color schemes work best with one light and one dark color, or two clashing or vibrating colors. But always be sure to use more of one color than the other.

In three, five and seven-color schemes use unequal numbers of light and dark colors, even if your design is built up of closely related tones of one color.

Shaded yarn

Shaded, 6-strand embroidery floss is dyed so that the colors vary from light to dark tones of one color throughout the skein. The wings of the pale blue and copper butterfly on the right have been worked to make good use of the dark tones in the center, running out to the lighter tones at the edge of each wing.

A butterfly makes a first-class motif for trying out colors and stitches. You can trace these simple outlines straight from the page and make a couple of butterflies flutter onto a scarf, hover on the sleeve or hem of a little girl's dress, or settle on a pocket. Either look up pictures of real butterflies to find color scheme inspiration, or invent your own scheme with the help of the color wheel.

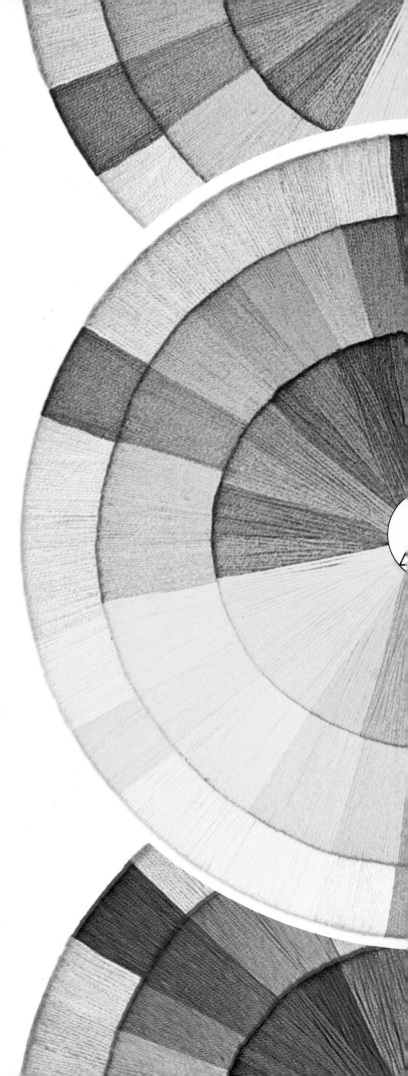

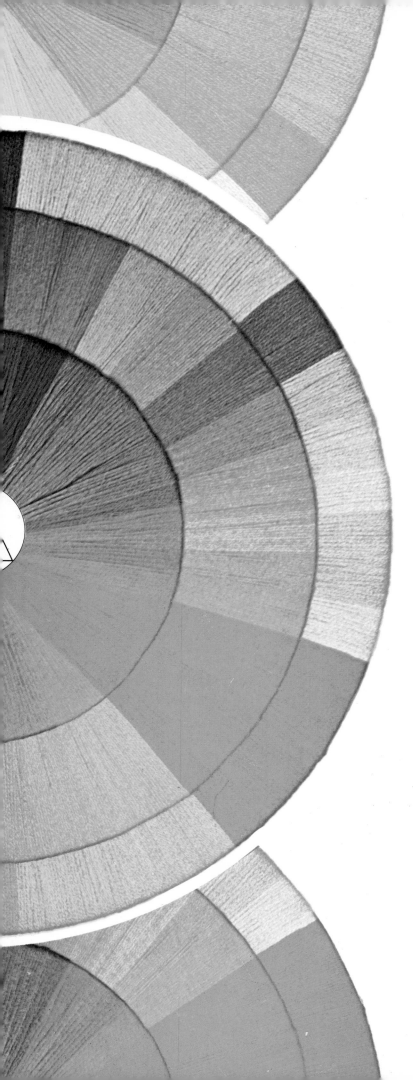

Use of the color wheel

Here are four ways to use this color wheel. Do remember though, a color includes all tones of that color.

1. Use several tones of the same color for subtle, harmonious schemes.

2. Use colors opposite each other for maximum-contrast schemes. These colors vibrate.

3. Use colors at the three corners of an equilateral triangle for rich harmony.

4. Use four colors from one half of the wheel, and a fifth color from the other half.

1. Toned color scheme

Purple butterfly.

Body—satin stitch, violet (three

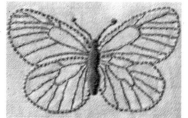

strands). *Wings*—outline: backstitch, lavender (two strands); veins: couching, lavender (one strand).

2. Two-color scheme

Pale blue and copper butterfly—using shaded yarns.
Body—satin stitch, copper (two strands). *Antennae*—stem stitch, burnt copper (one strand).

Wings—outline: two rows chain stitch, burnt copper (two strands); inner wings: satin stitch, light blue (three strands).

3. Three-color scheme

Orange butterfly.
Body—satin stitch, lilac (three strands). *Upper wings*—outlined in backstitch, lilac (two strands); filled in shadow work done on wrong side, orange (two strands). *Lower wings*—outlined in four rows of backstitch: outer, lilac (two strands); inner, orange (two strands). *Spots*—outer circles:

chain stitch, emerald (three strands); and inner contrasting color: satin stitch, lilac (three strands).

4. Five-color scheme

Fantasy butterfly—using magenta and orange as clashing colors.
Body—satin stitch, turquoise (three strands). *Wings*—outlined in chain stitch, magenta

(two strands). *Flashes*—satin stitch, leaf green (three strands). *Small spots*—satin stitch, tangerine (two strands). *Large spots*—inner: satin stitch, turquoise (two strands); and outer: three rows backstitch, yellow (two strands).

Chapter 3

How to enlarge and reduce designs

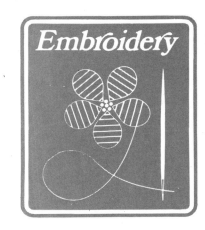

What you will need:
- [ ] Tracing paper
- [ ] Graph or squared paper
- [ ] Ruler
- [ ] Fine felt-tipped pen
- [ ] Soft pencil and eraser
- [ ] Carbon paper (optional)

Method

1. First trace the outline of the design onto tracing paper.

2. Carefully transfer tracing to graph or small-squared paper.

3. Draw a rectangle around the tracing.

4. Draw a diagonal through the rectangle. Extend two adjacent sides of the rectangle to the final size you want, then draw lines at right angles from the ends of the extended sides to meet at the diagonal. If it confuses you to have the rectangles inside one another, draw the larger to one side of the smaller one.

5. Count the total number of squares in the small rectangle and divide the larger rectangle into the same number of squares to form a grid. Draw this in pencil as you may want to erase and re-draw some of the lines of the design to improve its shape. Now in pen carefully copy this design onto the larger grid. It will help if you make tiny marks on each square where the lines of the design cross it, then you can join up these marks.

To reduce a design, use the same method in reverse.

Whether you create your own embroidery designs or adapt those you find in books or magazines, it is useful to know how to alter the size. With the method of enlarging or reducing explained in this chapter, you will no longer have to worry if the initial design is miniature or enormous—you will be able to alter it to the exact size you want. You will be surprised to find how easy it is to enlarge or reduce designs.

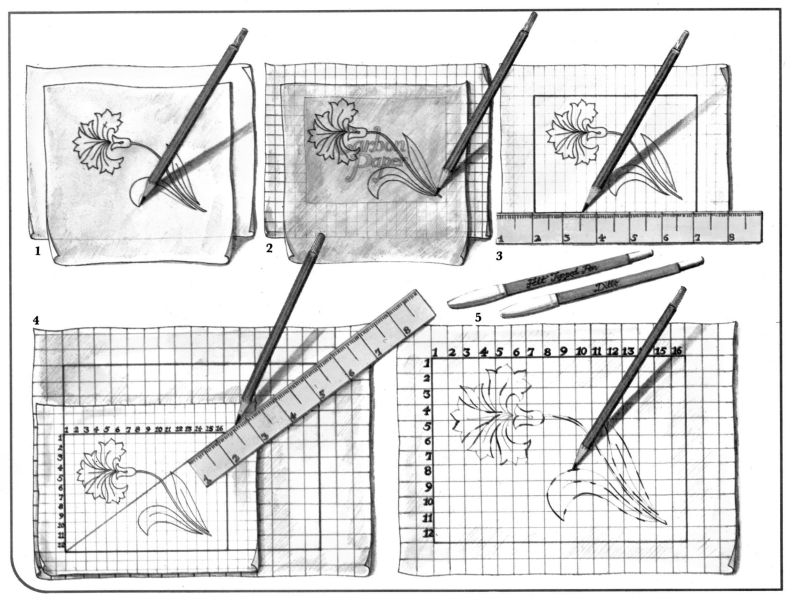

This anemone has been enlarged and reduced using the technique described opposite

Chapter 4

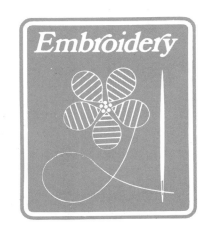

How to transfer a design

▲ *Ironing on the transfer*

The techique of transferring designs to fabric is one of the key steps in embroidery. When choosing your design, first consider the function of the finished object and also the weaving qualities required of the fabric and threads. You may wish to begin with a small surface such as a table mat, and progress to more elaborate designs.

Ironing method

Specially prepared transfers which can be ironed directly onto the fabric are easy to find. There are two types: single impression which can only be used once, and multiprint which gives up to eight impressions, depending on the weight of the fabric (more impressions can be made on a fine fabric than on a heavy one). With both types you have to work on a flat surface.

First establish the center of the transfer by folding it in half lengthwise, then crosswise. Now you are ready to begin. Decide where you want to put the design on the fabric and find the center of your chosen position in the same way. Baste in lines as in adjoining photograph. Match the center of the transfer with this point.

Single impression

Cut off any waste lettering from the transfer. Heat your iron to wool setting, and test transfer on a corner or scrap of the fabric you are using by placing the spare lettering face downward and applying the iron for a few seconds. If the transfer takes, you can begin to transfer the design itself.

Place it face downward on the fabric in the exact position you want and pin it at each corner. Protect the fabric not covered by the transfer with tissue paper. Then apply the iron for a few seconds and remove. Lift one corner carefully to see if the transfer has taken. If not, re-iron gently, making sure you haven't moved the transfer or fabric as this will give a double impression.

Multiprint transfers

You can use multiprint transfers in the same way as single impression ones, but with the iron on cotton setting. The only other difference is that if the transfer does not take the first time, you should allow it to cool before re-ironing.

Basting and Tracing methods

If you are working from a drawing, or from any design without a transfer, you have a choice of various methods. The following two are the quickest and easiest to do.

If the design consists of large shapes, basting is the best transferring method. Trace the design onto tissue paper and place this on the cloth, pinning it at each corner. Baste along each line with small running stitches. When you have finished, tear off the paper.

Find the center of the fabric by folding it in half lengthwise and crosswise. Mark with lines of basting.

Tracing designs

By far the quickest and easiest way of transferring designs is to use dressmaker's tracing (carbon) paper. Trace the design onto ordinary tracing paper, then place a sheet of the dressmaker's tracing paper between the design and the cloth, and trace over the design with a sharp pencil.

This method is fine for designs which will be embroidered quickly, but not quite so effective for really large designs because, with constant handling, the tracing on the cloth tends to smudge.

Opposite—transfers, thread and inspiration. Ferns come in all sorts of beautiful graphic shapes—and provide inspiring embroidery ideas for anyone with an eye for design and subtle color. We suggest stitches and colors for new ferns in Embroidery Chapter 6, but if you would like to give the ferns an individual touch, why not borrow a reference book with color plates of ferns from your local library and interpret your own color schemes? Or, for a more sophisticated effect, you could work them all in gold and silver threads on a cool gray silk background.

Parsley Fern (p. 36).
Cryptogramme crispa.

Pl. 24.

Chapter 5

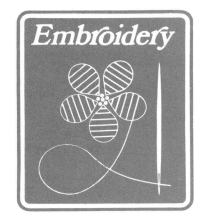

Basic running stitches

If you are new to embroidery, running stitches will provide a sound basis for developing your embroidery skills. These stitches are the easiest embroidery stitches to do. They all form lines—useful for outlining shapes, embroidering curved stems and working geometrical designs. Although running stitches are simple they should not be ignored, as they form exciting patterns when used imaginatively, and like many other simple stitches they can be used as the basis of more elaborate techniques.

Running stitch
Bring the needle through to the right side of the cloth and work stitches evenly along a straight line. Each stitch and interval should be of equal length.

Long and short running stitch
Work in the same way as running stitch but make the upper stitches alternately long and short, the short ones being equal in length to the stitches underneath.

Backstitch
Working from right to left, bring the needle through to the right side of the cloth and make a small stitch backward. Then bring the needle through again a little in front of the first stitch and take another backstitch to the front of the first stitch. Continue working across.

Backstitch—doubled
Make a stitch backward as for backstitch. Then, instead of bringing the needle through again in front of this stitch, bring it through where you started and make the stitch over again.
Continue as for backstitch, working each stitch twice.

Outline stitch
This is rather like backstitch, but is worked from left to right.
Make a slightly sloping stitch along the line of the design, and then take the needle back and bring it through again about halfway along the previous stitch, on the lower side.

Laced and whipped running stitch
Running stitch can be laced or whipped to give extra effect, either with the same or a contrasting colored thread. Take a tapestry needle and thread it in and out of the stitches as shown on the opposite page, without letting it catch in the cloth. Running stitch is used in the diagrams on the opposite page but these techniques can be used equally well with backstitch.

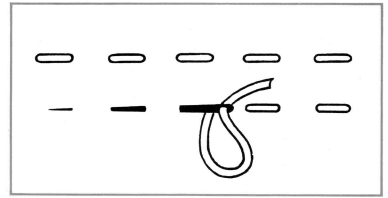

Running stitch

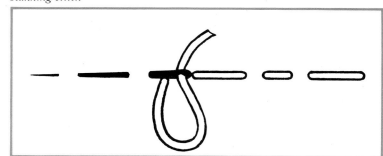

Long and short running stitch

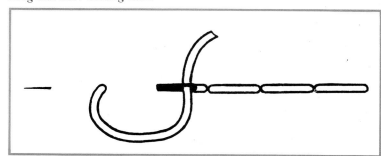

Backstitch

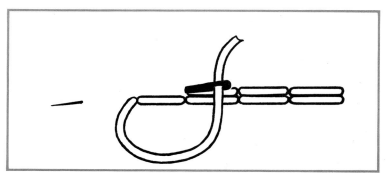

Backstitch—doubled

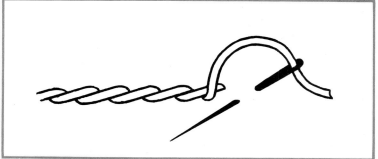

Outline stitch

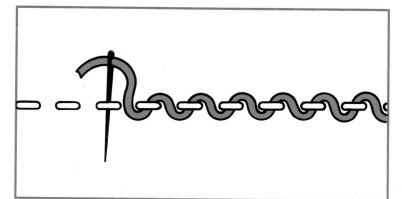

Whipped running stitch

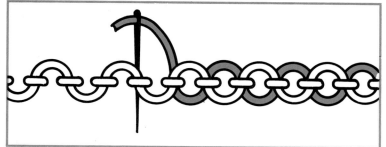

Laced effect

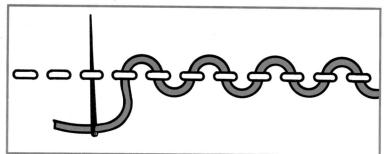

Double lacing

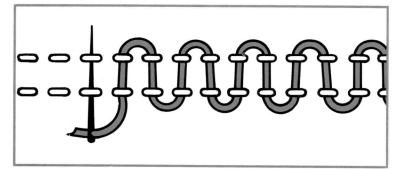

Interlacing

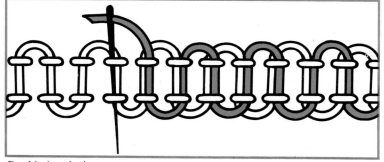

Double interlacing

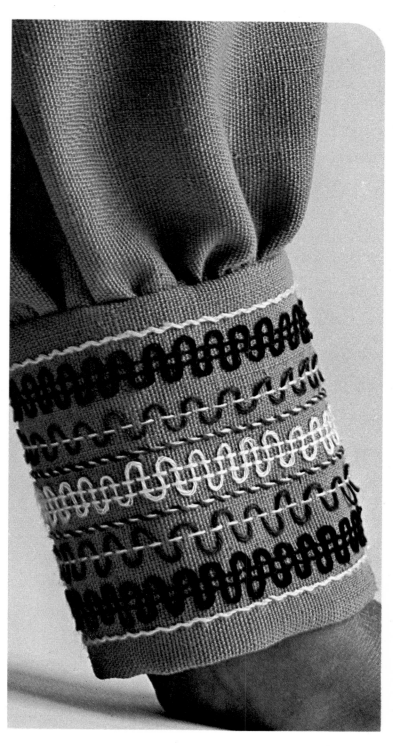

Embroidered borders

On the embroidered cuff shown above we have used a combination of the stitches illustrated in this chapter. It would look most effective on cuffs, collars, sleeves, yokes or worked around the hem of a little girl's skirt.

It isn't necessary to follow the pattern shown here. You can make up your own individual design and color schemes. But remember —for a sophisticated, high fashion effect, use only one or two colors at a time to let the stitches make their full impact. For a peasant effect, however, the more colorful the better!

Chapter 6

Straight stitches, knots and their application

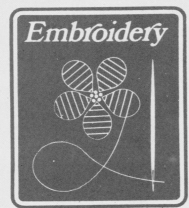

Once you have a repertoire of straight stitches and knots, and you know how to transfer designs and choose colors, you are then ready to start filling in shapes. So, why not try your hand at embroidering some of these filling stitches and knots on the beautiful botanical fern designs which are shown on the next twelve pages? The charts include detailed stitch references; locate the stitches you have not yet learned in the index.

Tracing and transferring the designs
Trace and transfer the fern designs from the transfers given on pages 26, 27, 28, 30, 34 and 35 to your fabric (see Embroidery Chapter 4). You can, if you wish, enlarge the designs at this stage and you will find full details of the technique for doing this in Embroidery Chapter 3.

Choosing your own color scheme
The color scheme chosen by the designer is by no means the only possibility, and you may well prefer to choose your own. The actual texture of the many lovely stitches will take on added importance if you work them all in one color. White on a dark background, perhaps navy or scarlet, would be particularly striking, or, again, dark threads on a light background. Black and white is always an extremely effective combination, whether you choose to embroider a black design on a white background or the other way around.

For a more sumptuous effect, perhaps for a caftan or an evening skirt with a matching stole, work the ferns in silver or gold threads on a rich purple textured silk.

Suggestions for using the fern designs
The original fern designs were worked with a single fern on each of six elegant place mats, with the Scolopendrium Officinarum and the Platycerium Alcicorne designs at each end of a table runner. There are, however, many other exciting ways to apply the designs. Here are some of them.

In the kitchen and dining room—on a wall hanging, apron or tablecloth; in the living room—on a table runner, pillows, or book covers, and as pictures with small gold frames, or as one large botanical print framed in silver or maple wood; in the bedroom—on a pajama case, headboard panel or as a frieze along a pair of curtains; in the bathroom—a single fern on a guest towel.

Ferns as place mats
The quickest and easiest way is to embroider the ferns onto a set of ready-made mats, but if you are expert enough to make your own, here is what you will need: For six place mats each 12in by 18in and a large center mat 12in by 36in, you will need 1¾yds of 54in wide linen. The ferns shown here are worked on natural, but there is a wide range of colors in dress-weight linen

to choose from and each fern can look quite different when worked on another color background. Use two strands of 6-strand embroidery floss either in similar shades to those chosen by the designer or a color combination of your own choice.

Satin stitch
Satin stitch is useful for solid fillings, and consists of straight stitches worked evenly and closely together. The illustration below shows how to fill in a leaf shape or a flower center. If you're working this stitch on an article which you use it is unwise to use a stitch more than ⅜in long, because it will not wear well. However, if the work is to be mounted as a picture or a wall panel, the stitches may be any length. When using a twisted yarn like pearl cotton, take care to keep it evenly twisted while working. Stranded floss is more difficult to use successfully with satin stitch as all strands must lie flat and parallel.

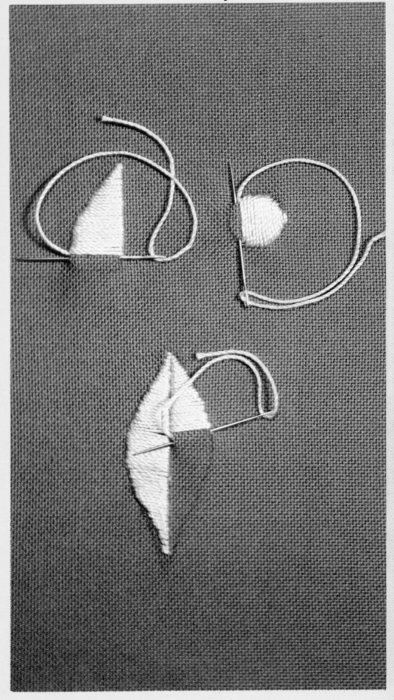

Stitch Library

Wheatear stitch

This is a versatile openwork stitch which is ideal for the filigree parts of the second fern, Platyloma Falcata. Worked in a chain, it looks very like an ear of wheat, from which the stitch takes its name. However, the effect can be changed completely if the stitch is worked in parallel rows.

Work two straight stitches at A and B, bringing the needle through below these stitches at C. Pass the needle under the two straight stitches without entering the fabric, insert the needle again at C, and bring it through at D. (The letters A–D apply to both methods of working the stitch).

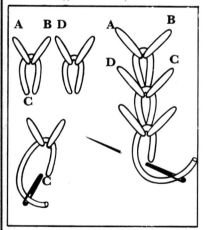

French knots

Bring the needle through to the right side of the material in the required position. Take the working thread in your left hand and wind it twice around the needle. Then, still holding the thread firmly in the left hand, insert it close to where it first emerged. Pull the needle through to the back and secure the knot, or bring the needle up in position for the next stitch. Each stitch should resemble a bead.

Use a thick needle with a small eye so it passes through the coiled thread easily. Choose a needle size depending on the thread used—a large crewel, or medium chenille for soft

embroidery cotton and wool, and a fine crewel for stranded floss.

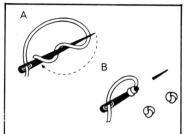

Bullion knots

Make a backstitch the length of the knot required, but do not pull the needle right through the fabric. Twist thread around the needle point as many times as needed to fill the length of the backstitch. Pull the needle through, holding the left thumb on the coiled thread. Then, still holding the coiled thread, and twisting the needle in the direction indicated, re-insert the needle at the point where it was first inserted. Pull the thread through until the bullion knot lies flat.

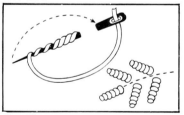

Seeding

Seeding stitches can be used to fill any area and to give a textured effect to a design. This simple filling is made up of many small straight stitches of equal length placed at random. To give greater relief, you can work one stitch over another.

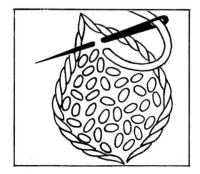

Woven spider web

Work straight stitches from the center of the circle, building up an uneven number of foundation threads. Then, working from the center, weave over one stitch, under one stitch until the circle is filled.

Ribbed or backstitched spider web

The base is formed by working two cross-stitches to form an eight-spoked star. Then cover with a continuous line of backstitch starting from the center.

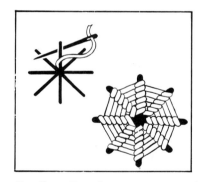

Surface darning

First make a foundation of closely worked satin stitch. Then, with either a matching or contrasting thread, weave over and under the foundation threads only and not through the fabric, except at the beginning and end of each row. If the foundation threads are slightly spaced, an open effect results.

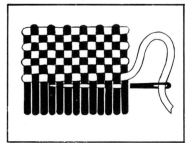

Double knot stitch

Make a small diagonal stitch over the line of design, bring the needle back and slip it under the thread once, then again under the same thread, making a buttonhole loop stitch. When this stitch is worked closely together it gives an attractive bold line.

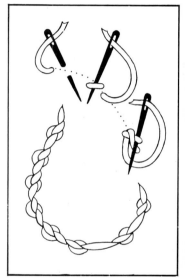

Butterfly chain stitch

First work a row of vertical straight stitches in groups of three, then bunch each group of stitches together with a chain stitch to make a butterfly. The chain stitch is not worked through the fabric.

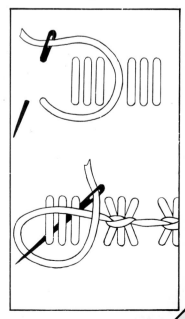

Ferns and fronds

The eight botanical fern designs on pages 24-35 provide an excellent substitute for the Victorian sampler as the embroiderer can try out many of the different stitches described in this book, beginning on page 21 and continuing throughout the Embroidery section. Illustrations and charts of all the ferns are included in this chapter, and you will be introduced to the stitches needed to complete them in later chapters. (Consult the index.) The first fern, Hermionitis Palmata, is designed to let you use some of the stitches you have just learned. Apart from providing beautiful shapes on which to practice new stitches, the ferns can be used to make a set of table mats or as motifs on a tablecloth. The complete set, with Latin names included, would make a magnificent botanical wall panel.

Threads and fabrics

Details of the stitches are provided beside each section of the ferns. Use two strands of six-strand floss throughout for the best effect. The colors in the photographs are those chosen by the designer and can be used as a guide, but you may of course choose to plan your own favorite color scheme. The background fabric can be fine embroidery linen, ready-made table mats, or plain cloths. If you are making a wall panel, finely slubbed or textured upholstery fabrics are ideal.

Hermionitis Palmata ►

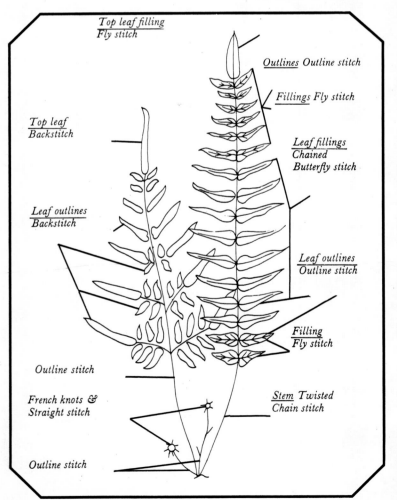

Top leaf filling
Fly stitch

Outlines Outline stitch

Fillings Fly stitch

Top leaf
Backstitch

Leaf fillings
Chained
Butterfly stitch

Leaf outlines
Backstitch

Leaf outlines
Outline stitch

Filling
Fly stitch

Outline stitch

French knots &
Straight stitch

Stem Twisted
Chain stitch

Outline stitch

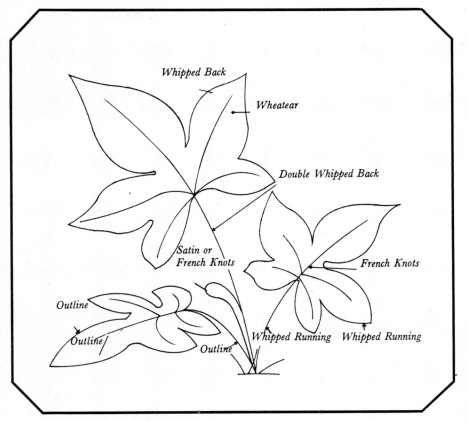

Whipped Back

Wheatear

Double Whipped Back

Satin or
French Knots

French Knots

Outline

Outline

Whipped Running

Whipped Running

Outline

▲ *Platyloma Falcata* ▼ *Scolopendrium Officinalis*

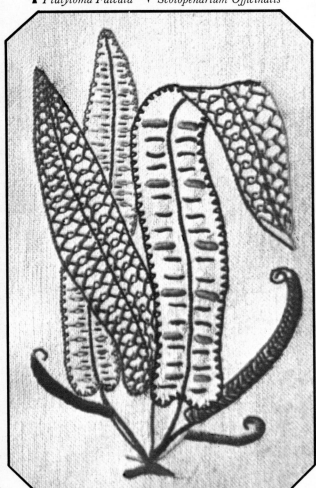

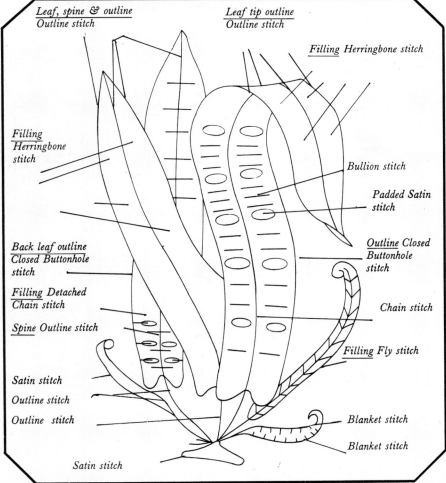

Leaf, spine & outline
Outline stitch

Leaf tip outline
Outline stitch

Filling Herringbone stitch

*Filling
Herringbone
stitch*

Bullion stitch

*Padded Satin
stitch*

*Back leaf outline
Closed Buttonhole
stitch*

*Outline Closed
Buttonhole
stitch*

*Filling Detached
Chain stitch*

Chain stitch

Spine Outline stitch

Filling Fly stitch

Satin stitch

Outline stitch

Outline stitch

Blanket stitch

Blanket stitch

Satin stitch

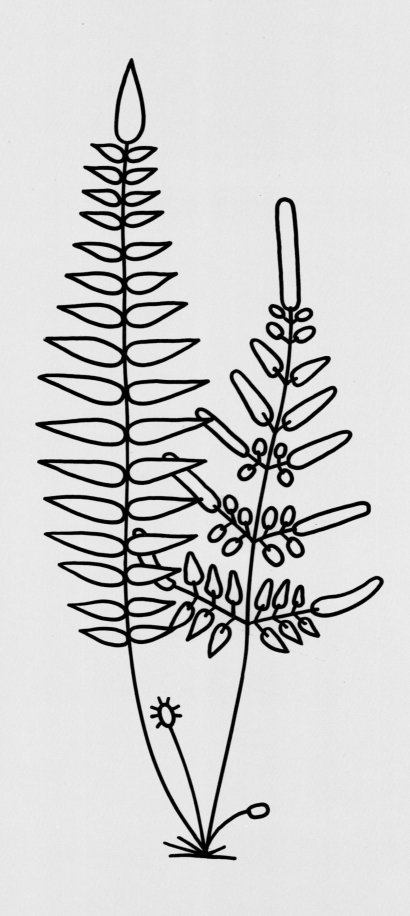

Hermionitis Palmata

Platyloma Falcata

Scolopendrium Officinalis

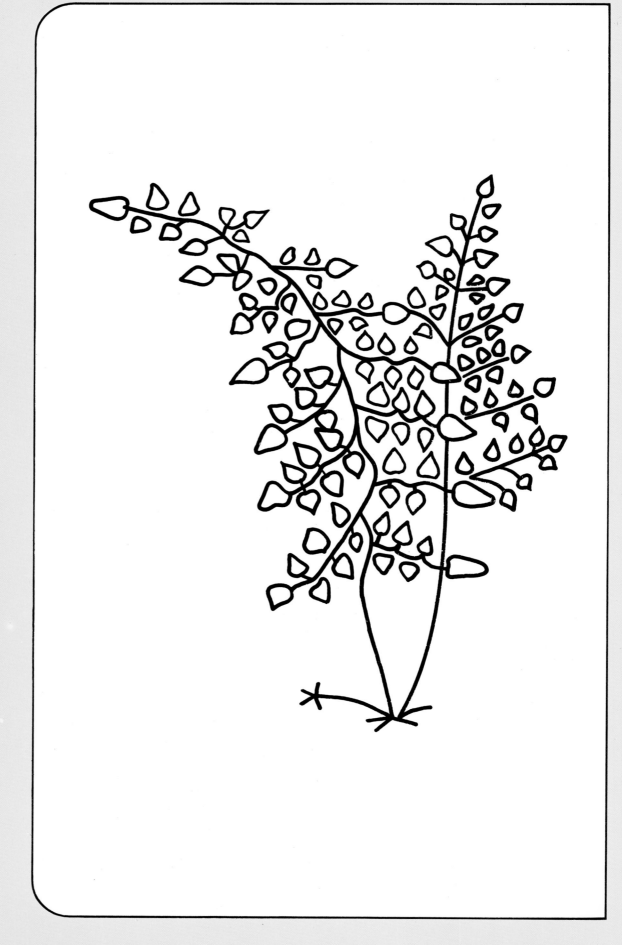

Platyloma Calomelanas

Fern No. 4: Platyloma Calomelanas, showing one of the stems worked in zigzag chain stitch

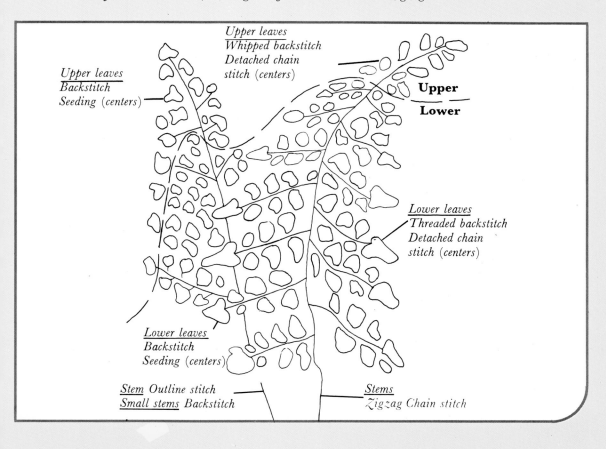

Upper leaves
Backstitch
Seeding (centers)

Upper leaves
Whipped backstitch
Detached chain
stitch (centers)

Upper

Lower

Lower leaves
Threaded backstitch
Detached chain
stitch (centers)

Lower leaves
Backstitch
Seeding (centers)

Stem Outline stitch
Small stems Backstitch

Stems
Zigzag Chain stitch

Adiantum Wilsoni

Dryopteris Pedata

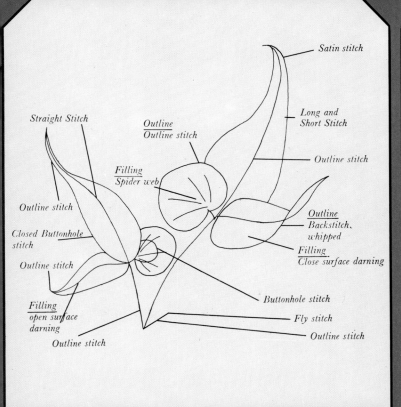

Design chart showing stitches for Adiantum Wilsoni (above) and Dryopteris Pedata (below)

Here you see the final embroidered versions of the ferns worked in the colors chosen by the designer

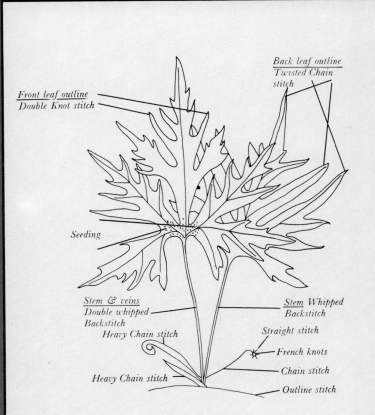

Ferns as pictures

On this page you'll see how decorative the ferns look mounted in gold frames. The names of these particular ferns are Platycerium Alcicorne and Woodwardia Areolata. If you prefer to plan a picture on a larger scale, work all eight designs on one large piece of fabric. Back firmly with woven interfacing and sew onto chunky bamboo rods to make an impressive botanical wall hanging.

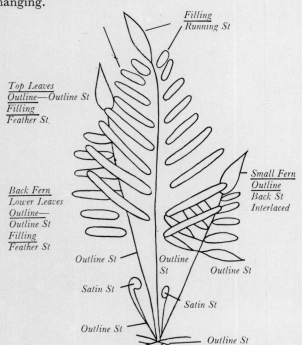

Filling
Running St

Top Leaves
Outline—Outline St
Filling
Feather St

Small Fern
Outline
Back St
Interlaced

Back Fern
Lower Leaves
Outline—
Outline St
Filling
Feather St

Outline St

Outline St

Outline St

Satin St

Satin St

Outline St

Outline St

In design form: ▲ *Woodwardia Areolata* ▼ *Platycerium Alcicorne*

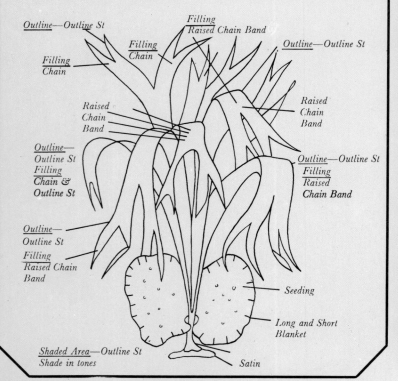

Outline—Outline St

Filling
Raised Chain Band

Filling
Chain

Outline—Outline St

Filling
Chain

Raised
Chain
Band

Raised
Chain
Band

Outline—
Outline St
Filling
Chain &
Outline St

Outline—Outline St
Filling
Raised
Chain Band

Outline—
Outline St
Filling
Raised Chain
Band

Seeding

Long and Short
Blanket

Shaded Area—Outline St
Shade in tones

Satin

Woodwardia Areolata

Platycerium Alcicorne

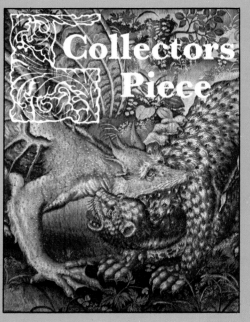

Dragons and griffins in embroidery

Rearing its ferocious head, the dragon has always been a popular motif in traditional embroideries. With its long twisting tail, scaly body and nostrils exhaling fire, the dragon is a particularly decorative monster whose shape lends itself well to a design.

The dragon (below) on this page is one of the many exotic animals which adorn a bed hanging, made by Abigail Pett, and now on display in the Victoria and Albert Museum, London.

Each curtain of the bed hanging is designed with six or seven motifs, showing mythical landscapes with trees, flowers and animals. The dragon is one of the larger motifs, and has been worked in bold stitches. Solid areas of embroidery are sewn in long and short, or split stitch, graduating from dark to light in definite stripes.

On other parts of the curtain, flower petals, leaves and hills are textured, made from various patterns such as laid or couched work, cross-stitch, satin, feather and herringbone stitch.

The griffins (opposite) have been delicately worked onto an 18th century hanging. These hangings were used to decorate the walls and must have looked very impressive indeed. The style and colors are typical of that period and it is made up of a great many stitches including long and short stitch, outline stitch, chain stitch, bullion and French knots, Cretan, detached Cretan, laid fillings and basket stitch. The hanging was originally found in pieces but has since been remounted on a natural linen ground.

A winged dragon displays savage characteristics as it grapples with a leopard. This magnificent tapestry (left) is at the Wawel Castello, Cracovia, in Poland.

37

Chapter 7

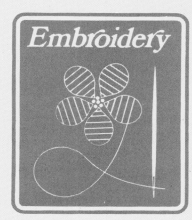

Filling~in and padded stitches

Long and short stitch, split stitch and Rumanian stitch are excellent filling stitches for feathery and furry textures and by introducing different tones of one color you can produce subtle and realistic shading for flowers, plants and animals. When you try out a new stitch it's a good idea to practice on a small motif first to get the "feel" of the stitch. Arrange one or two leaves or simple heart shapes on a table mat or napkin. Heighten the smooth flat surface of satin stitch with an underlayer of padding. Practice the stitch with the traditional cherry motifs in this chapter or create your own designs with padded straight lines interspersed with whipped and laced backstitches, velvet ribbons and cords.

Stitch Library

Long and short stitch

Long and short stitch is worked rather like satin stitch, and takes its name from the irregular method of starting the first row of stitches. This stitch should be worked in a frame for the best results.

Start at the outline and make the first row of stitches alternately long and short, following the outline of the shape closely. Then fill in the rest of the shape with rows of stitches of the same length, fitting them into the spaces left by the row before, to give a smooth texture. The

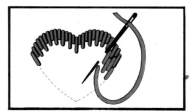

length of the stitch should only vary when you are filling in uneven shapes and you must take care in grading the stitches for these shapes to produce a neat finish. For a smoother effect, use split stitch rather than long and short stitch.

Split stitch

This stitch looks rather like chain stitch and is ideal for outlining. It can also be stitched in curving and spiral lines in close fillings as well as in straight lines.

Starting at A, make a stitch AB and bring the needle through again at C halfway along the stitch just made, splitting each thread into equal halves. The stitches can be gradually increased or decreased in length to fill the shape, but each should be brought up close to the center of the one before. When you are working curves use shorter stitches.

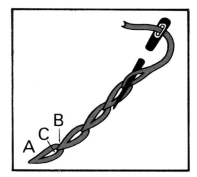

Padded straight lines

To pad straight lines and stems, first cover the line of the design with small running stitches. Then, cover these with a loose thread and stitch it to the fabric with small, close satin stitches. If you are working on even-weave linen you can use the threads of the fabric as a guide for the spacing of the stitches: they should not be too crowded, nor too far apart.

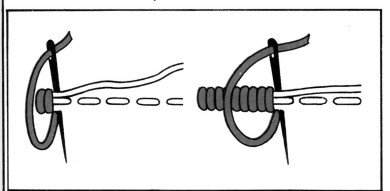

Rumanian stitch

This filling stitch can be used in many ways to give different effects. As it is shown in the diagram, it is useful for filling in leaf or petal shapes. It can also be worked between two parallel lines, either straight or curved, with the stitches placed closely together. For shading, work each stitch with slight spaces in between, then work the next row of stitches into the spaces.

Bring the needle out at the left of the shape at A, take the needle across and make a stitch on the right side of the shape with the thread below the needle.

Make a stitch at the left side at B with the thread above the needle. Continue until the shape is filled. The center crossing stitch can be varied to make a longer slanting stitch or a small straight stitch for different fillings.

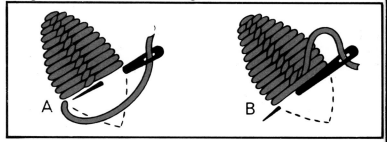

Double padding

More pronounced relief is given by padding twice. First fill in the shape with running stitches, cover with satin stitch in one direction and then work over the same area again at right angles to the first layer of satin stitch.

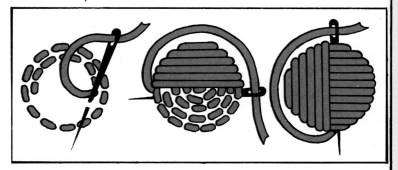

Flat stitch

Make small stitches alternately down each side of the shape with the needle emerging from the outside line. Guide lines can be drawn to insure the length of the filling stitches.

Chapter 8

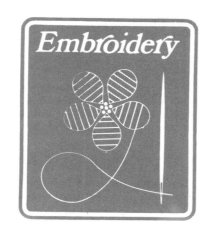

Flowered bag in wool embroidery

The effect of wool embroidery is bold, colorful and richly textured—and what's more, it's simple to work, producing results which are both quick and satisfying.

The shoulder bag shown here, beautifully embroidered in wool and suspended on a braided wool handle with tassels, has an exclusive boutique look about it. Worked in dazzling colors, it will add bright new life to any outfit.

Coming up in the next Embroidery chapter is a jacket embroidered in wool in a similar design. Stitched in co-ordinating colors, the two articles make an elegant set.

One of the joys of wool embroidery is that results are seen quickly, and although a wide variety of stitches can be used even the simplest stitches look extremely successful. This is particularly encouraging to people with a small repertoire of stitches.

Equipment

This type of embroidery should be worked in an embroidery hoop or frame, depending on the size of the work. A crewel needle is generally used for wool embroidery. This has a long, narrow eye for easy threading of wool, and a sharp point. However, a tapestry needle can be used equally well and the blunter point is less likely to split the yarn of stitches already worked.

Yarns

Crewel or tapestry yarns are best for wool embroidery, but color-fast knitting yarn makes a good substitute if you are looking for a particular fashion color. Two strands of crewel wool are generally used but more can be used for a particular effect. Tapestry yarn is used in single strands. When working with yarn, use short lengths to prevent excessive wear on the yarn while it is being pulled back and forth through the fabric. Worn yarn causes thin areas in the work.

Fabrics

Strong, firmly woven fabrics such as heavy quality linen or worsted-type woolen fabrics are ideal. Home furnishing fabrics in heavy linen or cotton are also suitable and these give a wide range of colors to choose from.

Finishing off

For small uncomplicated pieces of work, careful pressing under a damp cloth is sufficient.
Larger and more complicated pieces are best blocked into shape.

Method for blocking

Pin the work out, face downward, on a board covered with two or three layers of blotting paper. Use rustproof thumbtacks. Make sure the grain of the fabric is not distorted as you pin and that the piece is kept in shape. When pinning is completed, dampen the work well with cold water, using a sponge. To avoid uneven shrinkage it is best to dampen the outer edges first and work toward the center. This blocking method is used mainly on large items, such as wall panels and firescreen embroideries. It is not usually necessary with garments unless there is an obvious distortion in the shape of the piece.

To make the shoulder bag

Materials for a shoulder bag measuring approximately 7½in by 8in

- ☐ ⅓yd 36in wide fabric
- ☐ ⅓yd 36in wide lining
- ☐ ⅓yd ¼in ribbon, matched to the cord yarn
- ☐ Large snap fastener
- ☐ 1oz sports yarn in red for cord
- ☐ Spool transparent sewing thread
- ☐ Embroidery frame
- ☐ Spool sewing thread to match fabric
- ☐ Crewel needle size 5 or 6
- ☐ 3 skeins each of tapestry yarn in red, pink and orange

The entire design is worked in satin stitch (see Embroidery Chapter 6) with the direction of the stitches sloping toward the center of each flower petal. Details of the back and front of the bag are shown. Trace the outline of the bag and the design and transfer onto the fabric using the tracing method described in Embroidery Chapter 4. Complete all the embroidery before cutting out the bag. When all embroidery is completed, press on the back of the work using a damp cloth and a warm iron. Trim the fabric ⅝ inch from the traced outline of the bag and cut the lining to the same size.

Place the lining and bag piece right sides together and stitch on the marked outline, leaving A-B open. Trim and notch the seam allowance on the curves and turn the work to the right side. Baste seam allowances of the opening to the wrong side and slip stitch the opening A-B closed by stitching the lining to the bag. On the embroidery surface, baste around the edge of the bag and lining, easing the curves into shape and rolling the lining gently toward the back so that it does not show on the right side. Press the edges flat, working on the lining side. Fold up the front of the bag, matching C to C and D to D. Slip stitch the side seams. Fold down the flap along the center of the third row of flowers, counting from the edge of the flap.

Pin the narrow ribbon along the crease, centered under the flap, and hem along each edge. Approximately 2 inches will be left free at each end and this is used to make loops to support the shoulder cord. Do not stitch the loops at this stage.

To make the cord

Measure the length of shoulder strap you require and add on about 6 inches extra to allow for what is lost in braiding and enough for two long tassels. Cut the ounce of red yarn into approximately 48 lengths of this measurement. Divide the number of strands into three groups. Add a length of transparent thread to each group to prevent the yarn from stretching when it is braided. Braid the three groups together. Make a knot at each end of the braid, about 6 inches from the end, to make a long tassel. Bring a kettle of water to the boil and steam each tassel to straighten the yarn.

To attach the cord

Loop the ends of the ribbon, protruding from under the flap, around the cord just above the knot. Turn in the raw end and stitch the ribbon around the cord securely so that the knot lies below the loop and the tassels lie down each side of the bag. Fasten down the flap with a large snap fastener.

Left: close-up of bag back, showing ribbon loop holding cord in place
Right: bag front, the braided handle rolled into a sausage shape ►

Tracing pattern for the shoulder bag (actual size)

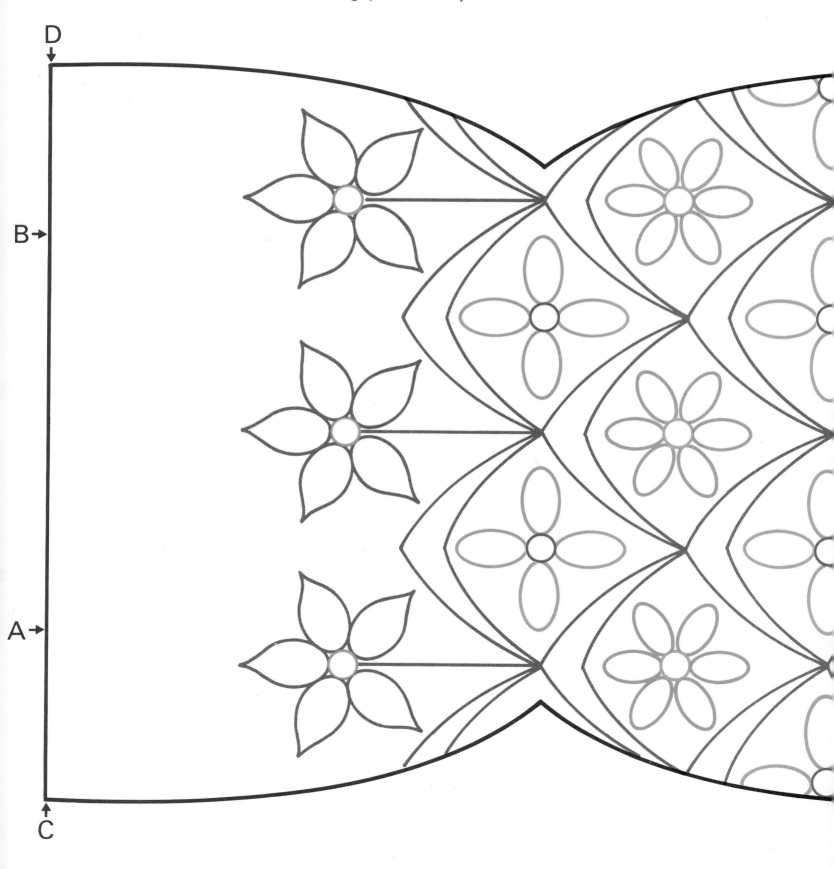

D

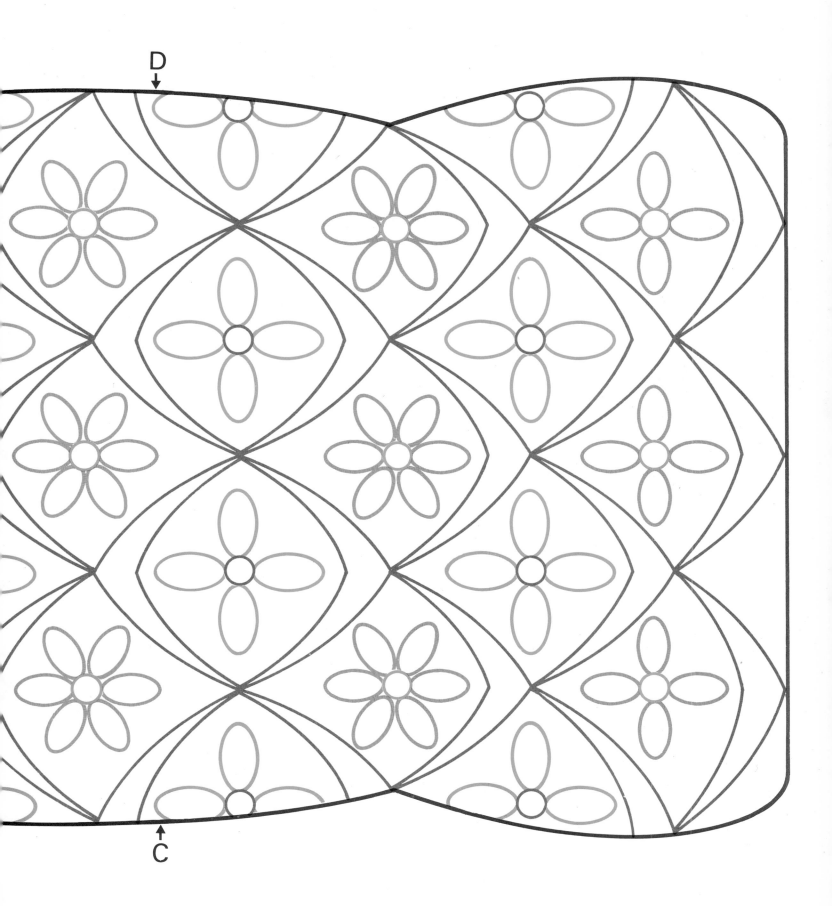

C

Chapter 9

Fashion vest in wool embroidery

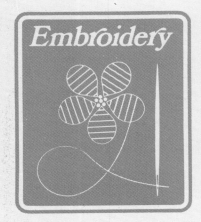

Match this vest with the bag in the previous chapter.

Vest

Measurements
The pattern is given in three sizes to fit 36, 38 or 40in bust.

Materials
- 54in wide fine wool or 36in wide heavy linen (adjust yardage for required length)
- Equivalent amount of lining
- Dressmakers' carbon paper
- Crewel yarn in following colors, 30 yard cards:
  Bolero length—red, 2 skeins; pink, 2 skeins; white, 1 skein; orange, 2 skeins.
  Hip length—red, 4 skeins; pink, 3 skeins; white, 1 skein; orange, 3 skeins.
  Midi length—red, 5 skeins; pink, 4 skeins; white, 1 skein; orange, 4 skeins.
  Long length—red, 5 skeins; pink, 5 skeins; white, 2 skeins; orange, 5 skeins.
- Crewel needle No.5
- Embroidery frame

Making the pattern
On 1 inch squared paper draw the pattern for the vest from the graph to the desired length. Cut out the pattern and pin it to the fabric. Mark around the outline of the back and both fronts with basting stitches. Do not cut into the shape of the pattern until the embroidery is completed. The pieces can be cut apart for easier working leaving a generous margin all around. When the embroidery is completed, trim the sections to within $\frac{5}{8}$ inch of the basting lines for seam allowances.

Transferring the design
Trace the design from the outline and transfer it to the fronts of the vest using the dressmakers' carbon paper method (see Embroidery Chapter 4). If you are working on a dark fabric use yellow carbon, blue or red on lighter shades. Place the design accurately, using the basting lines as a guide. The design can be continued around the back of the neck and back of the armhole if desired.

Working the design
It is essential to work this embroidery in an embroidery frame in order to keep the long stitches flat and even. The design is worked throughout in satin stitch using two strands of yarn, but long and short stitch can be used instead.
Begin the embroidery by working the white flower with two stems which lies at the joining of front and armhole borders, and then embroider every fourth flower in white with a red dot in the center. The remaining flowers are worked in pink with a white center dot.

Completing the garment
When the embroidery is completed, press the work carefully on the wrong side with a damp cloth and a warm iron. Sew together the bust dart, shoulder, side and center back seams. Baste the seam allowances on the front edges, neckline and armholes to the back of the work. Press.
Using the same pattern cut out and stitch a lining, allowing $\frac{5}{8}$ inch turnings on all edges. Baste the seam allowances on the front edges, neckline and armholes to the back of the work.
Pin the vest and lining together wrong sides facing.
Baste and slip stitch all around the edges. Turn up a hem to the required length, turning the surplus fabric to the inside, and slip stitch the edges together. This garment should be dry cleaned.

Choosing a color scheme
The vest illustrated is worked in vibrant colors to create a dramatic effect on the dark background. If you decide to choose another color scheme, remember that the best effect is achieved by using related colors and one contrasting color.

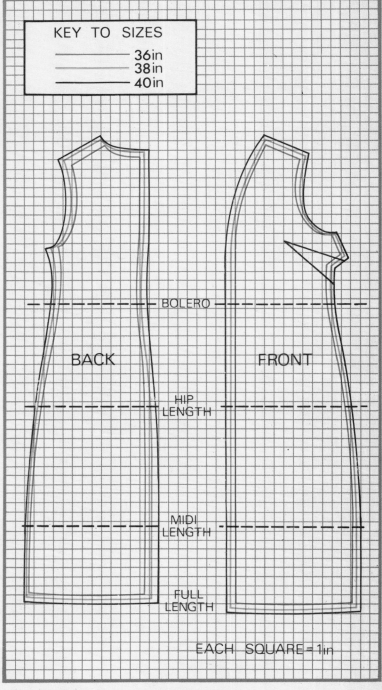

Above: Pattern graph in four fashion lengths. Right: The long vest.

Design outline to trace

The design is actual size and the outline should be extended when tracing off for the longer lengths.

Detail of the yarn embroidered flowers

Chapter 10

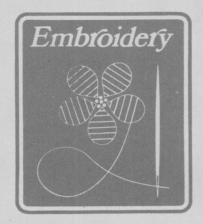

Flowered pillow in gingham

Flowers embroidered on gingham give a refreshing new look to furnishings, the softness of the design contrasting with the fabric background. Make this gay daisy-embroidered pillow to brighten a bedroom, to add a splash of color to a family or sun room, or for a set of garden chairs.

Materials you will need
- □ ½yd 36in wide gingham
- □ Pillow form 14in by 14in (finished pillow 13in by 13in)
- □ 10in zipper
- □ Crewel needle size 7
- □ Six-strand floss, 1 skein each dark yellow and bright green; 2 skeins each lemon yellow and brown; 6 skeins white

Stitches and threads
The stitches used in this design are outline stitch, chain stitch, long and short stitch, French knots and Rumanian stitch. The entire design is worked in six-strand floss using a varying number of strands for the different parts.

Transferring the design
First cut the fabric down the center fold and mark the center of one piece vertically and horizontally with lines of basting. Transfer the design by the tracing method (see Embroidery Chapter 4), centering it on the fabric.

Working the design
Flowers. The petals on the flowers are embroidered in long and short stitch using three strands of floss. The outlines of the petals are worked in outline stitch with two strands. Some of the petals on each flower can be stitched using five strands of floss to give a raised look.

Buds. Some of the buds are embroidered with brown and the rest with bright green, using four strands of floss. The edges of the buds are in outline stitch and filled with long and short stitch.

Bud petals. The petals on the buds are worked with two chain stitches, a small one inside a larger one, using four strands of floss.

Stems. Work the stems in outline stitch in brown and green alternately, using four strands of floss. The stems are caught together with three Rumanian stitches in yellow.

Centers. The centers of the daisies are first worked in outline stitch, working the outer edge of the circle first and working in to the center. Then several French knots are made over the outline stitch.

To make the pillow
When all the embroidery is complete, press carefully on the wrong side and trim the fabric to the size of the pillow, plus ⅝ inch seam allowances all around. Make the pillow according to the instructions in Embroidery Chapter 20, leaving a 10 inch opening for inserting the zipper.

The outline of the design to trace for the pillow

Stitch Library

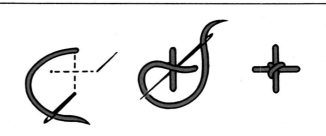

Four-legged knot stitch

When the second stitch of the cross is made a coral stitch knots it firmly in position. Then the fourth leg is completed. This stitch can be used as a powdered filling.

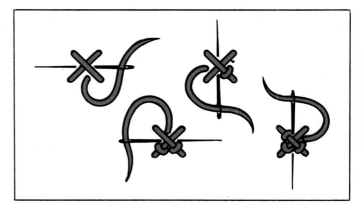

Raised knot or square boss stitch

A backstitch is worked over each arm of the cross to make a firm raised knot.

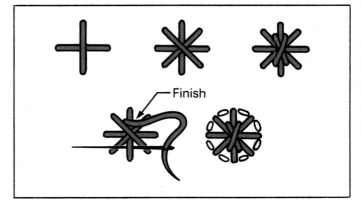

Star stitch

A useful stitch often arranged as a powdered filling. For backstitched star, both the backstitch and the central cross can be worked in a contrasting thread.

Chapter 11

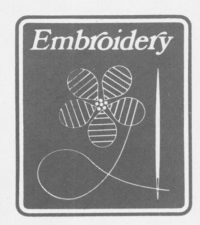

Buttonhole and chain stitch

Buttonhole stitch has many decorative uses besides the obvious practical one. It is the strongest way of doing appliqué and is also useful for binding raw edges in cut work and scalloping. Work buttonhole stitch motifs on a blouse, dress or handkerchief case. Each stitch can be threaded, knotted, whipped or worked in groups—there are countless variations to have fun with.

Chain stitch gives an even, regular line. It is perfect for outlines, and marvelous for flowing twists and turns.

Indian wall hanging with paillettes couched onto the fabric using buttonhole stitch

Buttonhole stitch or blanket stitch

Simple buttonhole or blanket stitch is worked from left to right. Bring the needle out on the lower line, then insert the needle above and a little to the right and make a straight downward stitch, pulling the needle through over the working thread. This forms a row of straight stitches with a closely knotted edge on the lower line.

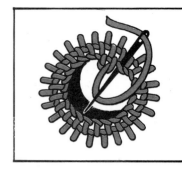

Buttonhole edging

The buttonhole stitch is worked before trimming away the fabric—not the other way around. Cut as close as possible to the edge of the stitching with a small, sharp pair of scissors, taking care not to cut into the stitching itself. The edges should be clean with no fraying visible.

Buttonhole wheel

Arrange the stitches in a circle taking each stitch into the same central hole so that they pull a hole in the fabric. On closely woven fabrics it is helpful to start the hole with an embroidery stiletto.

Paillettes and mirrors

Add another dimension to buttonhole stitch by fixing mirrors or paillettes onto material. Simply make a circle of buttonhole stitches so that the knots lie toward the center and frame the edge of the paillette. Then work buttonhole stitches into the looped edge of the last row of stitches, building up two or three rows. Always point the needle toward the center and pull the thread tight making a round, looped pocket to hold the mirror or paillette in place.

Closed buttonhole stitch

This is similar to simple buttonhole stitch with the stitches worked in groups of two or three to form triangles as shown in the diagram.

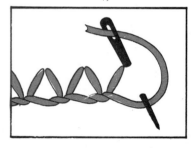

Padded buttonhole stitch

Prepare this in the same way as padded satin stitch. Then, work the buttonhole stitch over the padding. This is especially useful for strengthening any scalloped edges.

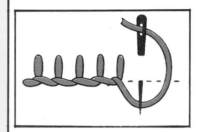

Stitch Library

Chain stitch

Work from the top down, making a chain of loops on the right side of the material and a line of backstitches at the back. Bring the needle through on the line of the design and hold the thread down with the left thumb. Insert the needle again at the point where it first emerged and bring the needle out a bit farther along the line.

Pull the needle through, keeping the thread under the point so that the next stitch holds it down in a loop. Continue working in the same way for the length of chain required.

Zigzag chain stitch

Work this in the same way as simple chain stitch, but position each stitch at an angle to the one before it to form a zigzag. Pierce the end of each loop before you take the needle through the fabric so that the loops stay in place.

Detached chain stitch

Make a chain stitch, then make a tiny stitch to hold the loop down. Leave a space and bring the needle out again to begin to make the next stitch.

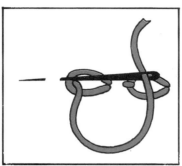 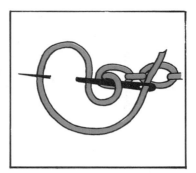

Cable chain stitch

Start with a simple chain stitch. Then, holding the thread down with your left thumb, pass the needle under the thread and twist the needle into a vertical position so that the point comes over the top of the thread. Insert the needle into the fabric so that the working thread is twisted around it, and make another chain stitch.

Daisy chain stitch (or lazy-daisy stitch)

This is worked in the same way as for detached chain stitch, but the detached chain is positioned to form a flower shape.

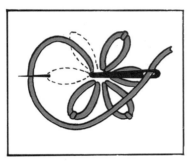 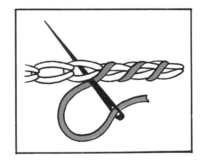

Whipped chain stitch

Chain stitch can be whipped to give it greater effect. Work either a single line, or two or three lines together, and whip with a contrasting thread for a braided effect.

Checkered chain stitch

Checkered chain stitch is another version. Simply thread

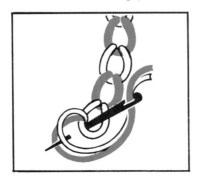

two yarns of different colors through the needle and use them for alternate stitches.

Twisted chain stitch

For this stitch variation the needle is inserted at an angle

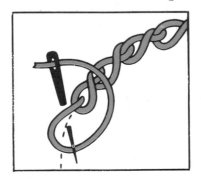

to form the twist as shown in the diagram, giving a slightly raised line.

Heavy chain stitch

First make a small running stitch at A then bring the needle out just beyond it at B. Thread the needle back under the running stitch and insert it again at B. Take another small stitch forward at C then thread the needle again under

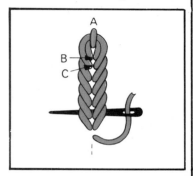

the first running stitch. Continue making the third and following stitches in the same way, always threading the needle under two stitches.

Russian chain stitch

Make a chain stitch. Then, instead of continuing in a straight line, make the next stitch at an angle pointing to the left, then another to the right, catching each down with a tiny stitch. Bring the needle out again farther along the line and repeat to make a line of stitches. This stitch can also be worked in groups as a filling stitch, or vertically in horizontal rows.

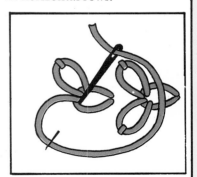

Backstitched chain

Backstitched chain is a very simple variation, worked with a row of backstitches over each of the chain stitches.

Chapter 12

A pillow in simple chain stitch

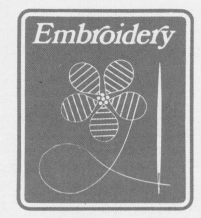

This succulent apple motif for a pillow in vibrant colors shows an interesting use of chain stitch for a bold effect.

To make the pillow 16 inches by 16 inches you will need:

☐ ½yd 36 inch wide even-weave linen
☐ Pillow form 1 inch larger than finished size of pillow
☐ Mercerized sewing thread to match background fabric
☐ D.M.C. Six-strand floss in the following colors: One skein orange 608; one skein dark green 700; two skeins green 3346
☐ D.M.C. Matte Embroidery cotton in the following colors: Four skeins red 2349; two skeins pink 2776
☐ 12 inch zipper
☐ Tracing paper
☐ Graph paper

To enlarge the design

Trace and enlarge the design to measure 11 inches from the tip of the top leaf to the lower edge of the apple. Trace the enlarged design onto tracing paper (see Embroidery Chapter 3).

Transferring the design

Fold the fabric and cut the piece in two. Mark the center with rows of basting stitches each way. Work a line of basting stitches 2 inches in from the outer edges to form a square measuring 16 inches by 16 inches, to mark the outer edges of the pillow. Pin the traced design in position $2\frac{3}{4}$ inches up from the lower line of basting stitches and centering the design between the two vertical lines. Using the matching sewing thread transfer the design to the background fabric, stitching all the lines of design through the tracing paper. When all the lines have been marked with basting the paper is torn away. If the basting stitches are well covered with embroidery they need not be removed when the design is completed.

Stitches

Begin with the orange shape. Use six strands of floss, and start the chain stitching (see Embroidery Chapter 11) from the outer edge of each shape, working toward the center. This insures a well defined outline. Work the deep pink area next and finally the red. Leave gaps in the chain stitch filling where indicated on the design and fill these with bullion knots. The bullion knots are also worked with six strands of floss and with three twists around the needle. Work the apple leaves in outline stitch filling with the veins in outline stitch, using four strands of floss. The calyx at the bottom of the apple is formed by working three detached chain stitches one inside the other starting with the outer. The stem is worked in four separate rows of outline stitch using four strands of floss.

To make the pillow

When the embroidery is completed, press the work lightly over a damp cloth and a thick, soft pad to avoid flattening the bullion knots.

Make the pillow according to the instructions given in Embroidery Chapter 20, and insert the pillow form.

▼ *Trace and enlarge this design to the required size*

Collector's Piece

Elizabethan pillow cover

Nowadays we cover up our pillows with a bedspread but the Elizabethans, it seems, intended their pillows to show. They embroidered delicious, garden-encrusted covers, called "pillow beres", for each pillow. The one illustrated here is part of a set in the Abingdon Collection at the Victoria and Albert Museum, London. The average size of these pillow cases was 35in by 20in. They were always made of white linen and their backs were plain and attached by an open seam of herringbone stitch. Unlike cushion covers of the same period, the pillow covers are nearly always found without a border. Such covers ceased to be made in the 17th century as the fashion had developed for embroidered drapes and curtains.

The flowers and fruits are those found in an Elizabethan garden, usually embroidered in their natural colors—carnation, rose, pansy, pomegranate, borage, pear, honeysuckle, campion and oak. Illuminators used them to decorate their manuscripts and calendars together with birds and small animals, providing models for the embroiderers to copy.

In the cover illustrated here, silk, silver and silver gilt threads have been used, but the stitchery has been kept simpler and flatter than much of the same sort of work found on Elizabethan garments. The stitches are all a variation on chain and buttonhole.

Photograph by courtesy of the Victoria & Albert Museum, London.

Ceylon stitch

Open Ceylon stitch

*Detached buttonhole filling—
taking the needle through a
different loop from usual*

*Left—chain stitch
Right—chain stitch—double*

*Left—buttonhole stitch
Right—detached buttonhole filling*

*Fancy buttonhole filling, smaller
and firmer than the other and
not worked over a ladder of
threads made beforehand*

Chapter 13

Tambour work

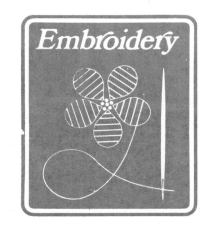

Tambour work first originated many centuries ago in the Orient. It reached Europe in the mid-18th century and was introduced to Britain during the early 19th century. As both hands have to be free to do the work the embroidery was worked in a circular tambour frame (hence the name) and was done on net or fine muslin. The stitch is similar to chain stitch in appearance, but it is formed by the use of a tambour hook, which is like a fine crochet hook.

The stitch can be used in various ways to create greatly contrasting effects. It can be used purely as an embroidery stitch as seen on traditional Indian embroidery, when it is worked in rich colors on fine silk or cotton fabric and frequently enriched with the addition of paillettes or mirrors (see Embroidery Chapter 11). A variety of yarns can be used such as very fine wools, cottons, and silk—yarns which come on a spool are preferable, as a free running thread is needed and too many joins should be avoided. Tambour stitch can also be used as a couching stitch with a fine thread such as machine embroidery cotton worked in a zigzag motion to secure heavier yarns in place. And the stitch is an ideal method for attaching beads and sequins.

The silver embroidery on the black caftan illustrated opposite is worked in tambour stitch. The embroidery itself was bought separately in the East and was then couched onto the caftan creating a garment of great originality and impact. You can see a motif from the tambour work on the left-hand side of this page.

Method of working tambour stitch

It is essential to work this type of embroidery in a frame with a stand as both hands need to be free, one to hold the hook, the other, the thread. The thread must be placed in a position where it can run freely off the spool. If you are using a frame assembled with cotter pins, replace one of the pins with a long nail, over which the spool of yarn can be placed. The hook is used in the same way as a crochet hook, but the chain stitches are made through the fabric. Hold the hook in the right hand and the yarn in the left hand and insert the hook into the fabric on the line of design. Pick up a loop through the fabric. Insert the hook a little distance ahead, depending on how long you want to make the stitches, and draw through another loop. Continue in this way until the work is finished. It is advisable to secure the starting and ending points of the work firmly, for if the ends work loose, the entire embroidery will come undone.

Broad or reversed chain stitch

Make a small running stitch then bring the needle out to the required depth of the stitch. Slide the needle back under the running stitch, inserting it once again where it last came through the fabric. Make another stitch, slide the needle under the two threads of the previous stitch and continue. This stitch is most effective worked in a thick thread with a small stitch.

Dress embroidery

Always plan dress embroidery to follow a neckline or a sleeve shape or a hem, as shown here, so that the design appears as an integral part of the garment.

A motif from the tambour work on the caftan

Chapter 14

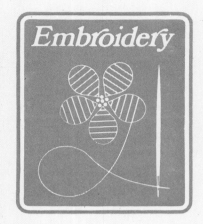

Feather stitches

Feather stitch is attractive as well as useful and can be worked in straight or curved lines. It is one of the main stitches used in the decorative panels of traditional smocks (see Collector's Piece pages 112-13).

The stitches shown here are all from the same family and are useful for either decoration or filling. Because of their realistically veined look, the lacy open feather stitches are ideal for filling leaf or fern shapes and they also look very pretty on hems and edges. When practicing feather stitches lightly draw a central spine and parallel outer guide lines until you achieve the even stitching which is this stitch family's main beauty.

Fly stitch

This stitch can be worked either horizontally or vertically but for both, the basic movement is from left to right. Bring the needle through on the left and, holding the thread down with the left thumb, insert the needle at the same level, a little to the right. Bring the needle up below, but exactly between, these two points, catching the thread under the needle. Take a tiny stitch just below this thread to hold it and bring the needle through in position for the next stitch. Continue in a horizontal or vertical line.

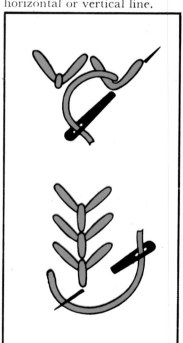

Quill or long-armed feather stitch

Work from the top down. Bring the needle through on the center line of the design. Make a long, slightly sloping backstitch, bringing the needle through again, a little in front of the previous stitch, catching the working thread under the needle. Repeat, taking the backstitch alternately to either side of the center line of the design, to form a quill.

Detail from an apron worked in feather stitch and buttonhole stitch

Stitch Library

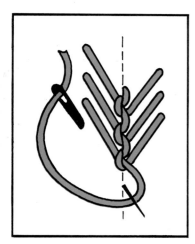

Feather stitch

Work from the top down. Bring the needle through to the right of the center line of the design. Take a small stitch to the left, catching the thread under the point of the needle. Continue making a series of stitches to the right and left of the central line, catching the thread under the needle each time. The result is parallel lines of stitches linked by a zigzag line.

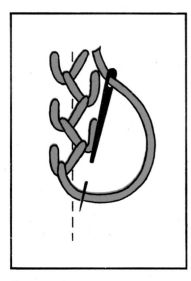

Double feather stitch

Work in the same way as feather stitch, but take two stitches in each direction instead of one. This rather geometric stitch is very popular on the European continent.

To achieve the more rounded, softer feather stitch favored by British embroiderers, angle each small stitch toward the center of the feather rather than working them absolutely parallel to each other.

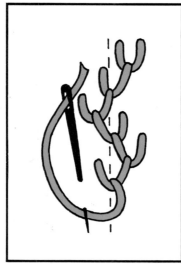

Cretan stitch

Work from left to right. Bring the needle through above the center line of the design. Take a deep stitch immediately below this point and bring the needle up toward the center line taking a small stitch and

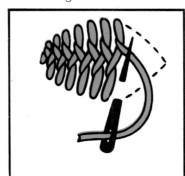

catching the thread under the needle. Make a second big stitch above the center line and a little to the right of the bottom stitch and take a small stitch toward the center of the design, catching the thread under the needle. Continue, taking great care that each stitch is as even as possible.

Because of its close, woven effect, Cretan stitch makes a very effective filling stitch.

Open Cretan stitch

Work this stitch in exactly the same way as Cretan stitch, spacing the stitching at regular intervals. It is very important to keep the spacing even.

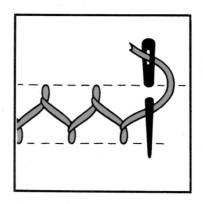

Herringbone stitch

Work from left to right. Bring the needle through below the center line of the design. Insert the needle above this line to the right, taking a small stitch to the left. Then insert the needle below the line a little to the right, taking a small stitch toward the left, making sure that the needle comes up in line with the previous stitch. Herringbone stitch looks best worked very evenly so that the small stitches and the spaces between them are of equal size.

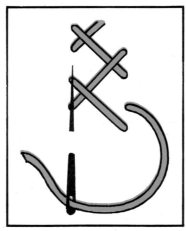

Threaded herringbone stitch

First work a foundation of simple herringbone stitch then, with a contrasting thread (use self color if you wish), pass the needle across the intersection of each stitch.

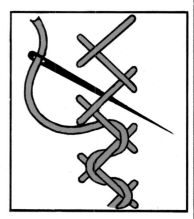

Laced herringbone stitch

This again is worked over a foundation of simple herringbone stitch. A surface thread is woven around the intersection of stitches to form the interlacing. The thread is woven twice around each intersection in the diagram but it can be worked around as many times as you wish depending on the effect you want to achieve.

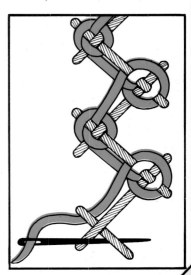

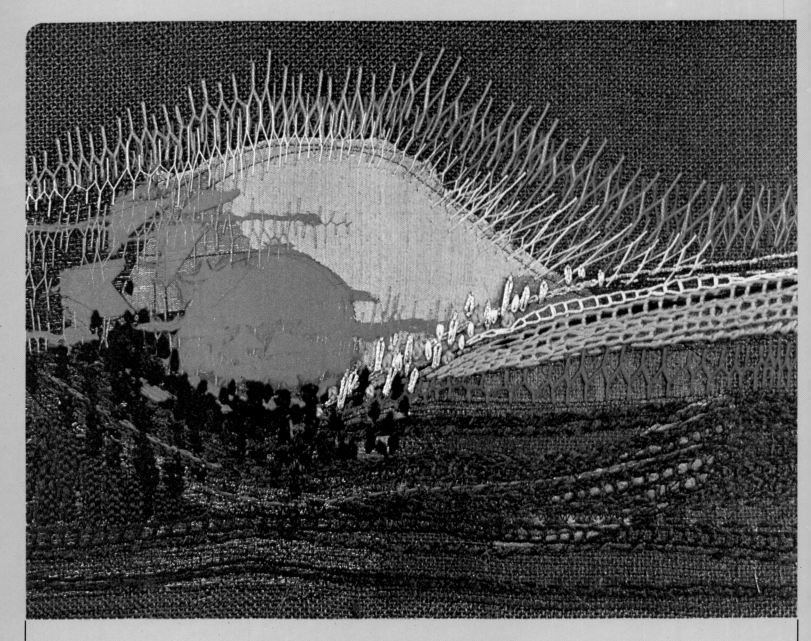

Collector's Piece

The Red Sun

The designer of this unusual example of abstract embroidery was inspired to reproduce, in fabric, the effects of dazzling sun on a landscape. The foreground depicts undulating hills and plowed fields, lit up in places by the sun's brilliant rays in the background. Contrasts in tone and texture are created by the careful choice of stitches and threads, producing interesting effects of light and glowing color.

Two main types of stitch have been used for this piece of work. The sun has been sewn in Cretan stitch, worked upright in blocks, while the stitches above the sun, also in Cretan, are slanted to give the effect of movement. The remainder of the embroidery has been worked in chain stitch: in the foreground, single chain stitches of gold and navy give the impression of

dappled light and shade produced by the sun.

The landscape of hills and plowed fields was achieved by lines of open and twisted chain stitch. Vertical lines of raised chain band in dark brown and navy counteract the horizontal flow of the other chain stitches, making the sun a focal point. This imaginative stitching is enhanced by contrasting areas of plain fabric, and by the use of shot fabrics which lend a glow to the entire work. A feeling of vitality and movement is given to the embroidery by the effect of light on the Cretan stitches. Throughout the composition, all the stitches and threads, the textures and colors of the fabrics, have been chosen carefully for their individual characteristics.

Valerie Tulloch designed and worked this embroidery.

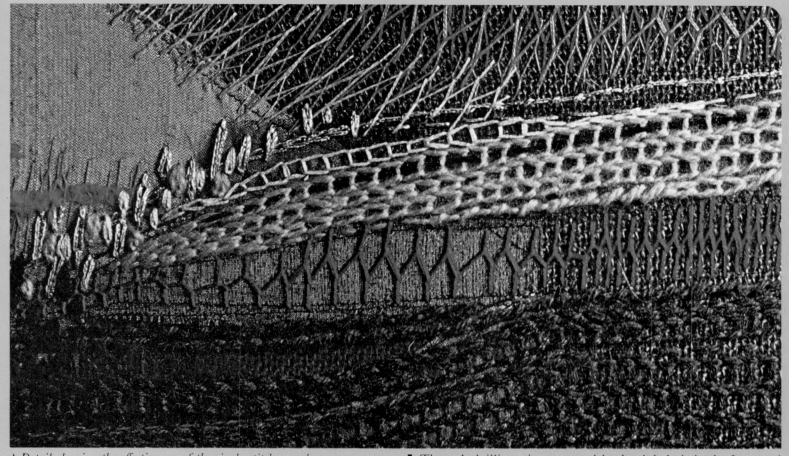

▲ *Detail showing the effectiveness of the single stitches used*　　　▼ *The sun's brilliance is accentuated by dappled shade in the foreground*

Chapter 15

Counted threadwork traycloth

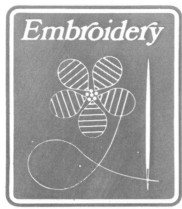

This attractive traycloth in brilliant colors is decorated in counted thread embroidery. It can be worked in six-strand floss or pearl cotton as desired. Although at first glance the design may appear complicated, the stitches used—satin stitch, raised chain band and fly stitch—are all simple to do. Full instructions are given for embroidering and finishing the cloth.

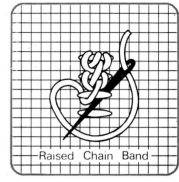

▲ *Method of working chain band*

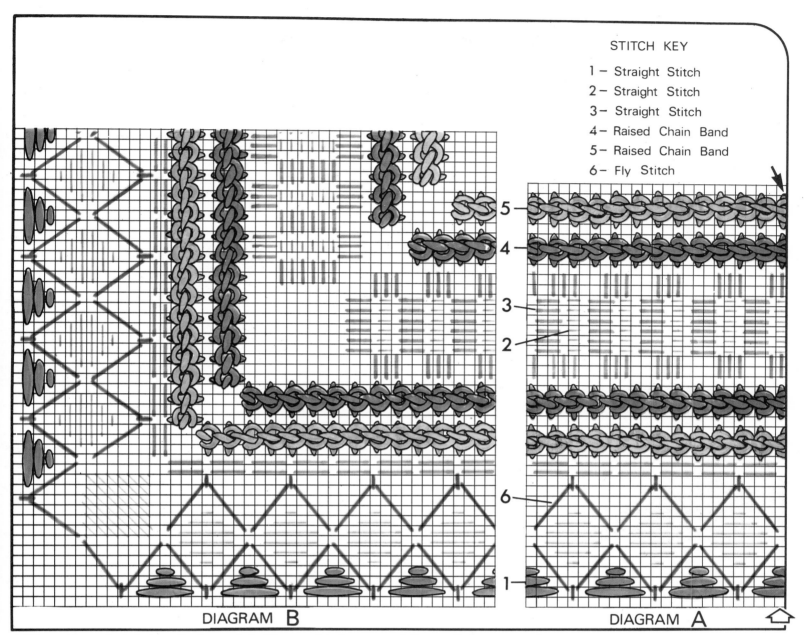

DIAGRAM B

DIAGRAM A

▲ *The working and stitch charts for the traycloth. Diagram A is the repeat and diagram B the corner turning*

Raised chain band
(see diagram on opposite page).

Work the required number of foundation stitches over 4 threads of the fabric and two threads apart. Bring the needle through at A, then pass the needle upward under the center of the first bar and to the left of A. With the thread under the needle, pass the needle downward to the right of A and pull up the chain loop thus formed.

To make the traycloth measuring 20 inches by 13½ inches you will need:

☐ ½yd pale blue even-weave linen 59 inches wide, with 20/21 threads to 1 inch

☐ Tapestry needle No.20

☐ D.M.C. six-strand floss in the following colors and amounts: 7 skeins violet 552; 5 skeins rose pink 956; 4 skeins orange 900 and 3 skeins cyclamen 554

As an alternative you can use:

☐ D.M.C. Pearl Cotton No.8: 1 ball each of violet 552; rose pink 956; flame 606 and cyclamen 554

To make the traycloth

Cut one piece of fabric measuring 15½ inches by 22½ inches following the grain, and mark the center both ways with a line of basting stitches. Diagram A gives a section of the repeat. The center is indicated by a white arrow which should coincide with the width-wise line of basting stitches. Diagram B is the corner turning. The diagrams also show the arrangement of the stitches on the fabric represented by the background grid lines. With the long side facing, commence the embroidery at the small black arrow, 81 threads down from the crossed basting stitches, and work section A following the colors and stitches as given in the key. Repeat section A five times more to the left and then work section B. To complete one quarter of the design turn the fabric and work as before along the short side to the lengthwise line of basting stitches. Work the other three quarters to correspond. Press the embroidery on the wrong side.

Finishing

Turn back ½ inch hems, miter corners and slip stitch.

Chapter 16

Garden pillows in wool embroidery

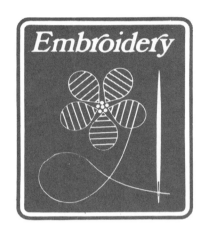

Brighten up your garden furniture with these brilliantly colored pillows. Embroider some and leave others plain. Using chunky tapestry yarn, the design is worked in simple stitches such as chain stitch, outline stitch and fly stitch. Use the stitches and colors suggested or experiment with your own choice. The same design could look interesting translated into appliqué.

To make a pillow measuring 17 inches in diameter you will need:

☐ ⅝yd 54in home furnishing fabric
☐ 2¾yds contrasting color piping
☐ Sewing thread to match fabric
☐ Pillow form 18 inches in diameter, 2½ inches deep
☐ Large tapestry needle
☐ 2 button molds 1 inch in diameter (plain pillow only)

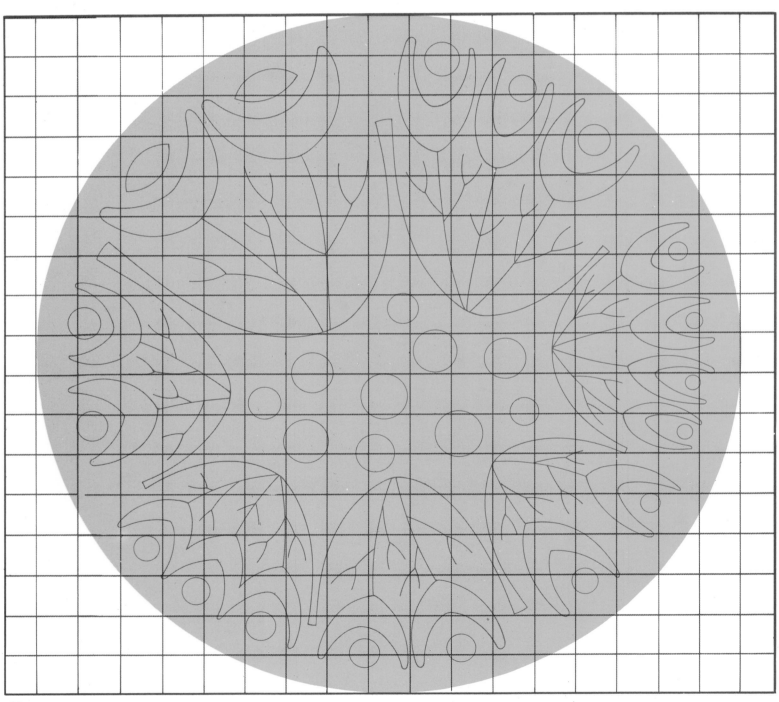

□ D.M.C. Heavy Tapestry Yarn No.13 in the following colors:
1 skein each of burgundy red 7110; wine red 7108; scarlet 7606 and yellow 7431

To transfer pattern and design

Enlarge the pattern and design from the chart and draw onto 1 inch squared paper. Trace the pattern and design onto tracing paper and cut out. Lay the pattern onto the folded fabric and cut out two circles for the top and bottom of the pillow, allowing $\frac{5}{8}$ inch turnings all around the edge. Cut a strip for the boxing strip measuring $49\frac{1}{4}$ inches long and $3\frac{3}{4}$ inches deep. Take one circle of the fabric and trace the outline only onto this. Now take the second circle of fabric and trace the outline and design onto the right side of the fabric, using carbon paper or small running stitches through the tracing paper and the fabric.

The stitches used

The central area of the design is worked in outlines of French knots in yellow. The stems are in chain stitch, outline stitch and fly stitches using scarlet and wine red. The stylized flower heads are worked in satin stitch in wine red and burgundy red.

To make the pillow

Pin and baste the piping around outline of pillow top and bottom. Pin the boxing strip to the top, easing it around the circle until both ends meet. Pin, baste and stitch the boxing strip seam. Baste the boxing strip to the top and stitch as close to the piping as possible. If stitching by machine use a cording foot. For a smooth finish, cut notches on seam allowance all around. Stitch bottom of pillow in same way but leave about 10 inches open to insert pillow form. Turn cover to right side and insert form. Stitch the 10 inch opening by hand.

◄ *The design to trace and enlarge*
Bright pillows for sunny days ►

Chapter 17

A wool embroidered panel

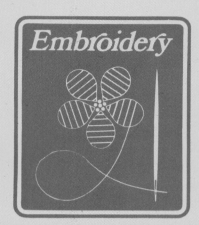

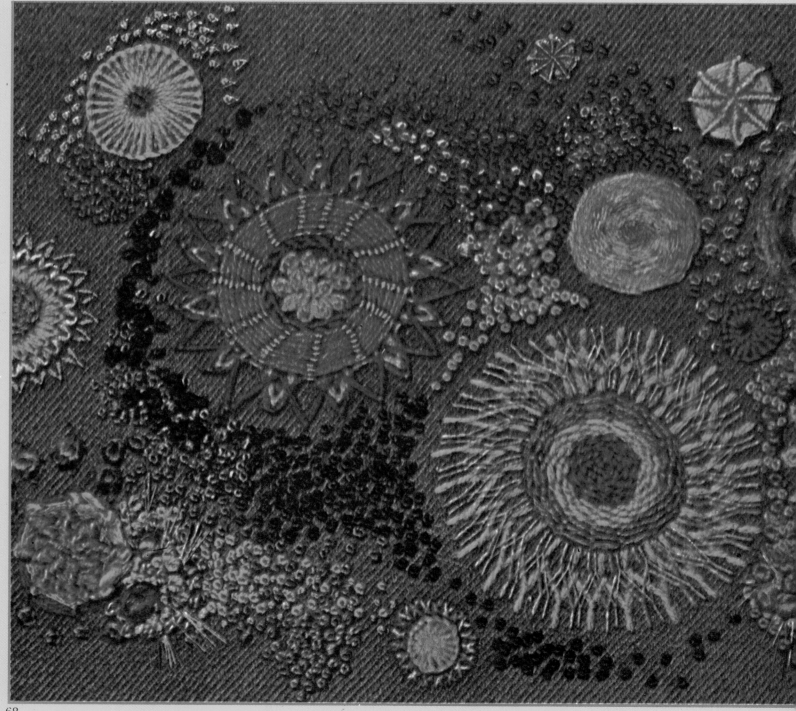

Color and stitch details are given for working this wool embroidered panel which is illustrated lifesize. Hang the panel framed or unframed.

The textural effects are achieved by using a variety of stitches and yarns woven onto a heavy home furnishing fabric. A color scheme could be worked in brighter colors to achieve a more exciting result. To make this panel, finished size 18in by 12in, you will need:

- ½yd unbleached muslin
- ½yd green-colored twill weave fabric
- Hardboard for mounting
- Tapestry needle No. 18
- Crewel needle No. 5 or 6
- D.M.C. Tapestry yarn colors (1 skein of each) 7603, 155, 317, 996, 576, 157, 769, 153, 547, 257, 708, 768, 595, 896, 135, 492, 542, 106, 895, 387

- Curtain rings
- D.M.C. Coton à Broder in colors (1 skein of each): 2227, 2825, 2572, 2209, 2570, 2595
- Rya wool (1 skein of each) in mauve, slate, turquoise and royal blue

Trace design from the color picture and use the key as a guide to the yarns and stitches.

Circles

Instructions and colors are worked from center of circles. Numbers refer to D.M.C. Tapestry yarn colors unless otherwise stated.
1. *Spiders web framework: coton à broder/backweaving, Rya wool mauve, turquoise edged 0708.* **2.** *Chain stitch 317/detached chain 996/fly stitch 153 and coton à broder 2595.* **3.** *Spiders web. Backweave 257 and 708.* **4.** *Buttonhole stitch 996/straight stitches 155.* **5.** *Detached rosette chain 7603/edged chain stitch 157.* **5a.** *Circular couching 155/with 996.* **5b.** *Overlapping fly stitches 157, 106.* **6.** *Buttonhole stitch 7603/herringbone stitch 155.* **7.** *Chain stitch 155/spider web weaving 996. 317/slanting Cretan stitch 576. 155/sewing thread bright pink.* **8.** *Spiders web, 708, 996, 896, 7603, 135.* **9.** *Curtain ring buttonholed 155/spiders web 153, 542.* **10.** *Spiders web 153/fly stitches 0708.* **11.** *Curtain ring covered Rya wool mauve/chain stitch slate/detached rosette chain 996.* **12.** *French knots 542, 996, 547, 2 strands Rya wool royal blue couched around 769.* **13.** *Spiders web 7603, 106, 155, 257.* **14.** *Backweave spiders web/French knots 7603/weaving 0708, 7603.* **15.** *French knots 542/chain stitch 7603 153.* **16.** *Spider web 542.* **17.** *French knots, 996, 595/weaving 0708/backweaving 153, 996.* **18.** *Curtain ring buttonholed 0708/spider web 7603, 317.*

French knot areas

The heaped areas of French knots are shaded on the chart. **A.** *Rya wool royal blue/fly stitch and French knots, coton à broder 2227, Rya wool mauve, turquoise.* **B.** *317, 157.* **C.** *Coton à broder 2825/sewing thread fly stitches.* **D.** *895, 996, 317.* **E.** *387, 547, 769, 768.* **F.** *153, 7603, 896.* **G.** *895/scattering 257.* **H.** *Rya wool mauve.* **J.** *Rya wool royal blue.* **K.** *106, 155, 0708.* **L.** *153, 0708, coton à broder 2570.* **M.** *The same.* **N.** *Spaced knots 996.* **O.** *769, 768, 547, 492.* **P.** *542, 576, 317, 996.* **Q.** *0708, 7603.* **R.** *0708, 7603.* **S.** *Rya wool royal blue, 7603, 542, 317, 157.*

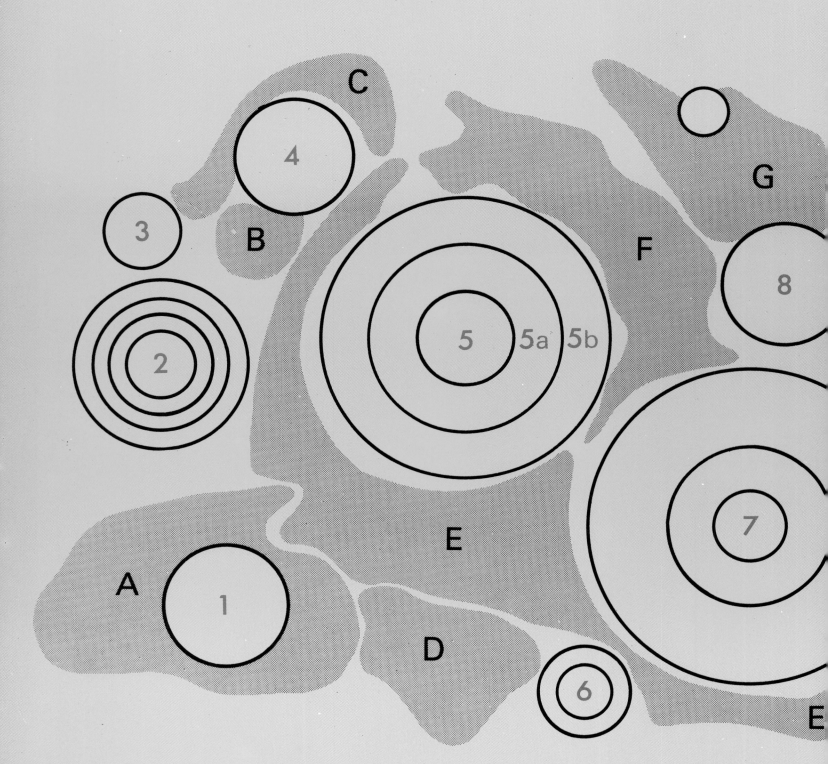

Yarn and stitch key for wool embroidered panel

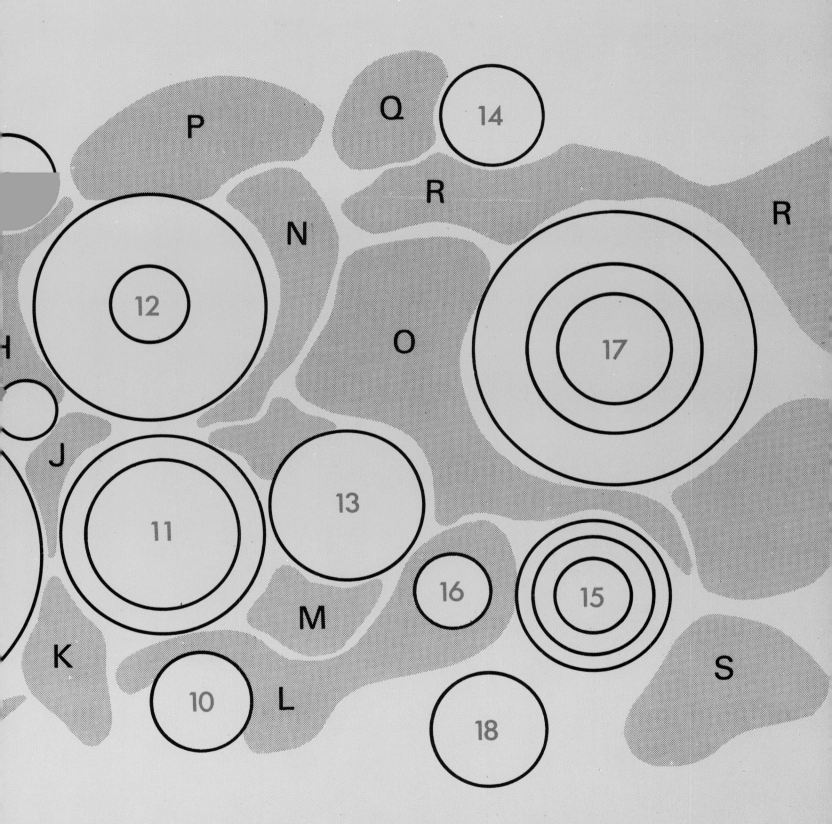

Collector's Piece

Wise old owls

Plump little owls are always fun to embroider and they can be made as simple or elaborate as you please. The owl's shape is uncomplicated, yet the outline can be filled in to depict feathers on the chest using a wide range of colors, textures and stitches. The two shy-looking owls perched on a branch have been worked in several decorative stitches to add detail to the embroidery without making it look too fussy or fragmentary. The feathers covering the owls' round chests are worked in patches of straight and chain stitch, some stitches varying in size, thickness and spacing. A more elaborate composition —the multi-colored owl— is worked all over in different stitches. French knots graduating into straight stitch give a dappled effect on the bird's chest, and the stitches form clearly defined feathers. The brown wings are boldly outlined in chain stitch and woven band and feathered in Rumanian stitch. The owl's eyes, head and ears are worked in straight stitch in assorted yarns, and the iris of the eye is made up of small iridescent beads. The woolly brown owl design adorning the opposite page is more a semi-collage than a pure embroidery. The owl's body is worked in delicate tawny shades of a special wool but the same effect can be achieved by taking yarns and twisting them. The eyes are large, flat black beads, the beak a shiny oval pearl, and the claws clasp a piece of tree bark matched to the colors of the wool.

Chapter 18

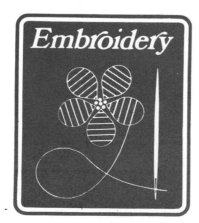

Introduction to appliqué

Appliqué is simply the technique of applying one fabric to another. It originated as an imaginative way of patching worn clothes, but it has become a highly developed form of decoration—its present-day popularity is probably due to the fact that it is quick to do and that it makes use of all sorts of fabric scraps. This chapter provides the essential tips on choice of fabrics and the methods of appliqué. Embroidery Chapter 19 suggests ways to create your own designs, and gives step-by-step instructions for basic appliqué.

Basic hints

Choosing materials

The applied materials should be of equal or lighter weight than the background material, but the background material can be mounted on strong cotton to add strength if desired. Non-fraying fabrics are the easiest to apply, as the edges don't have to be

Start with bold appliqué on nursery pillows or children's aprons

turned in. If you want to use an attractive material which might fray, iron on a woven adhesive interfacing to the wrong side of the fabric to prevent this.

Applying materials

If the appliqué is going to receive hard wear, remember to match the grain of the two fabrics to prevent puckering and splitting. Fabrics such as felt do not have a grain, so these can be applied in any position.

To work in the hand or in a frame

For appliqué it is best to work with the background material pulled taut, in a rectangular frame, an old picture frame or, for small items, an embroidery hoop on a stand (see Embroidery Chapter 1). Very small pieces may be worked in the hand if you wish, but whether you use a frame or not, be sure to stretch the fabric to be applied as much as the background material. If the fabrics are at different tensions it will eventually cause puckering and spoil the look of your work.

Using a rectangular frame

One type of frame is made up of four strips of wood—two strong cross bars joined by two side bars with peg holes to vary the size. Another type of rectangular frame works on the same principle, but differs from it in that the side bars are threaded for screwing the fabric taut.

The frame with peg holes is preferable to the other rectangular frame for anything but very lightweight fabrics, because the screw rings on the frame can work loose and relax the tension of the fabric while you stitch.

There are two kinds of rectangular frames on the market—hand frames and floor-standing frames. Hand frames adjust to 28in wide and floor frames to 40in wide. Whether you use a frame with a stand or not is up to you, but generally it is easier to work with a stand.

Mounting fabric on a frame

1. Mark the center of the webbing on the frame rollers with a basting line.
2. On the top and bottom of the fabric, make a $\frac{1}{2}$in turning to the wrong side, and hem it if it is likely to fray.
3. Mark the centers of these turned edges with pins. Place the center of the fabric to the center of the webbing and pin from the center outward.
4. Using very strong thread, whip the 2 edges together, always working from the center outward.
5. Repeat on second roller.
6. Adjust the side bars until the fabric is taut.
7. Baste 1in tape to the sides of the fabric, using small stitches.
8. Thread a large needle with strong string, and lace through the webbing and over the slats with stitches about 1in apart.
9. Leave about 18in of string at each end. Pull the string taut and wind it around the ends of the frame, then tie to secure.

Framing a fabric with backing

It is best to use a backing such as white (or unbleached) strong cotton or holland. Make sure the backing is pre-shrunk and at least one inch bigger all around than the fabric to be embroidered.
1. Baste a line down the center of the backing and of the fabric to be embroidered.
2. Place the fabric on the backing, matching the center lines. Pin it into place, working out from the center with the pins pointing inward to avoid puckering. Do not stretch either layer.
3. Firmly baste around the outside edge through both fabrics. Remove the pins.
4. Now mount the backed fabric in the frame according to the previous instructions.

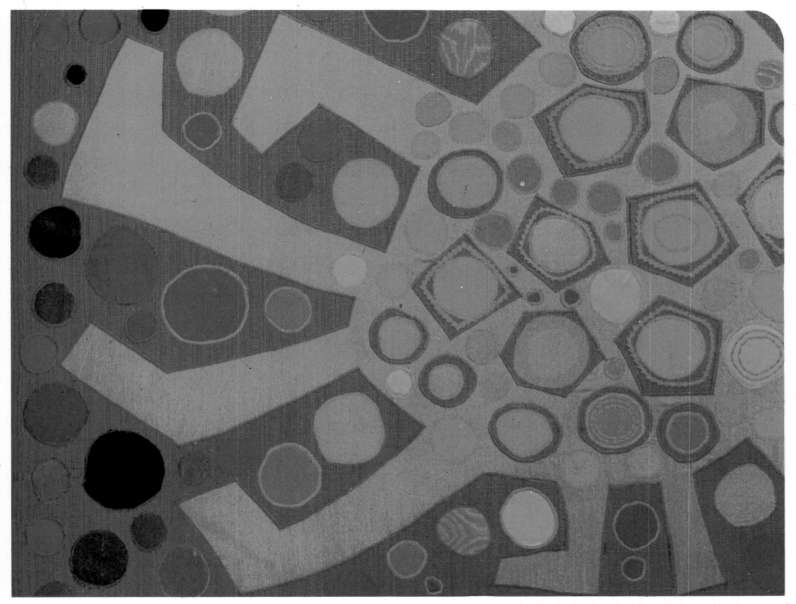

Part of a modern design, called Mexican Sun, which shows the stunning results of combining appliqué and simple embroidery stitches, using the cut and stitch method. Zigzag machining has been used to stitch the pieces to the background and couching and double knot stitch as surface decoration.

Which method do I choose?

There are several appliqué methods—it all depends on the type of materials you want to use or the effect you wish to achieve as to which one you choose. Here are the main methods.

Stick and stitch
This is the simplest form of appliqué. Simply stick cutouts of non-fraying materials with a fabric glue onto a fabric background and secure the edges with either hand or machine stitches.

Cut and stitch
This method is best used on firm non-fraying materials which you can safely cut to shape and slip stitch by hand or zigzag stitch on a swing-needle sewing machine over the raw edges. You can then decorate the applied areas with various kinds of stitching.

Stitch and cut
This method is used on thin fabrics which would fray if cut out before applying. Cut a larger area than you need, marking the

exact shape required, then either buttonhole stitch (see Embroidery Chapter 11) by hand or zigzag by machine onto the main fabric. Then trim off the surplus appliqué fabric very close to the stitching, using a pair of really sharp scissors.

Blind appliqué
This is another method for materials which fray easily. Turn the edges under and baste into position (around a cardboard template if it is a difficult shape), before applying. Press the turnings flat and slip stitch the shape into position. A bulky fabric will be easier to apply if you cut across corners and clip into curves. This will make the shapes neater and help them lie flat.

Cutouts
This is a reversed appliqué method. Baste two or more layers of fabric together and cut out the shapes to reveal the underneath layer or layers. Then, either buttonhole stitch the raw edges or stitch down a small turning with a slip stitch, or secure the shape with a straight or zigzag line of machine stitching. You can back the cutouts with different colored fabrics or ribbons.

Chapter 19

Designing for appliqué

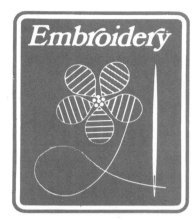

It is very surprising how many people become really expert at embroidering commercial patterns but who would never dream of attempting to create a design of their own. Designing for appliqué need not be difficult or complicated. In any case, bold, simple designs are often the most effective and you can always add to the interest and texture of the simplest design by your choice of embroidery stitches. Furthermore, if you try to do something so difficult that it is completely beyond you, you might easily be put off appliqué forever, whereas a successful first attempt will encourage you to go on to more intricate and exciting work.

Creative appliqué

You do not have to be an artist to be able to design for embroidery and appliqué is perhaps the easiest type to start on. The most important thing is to think in terms of large, simple shapes until you become more experienced. Small shapes are more difficult to handle, especially in materials which fray. Here are five easy ways to plan a design. And although they are for appliqué, they also apply to embroidery in general.

Folded and cut paper method

This is best used for non-fraying fabrics such as felt, suede, leather, synthetic leather, and plastic-coated materials. Fold a piece of paper twice to form a triangle and then twice more into smaller triangles. Cut out shapes (not too small), being careful not to cut away all the folded edges. Open out the paper and you have an instant design. Do not use the first one you make, but try several and choose the one you like best. Fold the paper in different ways to achieve different effects. Designs formed in this way can then be applied to a contrasting color background so that it shows up through the cutouts. For a more advanced piece of work, apply two or more contrasting colors behind the cutouts.

Transfer or trace method

This is suitable for all types of embroidery and the sources of designs are endless. The illustrations to be found in modern children's books, magazines, wallpaper patterns and greeting cards all make interesting designs to be traced and transferred onto fabric.

Exploding a design

This method is again suitable for both embroidery and appliqué and results in asymmetric, abstract designs.
Start with a rectangle of paper—a color page from a glossy magazine is ideal because this will also help with choosing your color scheme. With a ruler and pencil, divide the paper into sections of varying shapes and sizes. Then clearly number each section so that you can keep the shapes in the same order when they are all cut out. Now cut along the drawn lines carefully and arrange the pieces in numerical order on a plain sheet of paper, spreading them out in a slightly haphazard manner until you are pleased with the pattern they form. Stick the shapes down with glue. Trace the design and transfer it to the fabric. This method can be used on folded circular pieces of paper, cutting random shapes right into the folds. These designs usually require the addition of decorative embroidery stitches.

Drawing around a shape

This method can be used where a single motif is required, or to form all-over patterns using one or more motifs. Look around your home for items such as cookie cutters, ornaments with interesting-shaped bases, drinking glasses—in fact anything which has an attractive but simple shape will do. Just draw around the base with a pencil and you have an instant design.

Designing with ready-made motifs

Motifs can be purchased at large stores. Use one on its own or group several to form quick, easy designs. Ribbons and braids are also exciting materials for appliqué designs (see Embroidery Chapter 25) as there are so many different ways you can use them. They can be found in glorious colors and varying widths—just right for creating lively designs either on their own or as part of a larger scheme. Braids are also useful for adding interesting textures to the over-all effect.

Designing symmetrical patterns by cutting out shapes from folded paper

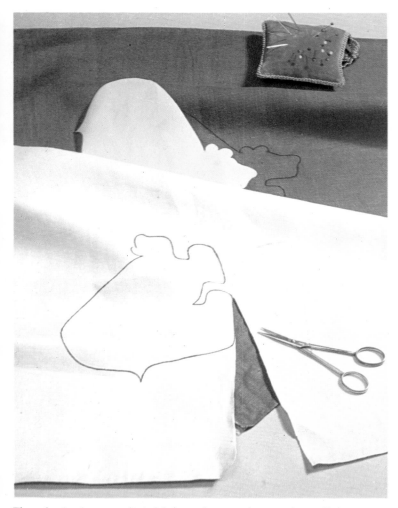

Transfer the shape onto both fabrics and cut out the one to be applied

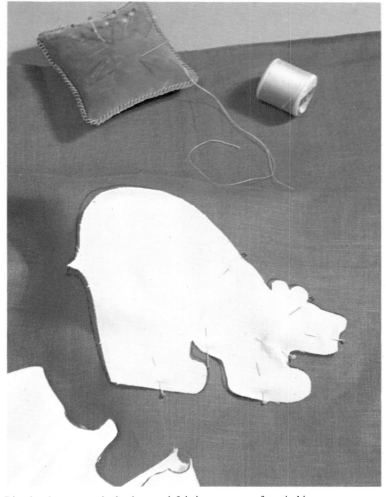

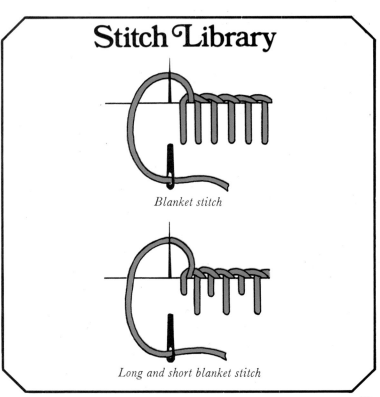

Pin the shape onto the background fabric to prepare for stitching

Appliqué step by step

1. Cut out the shapes used in the design in pieces of colored paper and place them in different positions on the background until you are satisfied with the color scheme and arrangement.
2. Transfer the outline of the design shapes onto the background fabric, using one of the methods described in Embroidery Chapter 4.
3. Transfer the outline of shapes onto the fabric to be applied.
4. Use one of the basic methods of application described in Embroidery Chapter 18.
5. Add further decoration, using hand or machine embroidery.

General hints

Whichever form of embroidery you prefer to use, it is important to be critical of your work, and a good way in which to view this objectively is to hold it in front of a mirror. You will be amazed how different your work looks—in fact it will appear very much as others see it. If the design is tilting to one side, or is too far up or down on the background, the faults will show more clearly in the mirror reflection than when you look directly at it.

Blanket stitch or buttonhole stitch

This stitch, for which instructions are given in Embroidery Chapter 11, is a good, strong stitch for sewing down applied shapes, either in its widely spaced form (blanket stitch) or in its closed-up form (buttonhole stitch). There are several variations, two of which are shown here. See Embroidery Chapter 11 for others.

Stitch Library

Blanket stitch

Long and short blanket stitch

77

COLLECTOR'S PIECE

Checkerboard Panel

This striking hand-embroidered panel is approximately 12in square. It was inspired by the use of two contrasting fabrics—one plain donkey-gray, the other printed. The plain fabric was chosen in a neutral color to intensify the pinks and mauves of the print. The idea was to link up the printed squares with stitchery reflecting the shapes and colors of the print. A first pattern was formed by arranging printed squares on the plain background and a second pattern was made from the background shapes. Solid pink squares were added to complete the scheme. The deliberate placing of the colored stitchery guides the eye easily from one color to another. Part of each line of stitchery was worked into the pattern on some printed squares. Each color has a varying impact since not every square is covered, nor is every color worked with a shiny thread.

Two stitches are used in this embroidery: simple couching to hold the threads on the surface, and outline stitch. The movement made by the tiny couching stitches when the rows are worked close together adds texture without complicating the pattern.

Chapter 20

Gay pillows in appliqué

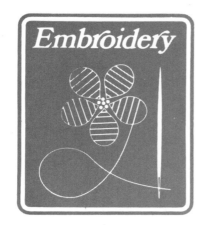

Felt is the easiest material for beginners who are trying appliqué. There is no problem of matching fabric weights and textures or of coping with fraying edges, which involves finishing the shapes before applying them. With felt you simply cut and stitch. It is stocked by most fabric departments and is available in a wide range of colors in 9 inch or 12 inch squares, or by the yard in varying widths. These brilliant pillows show ways of using cut and stitch appliqué.

Felt appliqué pillows

The two pillows shown in the photograph cleverly combine both the cut and stitch and the cutout methods.

Materials you will need:
- [ ] Four pieces of felt 20in by 20in, two in orange and two in yellow
- [ ] One piece of felt 20in by 20in in pink
- [ ] One piece of felt 12in by 12in in lavender
- [ ] Two pieces of paper 20in by 20in for making paper patterns (newspaper will do)
- [ ] Two pillow forms 20in by 20in or kapok for stuffing
  N.B. Felt should be dry-cleaned, but remember that if you use kapok—which is cheaper than pillow forms—the cushions cannot be dry-cleaned unless kapok is removed
- [ ] Two 12in zippers, one orange and one yellow (if you are using pillow forms)
- [ ] Matching sewing threads

How to cut out paper patterns

1. Fold each of the paper squares in half, then into quarters, and then diagonally, making a triangle.

2. On one of the folded triangles, draw cutting lines as indicated in the diagram. Cut evenly along these lines through all layers. Put aside the cutout pieces (4 of each pattern) and pin the large pattern cutout onto one piece of orange felt.

3. On the second folded paper triangle, draw cutting lines as indicated in the diagram. Cut out and keep only the cutout pieces (eight of one pattern and one center pattern), discarding the rest of the paper square.

4. Carefully unfold all paper patterns and label them A to D as shown.

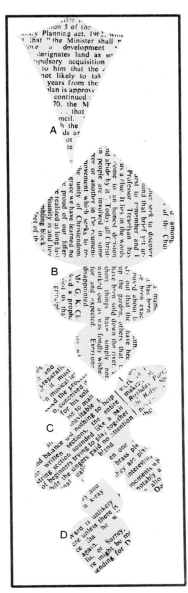

Cutting out the felt

5. Pin patterns to appropriate colors of felt, arranging them very carefully to follow the diagrams. As patterns A (lavender) and B (pink) will be used to fill in the cutouts of the orange pillow, leave $\frac{1}{4}$in seam allowance on these patterns. Cut all other patterns to the exact size.

Baste the pattern onto the felt and remove the pins. Use a small pair of scissors with very sharp points to begin cutting out each shape, then continue with normal cutting shears. If the raw edges are not smooth, trim with the small scissors. When cutting out is completed, you will have four lavender A with $\frac{1}{4}$in seam allowance, four pink B with $\frac{1}{4}$in seam allowance, four orange A, four orange B, one pink C, and eight pink D shapes. The orange felt will also have four A cutouts and four B cutouts.

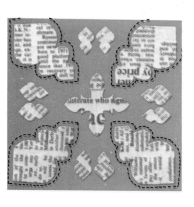

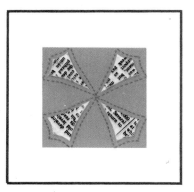

To make the orange pillow

6. Pin and baste four lavender A shapes and four pink B shapes to the wrong side of the orange felt, filling in the eight cutouts. Machine stitch with a straight stitch on the right side of the felt, as close to the raw edge as possible. (If you want a more decorative finish, use a zigzag stitch.) Next, still working on the right side, pin, baste and machine stitch in place

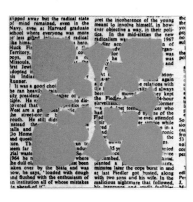

four pink D shapes.
Remove all basting threads.

To make the yellow pillow

7. Crisscross the yellow felt square with basting thread as shown in the diagram, which will enable you to place the shapes correctly. Pin, baste and machine stitch the remaining four orange A shapes and four orange B shapes onto the right side of the yellow felt. Then pin, baste and machine stitch the one pink C and the remaining four pink D shapes into position as shown.
Remove all basting threads.

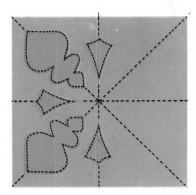

To finish pillows

8. Place plain orange and yellow felt pieces to appliquéd pieces with right sides facing. Baste and machine stitch around the sides with $\frac{1}{2}$in seam allowance, leaving a 12in opening along one side for inserting the zippers. Turn to the right side. Pin and baste, then stitch zippers into place. Insert pillow forms.

If you are stuffing with kapok, fluff it out first, then do not pack tight but fill gently.

On kapok-filled pillow, turn in seam allowance and sew the openings securely by hand.

Collector's Piece

Two details of the Fire of London picture showing some of the stitches and materials used

The Fire of London

This machine-embroidered picture by Joan Gilbert, "Musicians Escaping from the Great Fire of London", is based on a 17th-century engraving of the Great Fire by Visscher.

Joan Gilbert, who has had exhibitions of her embroidery, translated the engraving into appliquéd fabric worked over richly with cotton yarn and occasional gold and silver threads. It took her about a month to work, using an automatic electric sewing machine.

In 1666, as the picture shows, there was an apple orchard at Whitefriars, surrounded by the pleasant buildings of the Carmelite monastery, which were still standing. There was a fine water-gate with steps leading down to the broad highway of the Thames. Flames and smoke fill the background and give urgency to the hurrying figures. The musicians are carrying their lutes, harps and mandolins to safety. There is also a red hurdy-gurdy, a lyre and a baryton (pronounced bar-ee-tong, a member of the viol family,) in the rescue operation.

In the boat, a little figure in pink is gripping two big cheeses under his arms. (Cheeses could be almost as valuable as instruments. Pepys buried two cheeses in the cool river bank to avoid damage by fire.)

One fellow is carrying a bag of fine linen, and a pompous person bears away his casket full of jewels.

The lights of Hampstead can be seen through the flames.

In a sky obscured by smoke, the large gold braid stars stand still above the hullabaloo.

Instruments like those carried by the musicians can still be seen in special collections in some museums. Made of highly polished, often rare, woods, they are inlaid with bone, ivory, silver and gold.

Chapter 21

Picture making in appliqué

The appliqué clown design on pages 86-87 is adapted from an amusing gift tag—proof that design ideas can come from the most unexpected sources! Keep a scrapbook of ideas like this so that you will have a fund of inspiration whenever you need it. The clown incorporates simple surface decoration, which always makes basic appliqué shapes richer and also unites a design. Here are four stitches which are very suitable for appliqué.

Couching

If you use this form of surface decoration, do keep in mind that this stitch will not withstand washing.

Secure the threads to be couched at the back of the work, draw them through to the right side and then catch into place with another thread, using a small stitch.

Finally, take the ends through to the back of the work and secure in place. When couching two or more threads in place, care must be taken to prevent them from twisting.

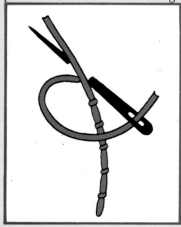

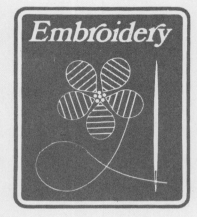

Overcasting

This is another attractive way of drawing or outlining shapes, but it, too, is not washable. First make a line of running

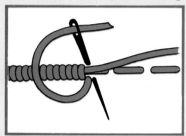

stitches. Draw one end of the cord to the back of the work and secure in place with a few stitches, then lay the cord along the line of the design and attach it by sewing it down with small stitches.

Finish off by taking the end of the cord through to the back of the work and sewing it securely in place. This technique is used alternatively as a padding stitch (see Embroidery Chapter 7).

Pin stitch

Basically this is a drawn fabric stitch, but it makes a strong neat finish when used for outlining appliqué. The diagrams show how the stitch is worked for a hem, but the same method is used for applying curved shapes, when each stitch is pulled firmly to make tiny holes between the stitches. Work this stitch from right to left or from top to bottom.

Bring the needle through the folded edge at A, insert the needle at B, and bring it out at C. Insert the needle again at B, bringing it out at C. Insert the needle once more at B and bring it out through the folded edge at D.

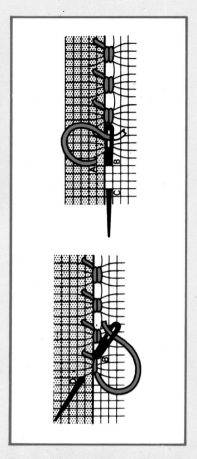

Repeat these steps, pulling all stitches firmly.

Up and down buttonhole stitch

This is an interesting variation of buttonhole stitch. Start as for plain buttonhole stitch and

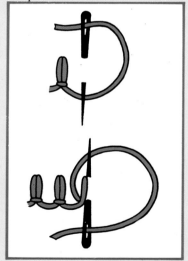

pull the thread through. Insert the needle on the bottom line, taking a straight upward stitch with the thread under the needle. Pull the thread in an upward movement, then downward to continue.

The clown appliqué

To make the clown panel you will need:

- ☐ 9in squares of felt in orange, amber, yellow, lime green, pink, deep pink, royal blue, black and white
- ☐ Medium-weight, firm-weave fabric for background, 29in by 14in
- ☐ Unbleached muslin or linen for backing, 25in by 10in
- ☐ Soft pencil
- ☐ A piece of hardboard or softboard for mounting, 25in by 10in (from most lumber yards)
- ☐ Fine string for lacing
- ☐ Squared paper
- ☐ Tracing paper
- ☐ Yarns: Tapestry yarn — 2 skeins black
  Soft embroidery cotton — 2 skeins black
  Six-strand embroidery floss — 2 skeins black
- ☐ Two needles — chenille No.19 and crewel No.3
- ☐ Transparent thread
- ☐ Sharp scissors

Making the clown appliqué

Copy the pattern for the design onto 1in squared paper from the graph overleaf. Then trace and transfer it onto the background fabric. Trace the various shapes onto the appropriate colored felts and cut them out. (To help you position the pieces of felt correctly, number the background fabric first, then number the back of each piece of felt to correspond.) Lay the shapes in the correct position on the background and baste in place. Stitch around the shapes lightly with small hemming stitches, using the transparent thread.

Now couch in between the applied felt shapes. Use 3 strands of floss in the needle and outline with 3 lengths of soft embroidery cotton (this should be the complete length required to outline the shape). To make sure the threads lie flat, bring each length of soft embroidery cotton separately through the material before you begin. Outline stitch the hair, nose, mouth and hands with soft embroidery cotton. Make pompons for the buttons down the front as follows:

Making the clown's pompon (see below)

First cut two circles of cardboard 1in in diameter, with a $\frac{5}{8}$in center hole. Place these two disks together, thread a bodkin with about 3 yds of black tapestry yarn, take it through the hole and wind it evenly all around the cardboard. Slip one scissors blade between the two disks and cut all around, through the yarn. Wind a double length of yarn between the disks twice and tie securely, leaving about 6in yarn to sew the pompon in place.

Now tear the cardboard disks and slip them off. Fluff up the pompon and trim into shape with sharp scissors. Make four more pompons in the same way. Stitch pompons in place.

Mounting the finished work

Mount the completed panel on a piece of hardboard or softboard cut exactly to the required finished size of the panel. Lay the piece of board centrally over the back of the work and with fine string (or very strong thread), lace the fabric (not too near the edge) at the back from side to side and then from top to bottom. Pull the lacing firmly until the work is evenly stretched without being puckered. Secure

the ends of the lacing thread by knotting several times.

Then finish the back of the work by stitching the un-bleached muslin or linen over it to conceal the lacing. Simply take the piece of backing fabric, turn under edges $\frac{1}{2}$in all around, baste, then slip stitch firmly in place to cover the lacing. Remove basting threads.

This method of mounting is suitable for most forms of embroidery, and you can then frame the embroidery if you wish. Or you can sew two plastic curtain rings to the back of the work on each side and not quite halfway down to hold a cord for hanging the panel on the wall.

Making the clown's pompon

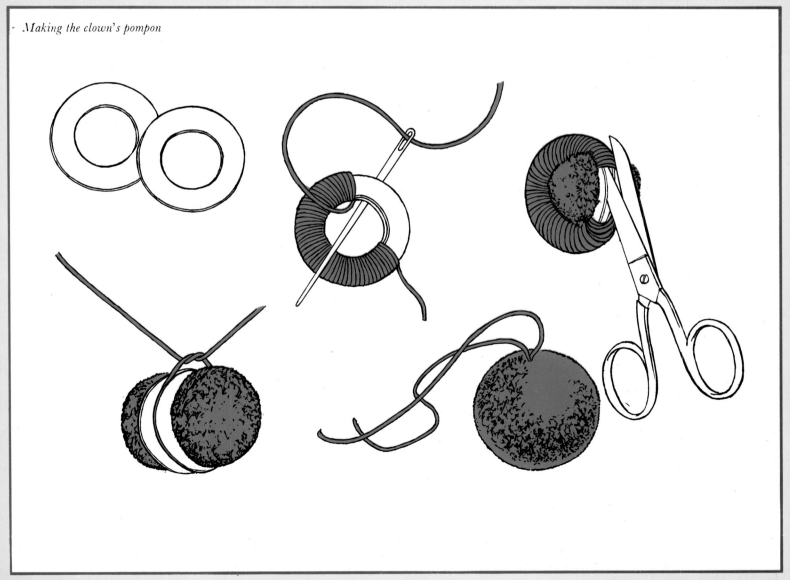

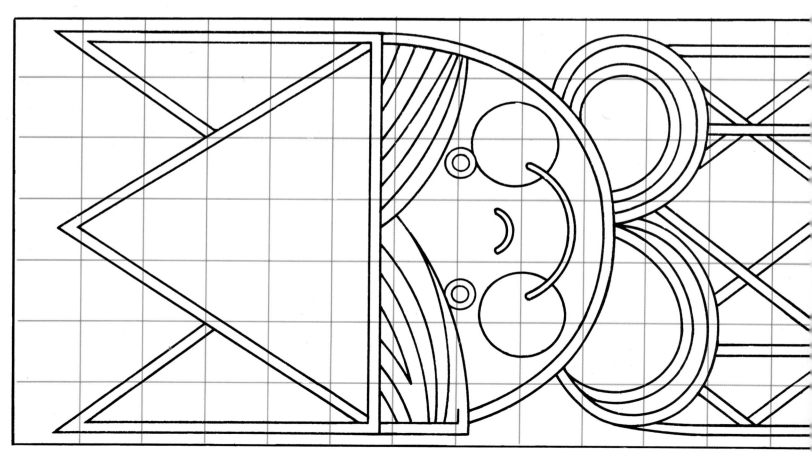

Appliqué clown panel

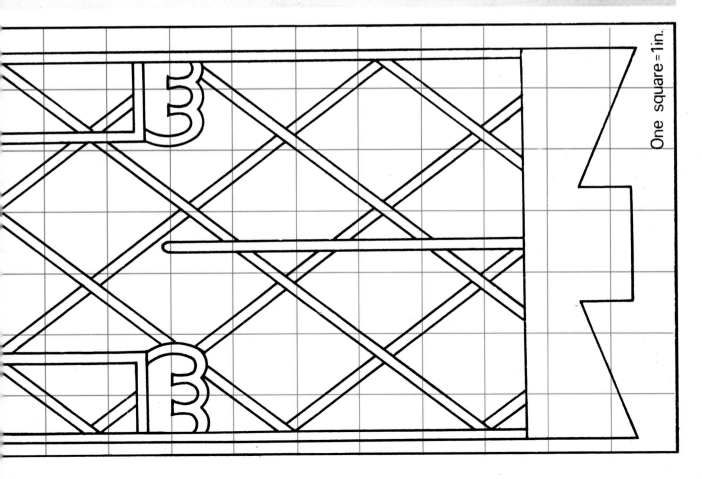

Graph pattern for appliqué clown

One square = 1 in.

Collector's Piece

Autumn flowers

This wall panel appears, at first sight,
to break the basic rules of good design.
The three dominating flowers are
equidistantly placed immediately above
one another.

The designer has, however, used various
techniques, together with a limited
color range, to make this an unusually
effective and interesting piece of
embroidery. Most of the panel has been
worked by hand but some machine
embroidery has been included.

The background is a natural beige-
colored wool which makes an interesting
contrast to the shiny, silky looking fabrics
applied to it. The shapes of the leaves
throughout the design are flowing and
have tremendous movement. This effect
is helped by the choice of embroidery
stitches. The heavier, dark leaves are
worked in twisted chain stitch and the
paler leaves, which have a softer look,
are worked in Cretan stitch over applied
pieces of net. Other leaf shapes are made
up of pieces of padded gold kid, but the
stitching has been done inside the shape
leaving the pointed ends free from the
background. This unusual technique
results in the pieces catching the light in
a more interesting manner than they
would stitched in the conventional way.
Each of the flowers is made up of layers
of applied net with blocks of Cretan stitch
on the larger petals and sorbello stitch,
twisted chain stitch and knotted chain
stitch around the beaded centers.

Groups of French knots and bullion knots
in toning colors have been used to fill
the spaces between the flowers and leaves,
adding texture to the design. The glass
beads added to the leaf shapes and
enriching the flower centers have been
placed with restraint and sensitivity.

Chapter 22

Lion panel in appliqué

Appliqué this corduroy lion onto a panel.

Materials

To make a picture 12 inches wide by 10 inches deep, you will need:

- [ ] Scraps of russet-colored corduroy
- [ ] Scraps of pink and green felt
- [ ] Purple felt, 14 inches wide by 12 inches deep

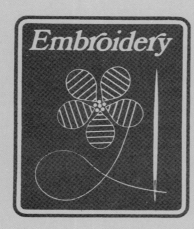

- [ ] Sewing thread to match corduroy
- [ ] Wool yarn, black and russet
- [ ] 6-strand embroidery floss, yellow, black, green and russet
- [ ] Piece of hardboard, 12 inches by 10 inches
- [ ] White glue

Preparing for appliqué

There are eleven pattern pieces in the lion's body: the main body, back leg and tail, two front paws, one back paw, chin, two cheeks, the nose and two ears. Each piece is marked with the grain line and numbered according to the order in which the pieces are to be stitched into position.

Trace each outline separately onto paper, mark the grain lines, and cut out.

Pin each piece of the pattern on the corduroy, matching the grain line to the ridges of the fabric. Cut out each shape, leaving $\frac{1}{4}$-inch turnings all around. Fold the turnings to the back of the fabric and baste, except those edges which are marked on the diagram with a red line. These seam allowances are left flat, the next section being placed on top.

Place the pieces on the purple felt background in the order indicated by the numbers on each piece in the diagram—

the main body piece, for instance, is marked number one and so are the ears and nose. Baste and sew each piece into position separately, using backstitch or slip stitch. Work the tail and the mane in long straight stitches using russet yarn and then finish the end of the tail and the edge of the mane with long stitches, using matching floss.

Embroider the eyes, the nose, jawline and claws in satin stitch using black and yellow yarn. French knots are used for the whiskers and backstitch for the outline of the tail, worked in black floss. Embroider the stems of the plants in green, using outline stitch or chain stitch. Cut out the pink flowers and green leaves from felt and fix them to the background, using just a touch of glue.

When the lion is completed, mount the picture on hardboard and then frame.

▼ A clever use of corduroy to achieve a three-dimensional effect

Diagram of pattern showing eleven pieces marked with grain of fabric ▶

PLACE ON STRAIGHT GRAIN OF FABRIC

91

Collector's Piece

Flowers in fabric

The designer of these appliqué and embroidery pictures has used the colors, textures and surface patterns of fabrics as a graphic artist uses pigments and brush strokes to achieve an effect. The poppy picture, for instance, uses for the background a gold colored stripe weaved curtain fabric which produces an effect of wheat stalks in sunshine. In each of the designs, the petal edges and the leaf edges have been left free of the background fabric to give a more life-like impression, and this technique is very noticeable in the poppy design. The Christmas roses are worked on a background of Moygashel dress fabric with the flower petals made of white satin, white velvet and pink grosgrain. The petals are applied to the background with long basting stitches, reproducing the natural crumpled look of the rose petals themselves. The rose centers are padded and decorated with seed pearls and French knots worked in plastic raffia and silk.

▼ *Christmas roses using satin, velvet and grosgrain for the petals*　　　　　*Brilliant poppy heads against an effect of sunlit wheat stalks* ►

Chapter 23

Children's panel in appliqué

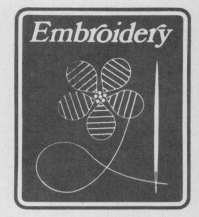

Hans Christian Andersen couldn't have dreamed up a more charming fairy-tale prince and princess than these embroidered appliqué panels. In addition to being attractive to look at when completed, they are also a delightful and satisfying project to work.

The panels illustrated each measure 17 inches by 12 inches.

You will need
For both panels
☐ ½yd cream even-weave linen for background
☐ Scraps of pink felt for faces
☐ 1 card Penelope gold lurex thread
☐ Dressmakers' carbon paper
☐ Tracing paper
☐ White glue (optional)
☐ Crewel needle size 7 or 8
☐ Hardboard 17in by 12in
For princess panel
☐ 11in by 11in blue material or felt for dress
☐ 5in by 8½in navy material for hem border
☐ 40 white sequins
☐ 40 small pearls
☐ 1 skein 6-strand floss in each of light blue, dark blue, white, deep beige, brown, red, turquoise, pink
For prince panel
☐ 10in by 12in blue material or felt for cloak
☐ 3 blue sequins
☐ 3 small pearls
☐ 1 skein 6-strand floss in each of white, light blue, brown, red, black, turquoise

To work the panels
Trace the actual size outlines given on pages 98-101. Copy the details of the figures from pages 96 and 97 (the stitch guide can also be found on these pages).

Using dressmakers' carbon, transfer the outline of the figure only onto the background. Trace the outlines and embroidery details onto the pieces of fabric to be applied.

Embroider the pieces before the shapes are cut out and stitched to the background. Follow the stitch guide and apply the face first, then the dress or cloak. The navy border is applied over the dress section. Felt can be stuck down or stitched, fabric should be applied with small slip stitches. When all the embroidery and appliqué is completed, work running stitches in gold lurex thread on the background, following the fabric grain.

Special techniques
Princess panel. Use three strands of floss for all the embroidery except the bullion knots on the headdress, which are made using one strand of floss twisted three times around the needle. The couching is worked with six strands couched down with two strands. The sequins are stitched and held in place with a small pearl, worked after pressing and before mounting.

Prince panel. The French knots decorating the cloak are worked with two strands of floss, and the rest of the embroidery is worked in three strands. The double rows of couching down the front edges of the cloak and all sequins are worked in the same way as for the princess panel.

94

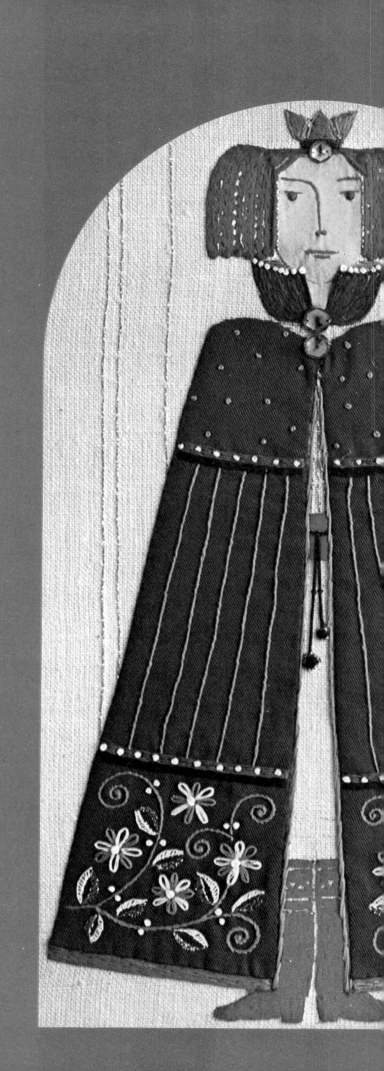

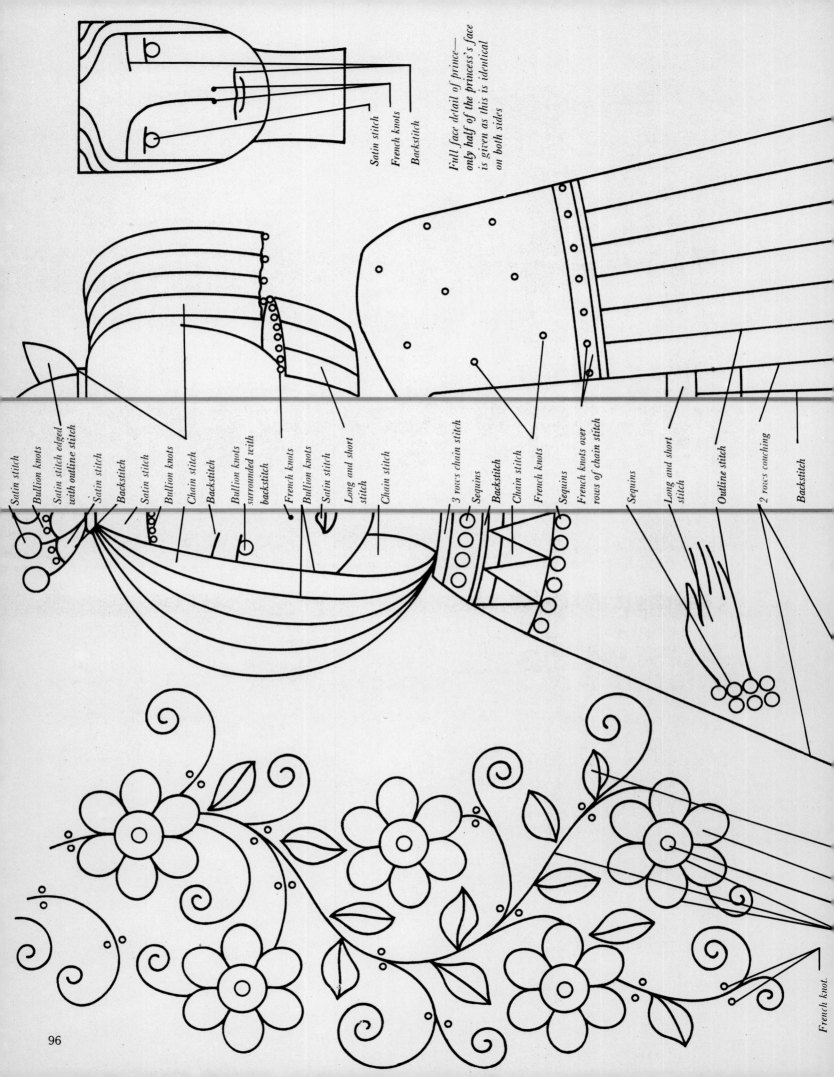

Satin stitch

French knots

Backstitch

Full face detail of prince—only half of the princess's face is given as this is identical on both sides

Satin stitch

Bullion knots

Satin stitch edged with outline stitch

Satin stitch

Backstitch

Satin stitch

Bullion knots

Chain stitch

Backstitch

Bullion knots surrounded with backstitch

French knots

Bullion knots

Satin stitch

Long and short stitch

Chain stitch

3 rows chain stitch

Sequins

Backstitch

Chain stitch

French knots

Sequins

French knots over rows of chain stitch

Sequins

Long and short stitch

Outline stitch

2 rows couching

Backstitch

French knot.

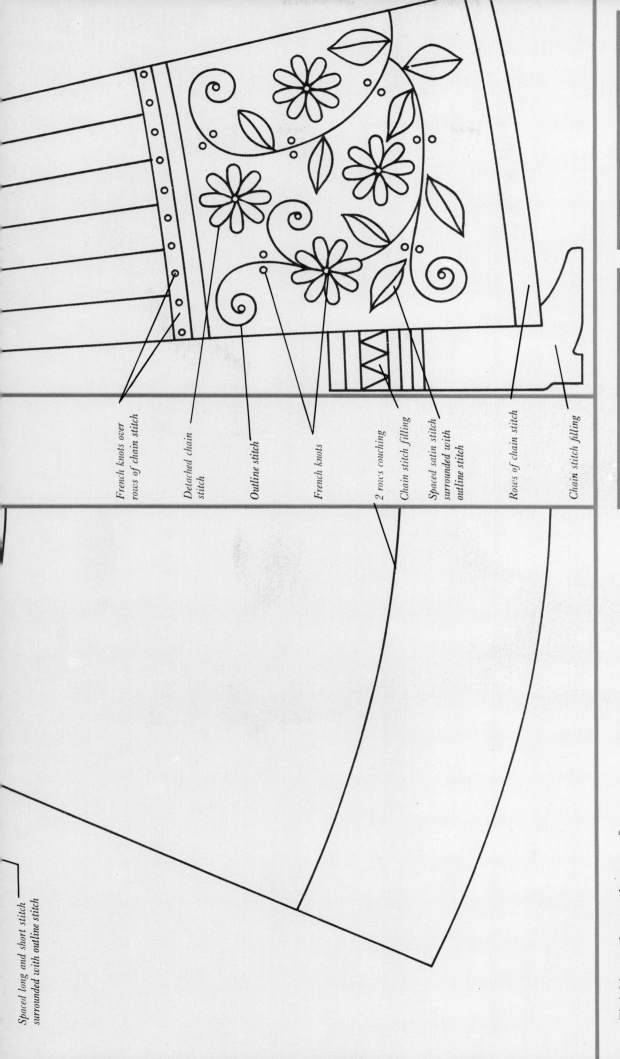

*Spaced long and short stitch
surrounded with outline stitch*

*French knots over
rows of chain stitch*

*Detached chain
stitch*

Outline stitch

French knots

2 rows couching

Chain stitch filling

*Spaced satin stitch
surrounded with
outline stitch*

Rows of chain stitch

Chain stitch filling

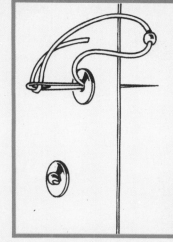

Stitching down a sequin with a bead

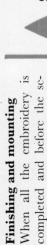

Work left hand the same as right

▲ **Stitch guide**

Finishing and mounting

When all the embroidery is completed and before the sequins are attached, press the work lightly on the wrong side over a well padded surface using a medium hot iron over a damp cloth. Attach sequins and mount the panels over hardboard (see Embroidery Chapter 21).

Tracing outline of prince

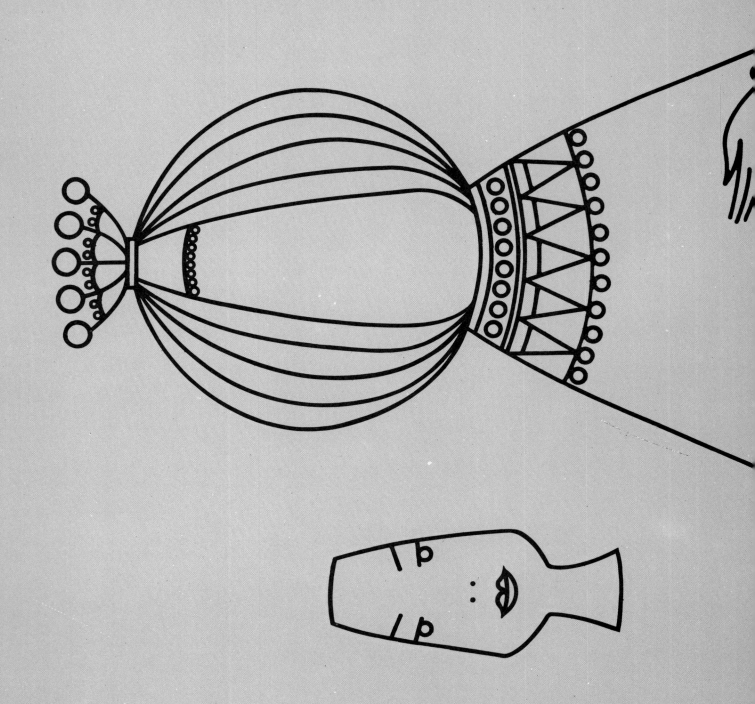

Tracing outline of princess

Chapter 24

San Blas appliqué

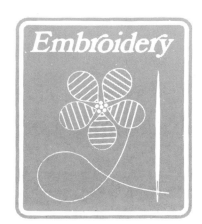

San Blas appliqué

Bold, brilliant colors are used in this unique method of appliqué, worked by the Indian women of the San Blas Islands off the coast of Panama. The appliqué designs are now worked in two pieces measuring about 14 inches by 20 inches and are made into blouses called molas.

When the Indians first moved to the islands in about 1850, the molas were simple affairs, made only of dark blue material with a single band of red cloth around the bottom. The designs developed to decorate the lower half of the mola and then developed further to form a major part of the blouse. Later, when traders brought fabrics of brighter colors to the islands, the designs became more elaborate, involving up to five or six layers of fabric in as many colors.

Mola designs

The designs themselves are primitive and gay, representing forms and figures from everyday life on the islands. Gods, goddesses, shapes from nature such as animals and plants and important people are all featured in bold, primitive stylized shapes. Often the designs are copied from pictures in magazines, comic books, calendars and even labels on canned foods. The designs often include English words or letters which are not understood by the Spanish speaking Indians and used with complete disregard of their meaning, but which look decorative and important. The stylized designs of the molas reflect the style of the wooden figures called "nuchus", carved by the Sans Blas men. The layers of fabric are first basted together and then cut away, and the result very much resembles the enamel work of some Mexicans, where layers of color are applied (painted) then incised to reveal color on color.

The molas are an important status symbol amongst the Indians and in some places it is considered improper for a San Blas Indian girl to be married without possessing at least twelve or more unworn molas as part of her dowry.

Fabrics

For the traditional style San Blas appliqué, plain dyed fabrics such as poplin or

▲ *San Blas appliqué worked on the hem of a simple wrapover evening skirt*

sail cloth are ideal. However, pure silks or shantung would lend themselves beautifully to the technique. For the more ambitious, experiments with textured fabrics such as corduroy or tweed could prove interesting. Felt, suede or leather could also be used but no turnings would be needed.

Uses

This appliqué technique is ideal for fashion where rich, bold effects are required. It would look good worked as a border on a skirt, on an evening cape, on inset panels or on a yoke on a dress or a blouse.

Mola work on curtains would look dramatic, and pillow covers, bedspreads, pictures and wall hangings are all suitable subjects.

Method

This appliqué technique is more a method of cutting away than applying pieces of fabric. Parts of the top layers of fabric are cut away to reveal a section of the color below. One, two or three layers of fabric may have to be cut through at the same time to get to the desired color for a particular part of the design. However, if the colors are arranged well, it should not be necessary to have to cut through more than one layer of fabric at a time. Pieces of different colors can be placed under only certain parts of the design.

Experiment with two or three layers of fabric to start with, introducing extra color by applying small areas of fabric

to highlight the design.

Place the fabrics in the desired arrangement of colors then baste the layers of fabric together all around the edge and also diagonally across each way to hold them securely.

To reveal the first color under the top layer, use a pair of sharp embroidery scissors and cut away a portion of the top fabric in the desired shape. Clip the edges of the fabric to be turned under on all curves and into all corners and turn in ⅛ inch. Using a matching color sewing thread, slip stitch the edge to the layer of fabric below. Small appliqués of another color can be added in one, two or more layers using the same technique of cutting out to reveal the color below.

Collector's Piece

Embroidery for a dream

Romantic in concept and evocative of another age, the embroidered clothes illustrated on these pages were designed and made by Angela Salmon, a dress design student at London's St Martin's School of Art, for her final diploma exhibition. Although painstaking embroidery is not commercially viable in the ready-made clothing industry, it is comforting to know that students of design continue to produce exquisite work such as this, adapting traditional techniques to modern design concepts.

The lilac silk and black velvet dress, worn with pantaloons, has flowers and leaves of machine-embroidered organza applied to the bodice with realistic-looking plastic blackberries to complete the motif. The caped coat-dress, made of olive-colored chiffon, is worn over a strawberry printed chiffon dress. Strawberry flowers, leaves and fruit motifs, made of matte satin and machine-embroidered organza, are applied with some of the edges lying free of the background fabric.

The blue and white ensemble consists of a blue organza apron worn over a full-sleeved chiffon dress. The designer has chosen field flowers for her inspiration—poppies, buttercups, speedwell and wheat stalks—embroidered and applied to the background fabric. Surface embroidery has been added to enrich the design.

▼ *HRH Princess Anne, photographed for her 21st birthday in a dress made of a fabric pattern designed by Susan Grist of St Martin's School*

Chapter 25

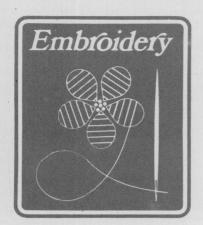

Embroidery with braid and ribbon

Braid embroidery is a simple form of appliqué. Dimension and texture are added by using ribbons, beads and sequins.

When braid embroidery is combined with other forms of appliqué and embroidery, the possible effects are many and varied. The richly raised finish is ideal for clothes, table linen and wall panels. When working braid embroidery on table linen, remember to position the design so that unworked areas are left for plates and glasses when the table is set.

Materials and yarns

This type of embroidery is worked with a narrow braid of wool, cotton or synthetic yarn. The width of braid you choose will depend on the final effect desired and can measure from $\frac{1}{4}$ inch to 2 inches.

The textures can be varied by the introduction of leather, suede, felt, plastic, cord, metallic yarn, beads or sequins, intermingling these with the braid. Ribbon creates a pretty effect, whether you use nylon, satin or velvet, and if you are very enthusiastic, you may want to make your own braids in crochet, knitting or macramé. If the braid is held down with a decorative stitch, the decoration is sewed in place with sewing thread, invisible thread or embroidery thread. Additional embroidery stitches are then used to add detail.

The background fabric should be a firmly woven material such as velvet, upholstery fabric or a strong linen.

Designs for braid embroidery

Designs should be basically simple. The technique lends itself well to modern geometric and abstract designs formed by straight lines or free flowing curves. Detail can be added in the form of embroidery stitches or beading.

Method of working

Trace the design onto the right side of the background fabric (see Embroidery Chapter 4). Sew the outline braid around the design (see diagram), using a simple running stitch or small backstitch about an $\frac{1}{8}$ inch long and worked at $\frac{3}{8}$ inch intervals along the center of the braid. Machine stitching can be used provided that the braid is first basted firmly in place.

When working around corners, ease the braid so that the inside edge is slightly fuller than the outside one. The curves are then pressed into shape to lie smooth and flat.

Effects with braid

Braid flowers are made by looping the braid into the shape of individual petals (see illustration). Secure the end of each loop with several stitches.

The centers of these looped flowers are decorated with embroidery stitches.

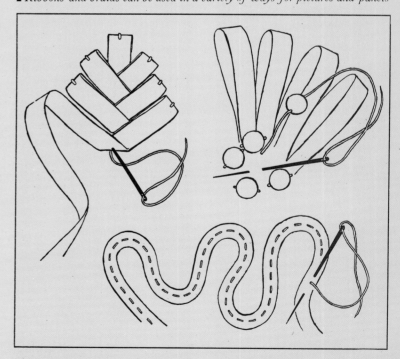

▲ *Ribbons and braids can be used in a variety of ways for pictures and panels*

▲ *Sewing the braid, and detail showing how stalk of wheat is worked*

Stalks of wheat are quick to make. Mark a center line on the background and work a line of double loops going to right and left of this center line, sewing the loops down at the center as you work. A single line of outline stitch forms the beard and smaller ones are made between the ends of the loops.

Complete the design by couching lengths of cord, or work embroidery stitches for stems and leaves.

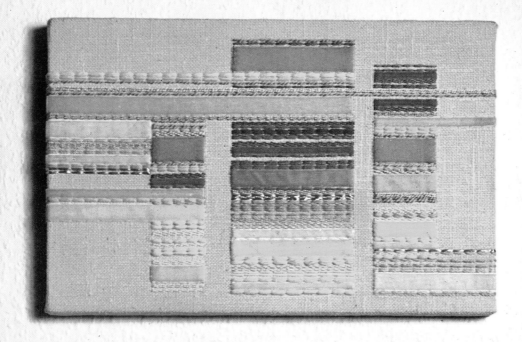

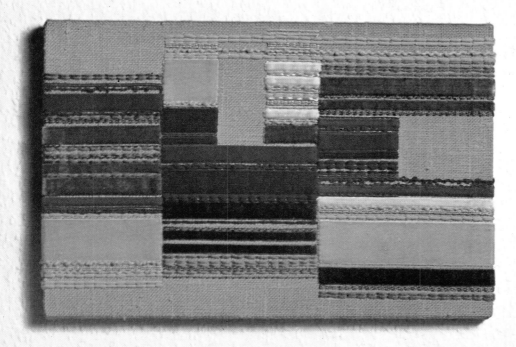

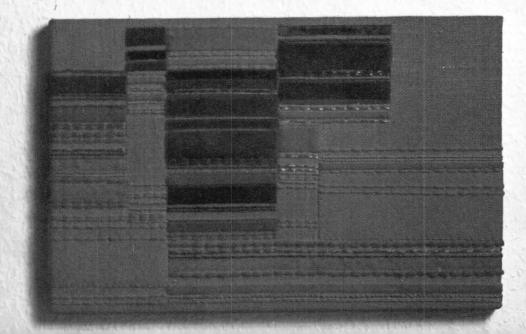

Seasons in color

These three panels show an interesting modern interpretation of braid embroidery using a variety of widths of velvet ribbon mounted on heavy dress linen. They form part of a set of four, each measuring 10 inches by 15 inches. The panels depict the four seasons and the three pictured here are (from top to bottom) spring, summer and autumn. The background color in each panel relates in general terms to the season.

Yellow stands for spring with the joyous colors of crocuses, daffodils, jasmine, pink hyacinths and tulips, all blending with the more subtle shades of lilac.

Green represents summer with its green grass, trees and red flowers, bright and clear as on a midsummer's day.

Pink brings to mind autumn sunsets and complements the richness of the browns which suggest dying leaves and dark wet roofs.

However, only the color categories were suggested by each season. The individual shades were dictated by working them together as a scheme within each panel and it is the use of some form of pink in each panel which unites them.

The main object of the panels is to create an experiment in color, and the design, materials and stitchery are simple to avoid detracting from this. While the various aspects of the seasons influence the colors, it is the rectangular outlines of modern architecture which inspire the symmetry of the design.

Only two stitches are used—couching and outline stitch. Plastic raffia, pearl cotton, knitting wool and 6-strand embroidery floss are couched in their own color of mercerized sewing thread so that only indentations are seen.

The couching stitches are placed exactly in line with one another throughout the rows to follow through the idea of stark simplicity. All the ends of the couched threads are taken to the back of the work.

107

Collector's Piece

Yugoslavian vests

These two gaily colored vests were made in Yugoslavia early this century. The braid is couched onto the material in simplified, traditional designs, reminiscent of Yugoslavian folk costume. One piece of braid is used for an entire design. It is simply curled or laid into positions to create shapes and patterns.

The vests would be worn by men, probably on holidays or any other festive occasion.

Embroiderers' Guild, London.

Chapter 26

Introduction to smocking

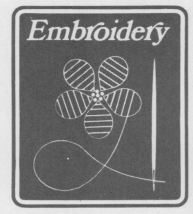

Smocks were originally worn as cover-ups by manual laborers. The smocking was not only decorative but served the practical purpose of holding the fabric together in tight, tiny pleats. Smocking is now used on garments wherever fullness needs to be controlled and for purely decorative effects. The basis of smocking is the gathering which forms the pleats. Once this is completed, there is a variety of decorative stitches which can be applied.

Fabrics

Smooth and even-textured fabrics are best for smocking: cotton, silk, cotton and wool mixtures or fine woolens. Very fine fabrics, such as voile and lawn, are exquisite when they are smocked but need a little more practice. Thick materials are not suitable for smocking.

Yarns

Soft embroidery cotton or pearl cotton are ideal yarns for smocking embroidery. Six-strand floss is not strong enough and is inclined to twist.

Smocking transfers

It is essential to keep smocking pleats even and regular, and transfers for planning the gathering dots are invaluable. Several different gauges are available: Dots close together give small pleats and are suitable for baby clothes and fine fabrics, while widely spaced dots which give a deep pleat are better for heavier materials. Transfers with dots about $\frac{1}{4}$ to $\frac{3}{8}$ inch apart are suitable for most fabrics.

How much material?

As a rough guide, fabric before smocking should measure about three times the required finished length, but it depends on the space between the dots, the firmness of the particular stitches used, and the tension of the work which varies from person to person. In dressmaking, it is important to remember that smocking should be completed before the garment is sewed together. It is not possible to smock ready-made clothes.

Smocking on a garment is easy to do once you have learned the basic principles of gathering and the basic stitches. Try a simple frill to begin with.

Ruffles and frills

Narrow, delicate frills look charming down the front of a shirt or blouse or around a cuff or neck edge. Quick and simple to do, frills are ideal for beginners. The frill illustrated is 2 inches wide with $1\frac{1}{2}$ rows of diamond stitch outlined with cable stitch. The edging can be buttonhole stitched or embroidered on a zigzag sewing machine.

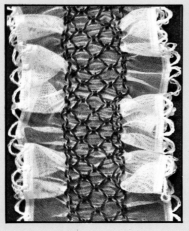

Smocking step-by-step

Cut the transfer to the length and depth required and iron it onto the wrong side of the material. Beginning at the first right-hand dot, on wrong side of the fabric, secure the thread firmly with a good

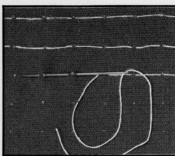

knot and a backstitch. Work from right to left and carefully pick up each dot along the line, leaving a few inches of the thread hanging loose at the end of the row.

Repeat until all the rows are completed. Pull all the threads together, not too tightly. (If you smock tightly, slacken the gathers; if loosely, pull them a

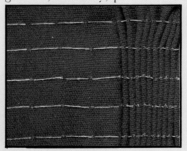

little tighter.) Knot the ends together in pairs, sliding the knot along the thread on a pin, and cut the threads to within two inches of the knots. Leave the gathering threads in place and remove them when smocking is completed. Use gathering lines as a guide to keep smocking stitches straight.

Smocking on patterns

Spotted, striped or checked fabrics with a regular pattern will not necessarily need gathering transfers, but it is important to decide which area of the pattern is required on the surface of the finished smocking.

Smocking on stripes

Make rows of guide dots on the wrong side of the fabric with a pencil. The dot should come in the middle of a light stripe if smocking is to appear on a dark area, and in the middle of a dark stripe if a light background to smocking is preferred.

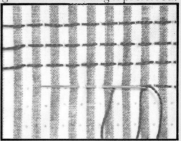

Smocking on spots

Gather each spot as if a transfer were being used. On the second and subsequent rows, use spots directly under those in the first row or pick up a stitch immediately under a spot.

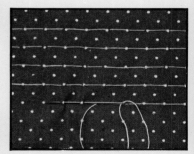

Smocking on checks

If you choose a dark background for your smocking, pick up the center threads of the palest squares; for a light background, pick up the center threads of the darkest squares.

Simple stitches

Diamond stitch

Diamond stitch is one of the larger smocking stitches, and care should be taken not to make it too large or the finished smocking will lack firmness. The stitch is worked from left to right in two stages and each stage is worked between two rows of gathering threads; (if the rows of gathering threads are $\frac{1}{4}$ inch apart, the finished depth of the entire stitch will be $\frac{1}{2}$ inch).

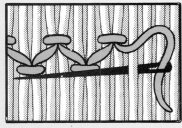

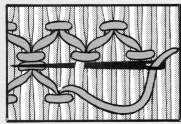

Cable stitch

Cable stitch is a firm control stitch and two rows worked closely together at the top and bottom of a band of smocking prevent the piece from fanning or spreading out too much. Cable stitch can be used as a single line, or in several rows, worked closely together between rows of freer stitches, to add strength to a design.

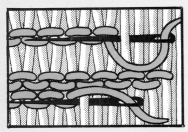

Smocking on fashion garments usually takes the form of reducing fullness across the bodice, down the sleeves or across waistlines and wide-skirted hems.
Effective, yet simple to do, smocked panels are worked on the same body fabric separately and then inserted into the garment ▶

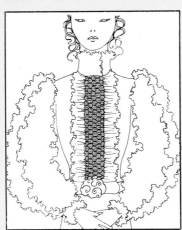

Collector's Piece

Traditional smocks

This smock was made in rural England in 1820. It might well have been stitched by a peasant's wife and worn either for working in the weekday or set aside "for best" on Sunday. All the smocks at this time were made of heavy, thick materials including cottons, linens and twills. The stitches used included feather stitch, chain stitch, faggot stitch and outline stitch.

Some smocks were worked in different designs showing the wearer's profession. For instance, trees and leaves stitched into the garment indicated that the peasant was a woodman. Crooks, sheep pens and hurdles meant that the peasant was a shepherd and so on. It is also possible to tell from the designs where the peasant came from, each county having its own particular pattern.

Colors, too, are associated with certain counties, although the most common colors were white, cream and brown. Green and black existed but few of these survive today.

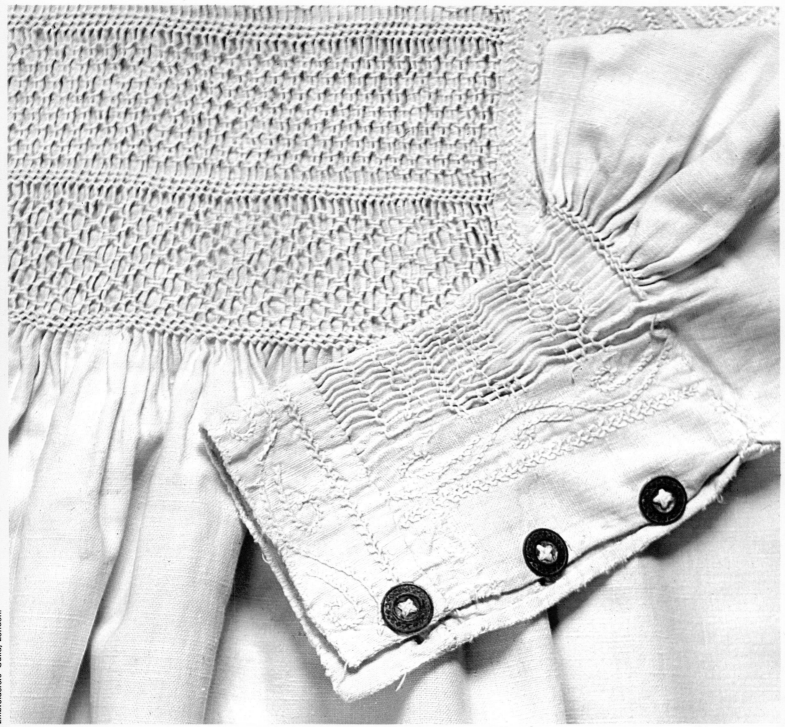

Chapter 27

Smocking an angel top

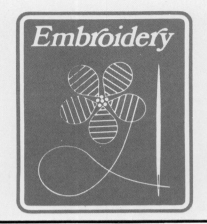

Embroidery

Children of all ages look delightful in smocked clothes —babies in angel tops, nine year-olds in frilled blouses and gadabout growing girls in smocked party dresses. This chapter gives instructions for making a smocked angel top from a graph pattern, to fit babies from birth to six months old. The neckline and cuffs are smocked with two of the three stitches illustrated, trellis stitch and outline stitch (in groups). Smocking stitches vary in their degree of fabric control: some have tight control, others have medium or loose control. It is important when planning smocking to note the control of the stitches selected. This angel top, for instance, uses a loose control stitch—trellis stitch—on the bottom edge of the smocking, so that the material flares.

Outline stitch. Similar to ordinary outline stitch (see diagram), each stitch picks up one tube of the fabric. A firm control stitch, two rows worked closely together at the top or base of smocking will hold gathers firmly in place. It is not advisable to use this stitch at the base of smocking where a loose flare is required (such as an angel top).

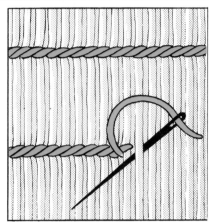

Honeycomb stitch. This is a medium control stitch and is worked from left to right. Bring the needle up at the top of the first tube and make a backstitch picking up the next tube on the right. Take a second backstitch, slipping the needle down through the tube and bring it to the right side ready to make the next double backstitch.

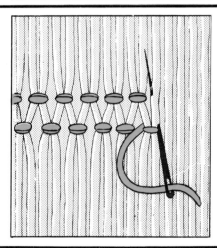

Trellis stitch. Worked in zigzag lines, this stitch is shown on the illustrated angel top and is on the cuffs. It is a loose control stitch and could be used for the last row of smocking where a flare is required.

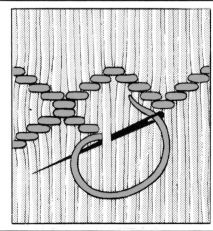

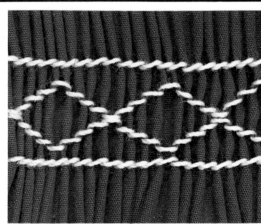

Making a smocked angel top

You will need

- 2½yds of washable fabric such as Dacron and cotton, cotton, or wool and cotton mixtures.
- Length of gathering dots transfer
- Pearl cotton embroidery thread

Preparing for smocking

Make a paper pattern from the angel top graph and pin this to the fabric. Cut out the pieces and iron the required length and depth of gathering dots transfer to the wrong side of the fabric. Gather on the **wrong side** (see Embroidery Chapter 26) and complete the smocking on each part of the angel top before sewing the garment together.

Making the top

Join sleeves to dress, trimming seams to ¼ inch depth. Overcast or bind the seams with bias binding or binding bias cut from the same fabric. Cut a neckband and two cuffs on the cross of the fabric to fit the child's neck and wrists. The neckband and cuffs should always be attached to the garment with hand sewing because if machine stitching is used, the pleats or "tubes" of smocked fabric would be pushed flat.

Make two rows of gathering ¼ inch above the top line of smocking stitches. The rows of gathering stitches should be placed exactly in line, one stitch above the other, and evenly through each "tube" of fabric. Draw up the gathering to fit the length of the neckband. Turn under the seam allowance of the neckband along one edge and baste. Place the wrong side of the basted edge ¼ inch above the top line of smocking on the right side of the angel top. Pin and baste. With the right side of the work facing, slip stitch each tube to the neckband evenly. Turn the work to the wrong side. Turn under the seam allowance on the other side of the neckband

and baste to the inside neckline ¼ inch above the top row of smocking. Hem to the backs of the tubes, using small neat stitches. Make sure that the stitches do not show through to the right side of the tubes. Stitch the sleeve and side seams carefully.

Adapting a yoked pattern for smocking

To adapt a nightie or dress pattern so that smocking can be included, choose a pattern with a straight or slightly curved yoke and cut the front three times the width of the actual pattern piece. Attach the yoke to the smocked areas as instructed for applying the crossway edgings to the top.

Angel top with a front fastening

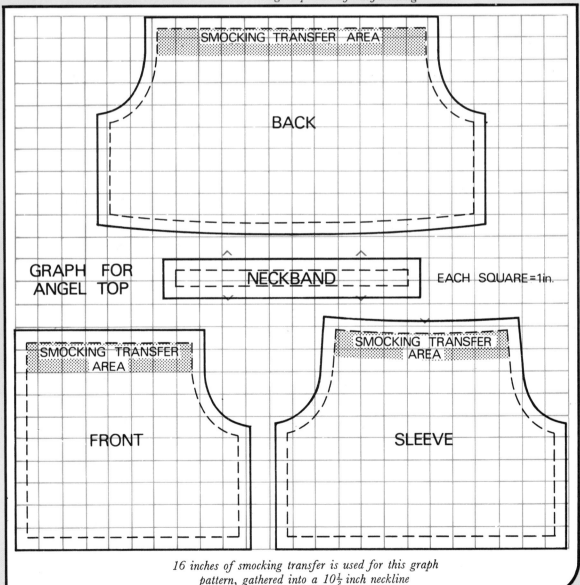

GRAPH FOR ANGEL TOP

SMOCKING TRANSFER AREA

BACK

NECKBAND

EACH SQUARE=1in.

SMOCKING TRANSFER AREA

FRONT

SMOCKING TRANSFER AREA

SLEEVE

16 inches of smocking transfer is used for this graph pattern, gathered into a 10½ inch neckline

Chapter 28

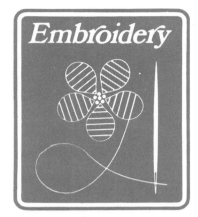

Smocking in fashion

Frills make a charming and feminine decoration for most clothes—smocked frills are even prettier. What was once a decoration solely for children's clothes has now become a fashion note for adults, lifting dresses and blouses to a new elegance. Add smocking at necklines, cuffs or in panels down the front of classically styled garments, working and insetting the panels before sewing the garment together.

Decorative smocking stitches

Surface honeycomb stitch
This is worked in the same way as honeycomb stitch (see Embroidery Chapter 27) except that the thread lies on the right side of the work all the time instead of being taken through to the back. It is worked from left to right as shown.

Double feather stitch
This is a fairly tight stitch which is worked like ordinary feather stitch, picking up two tubes of the fabric for each stitch and working from right to left. This stitch needs a little practice to achieve the even effect required for smocking.

Vandyke stitch
This is a small, tight stitch worked from right to left. Bring the needle through from the back of the work at the second tube from the right. Then work a backstitch over the first two tubes. Go down to the second row, take the needle through the second and third tubes and work a backstitch over them. Go back up to the first row and work as before with the third and fourth tubes. Continue in this way across the width of the work.

The next row is worked similarly, starting on the third row and working up to the second row. Simply thread the needle behind the previously worked backstitches of the second row, as shown. Continue working in the same manner.

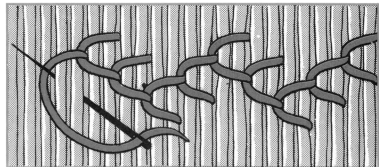

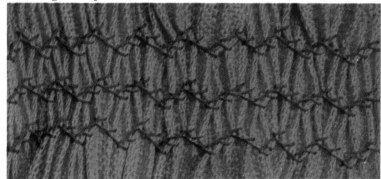

▲ *Working double feather stitch*　▼ *Three completed rows*

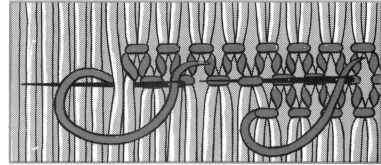

▲ *Working Vandyke stitch*　▼ *Four completed rows*

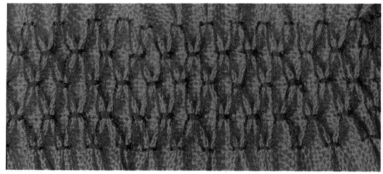

▼ *Surface honeycomb stitch*

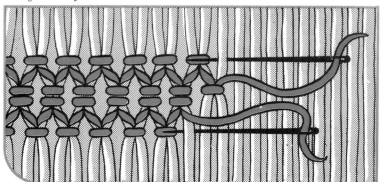

▼ *Crossed diamond stitch*

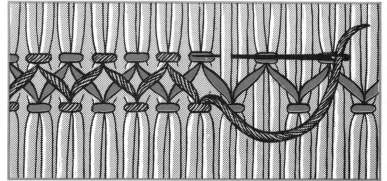

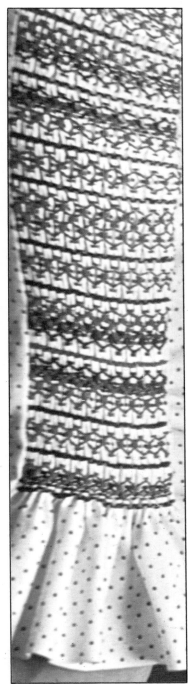

▲ *Detail of inset sleeve panel*

▲ *Inset smocked panels on the sleeves and a smocked neckline make a simple dress pretty*

Putting smocking to work

Smocking stitches are never really complicated and once you have mastered the basic ones it is simply a matter of combining several stitches as in this spotted dress. It may look like an ambitious project but you will be amazed at how easy it is once you break down the pattern to individual stitches.

This simple dress has been given a touch of glamour by inserting a panel of smocking into the sleeves and adding a smocked collar. You can decorate a handmade dress by inserting a smocked panel, remembering to cut the fabric three times the actual width of the finished panel, plus seam allowances. Once the smocking is completed, stitch the panel in place.

The stitches used on the sleeve from the top downward are:

Crossed diamond stitch rows 1, 8, 12, 29, 33, 50, 54, 61.
Cable stitch rows 2, 5, 10, 15, 18, 23, 26, 31, 36, 39, 44, 47, 52, 56, 59, 62.
Diamond stitch rows 3, 4, 6, 7, 9, 11, 13, 14, 16, 17, 19, 20, 21, 22, 24, 25, 27, 28, 30, 32, 34, 35, 37, 38, 40, 41, 42, 43, 45, 46, 48, 49, 51, 53, 55, 57, 58, 60.

Crossed diamond stitch is worked with two rows of diamond stitch immediately over each other, interlocking one row with the other by working in contrasting colors on alternate sets of tubes (see diagram).

The stitches used on the collar are:
Cable stitch rows 1, 4, 7.
Crossed diamond stitch rows 2, 9.
Diamond stitch rows 3, 5, 6, 8.

117

Chapter 29

Dress pattern to smock for 6-10 year olds

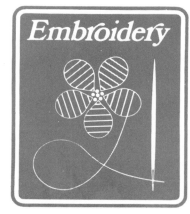

It should only take a few evenings to complete this charming child's dress with its pretty smocked collar and cuffs. It is made in a crisp, fresh gingham so that the small checks can be used as a guide for working the smocking panels. The same pattern will also make a lovely little nightgown.

Measurements

To fit a size 6-8 (9-10) year old

Materials you will need

Short-sleeved version
- ☐ 1½ (2)yds small check 36in gingham (¾ inch across each square)

Long-sleeved version
- ☐ 1¾ (2¼)yds gingham

Both versions
- ☐ 1 ball orange pearl cotton No.8
- ☐ 1 ball white pearl cotton No.8
- ☐ Snap fasteners or small buttons for back fastening

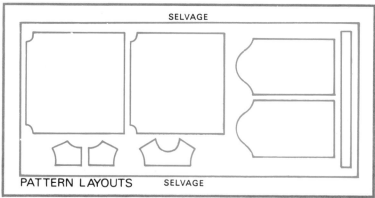

▲ *Size 6-8 years, long sleeves*　　▼ *Size 9-10 years, long sleeves*

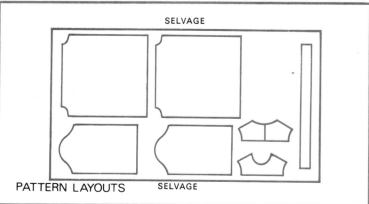

▼ *Detail shows effect of working three patterns for a deeper panel*

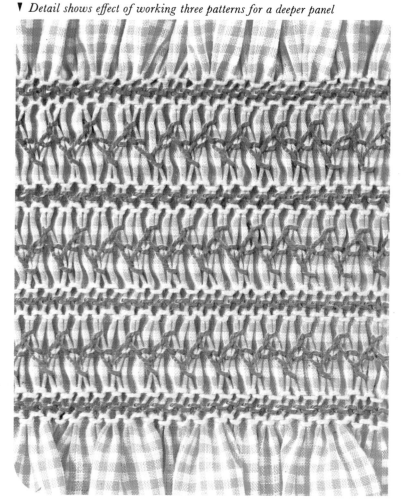

▼ *Blue: size 6-8 years; red: size 9-10 years, short-sleeved version*

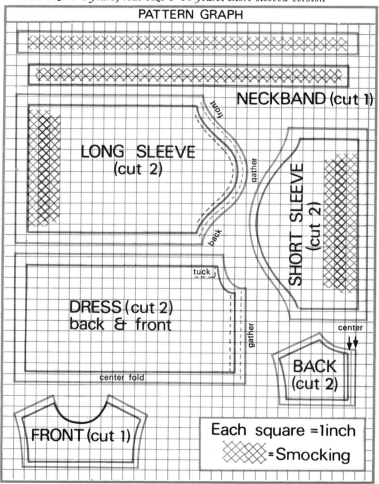

To make the pattern

Mark up a large sheet of brown paper in 1 inch squares and copy the pattern graph onto it, square by square.
Cut out the pattern pieces.

To cut out

When cutting out the dress, allow $\frac{5}{8}$ inch seam allowances and 4 inches for the hem. Lay the material flat and pin the pattern pieces to it as shown in the pattern layout.

To make the dress

Make a small hem at the top of the neckband and at each end of it, either by hand or machine. Gather up the smocking bands on the collar and sleeves by picking up the white squares on the wrong side of the work. Pull up the threads quite tightly so that the right side of the work is firm and evenly pleated. Smock three rows of cable stitch, one of feather stitch, three of cable stitch, one of feather stitch and three of cable stitch (see detail) on neck and sleeves.

Join the shoulder seams of front and back yokes. Cut a 4 inch opening down the center back of skirt top. Gather the top of the skirt to measure the same as across yokes. Join the side seams, then mark one inch out to either side of the seam and bring these two points together over the seam to make a pleat. Turn the pleat to the front of the dress (see diagram).

Slip stitch the neckband by hand to the neck of the yoke, picking up each tube separately, leaving seam allowance plus $\frac{3}{4}$ inch at the back of the yoke to be hemmed for opening. Machine stitch around edge of yoke to secure the neckband turning. Hem neck opening as in diagram and finish with snaps or tiny buttons, making buttonhole loops to fasten. Stitch the sleeve seam, then gather around the top of the sleeve to fit the armhole and set the sleeves into armholes. Make a narrow hem on sleeve cuffs. Overcast all raw edges or finish with machine zigzagging. Turn up hem.

▲ *No worries about washing her dress, made of small check gingham and decorated with pretty panels of smocking*

▼ *Making a pleat in the side seam* ▼ *Basting the neckband to the yoke* ▼ *A detail of the back opening*

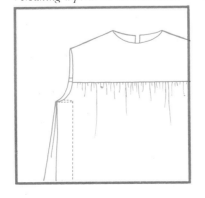 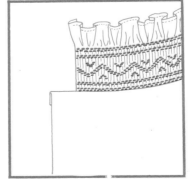 

Chapter 30

Italian smocking for a negligee

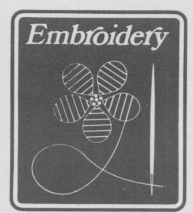

This pretty method of decorating gathers is really smocking in reverse. Rows of firm smocking stitches are worked on the back of the fabric to control the gathers, then the embroidery is worked on the right side over the surface of the tiny pleats, giving a firm control to the fabric. A graph pattern and full instructions for making the negligee illustrated are given in this chapter. The same pattern can be used for ordinary smocking if desired.

▼ *The tracing outline for the embroidery design*

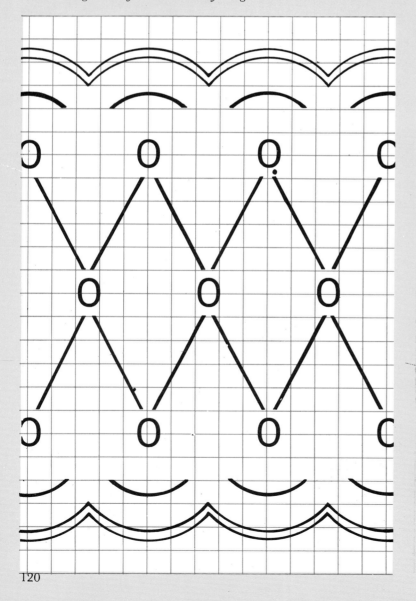

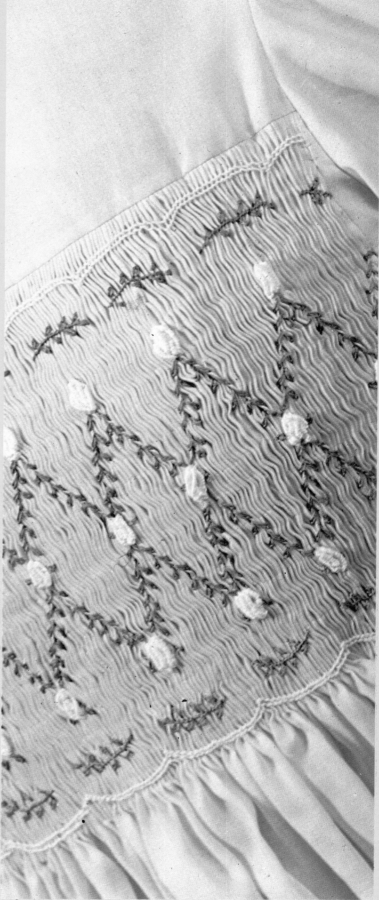

Working the smocking

Work the foundation of smocking on the wrong side, exactly over the dots so that they are covered with stitches and do not show through to the right side of the sheer fabric. Using pink pearl cotton, pick up the transfer dots using cable stitch. This is important as the embroidery on the right side will not keep the pleats firm without this backing work. Work across each row of dots until the whole panel is covered. When all the foundation smocking is completed pull out the gathering threads. Referring to the diagram, copy the design onto the right side of the work with basting thread. Embroider the design as shown in the illustration using chain stitch for the leaves, outline stitch for the stalks, bullion knots for the roses and two lines of outline stitch for the scalloped edge.

Full length view, showing the simple ribbon bow neck fastening ►
▼ *Back view of negligee showing the effect of the smocked panel*

▼ *A negligee to daydream in*

121

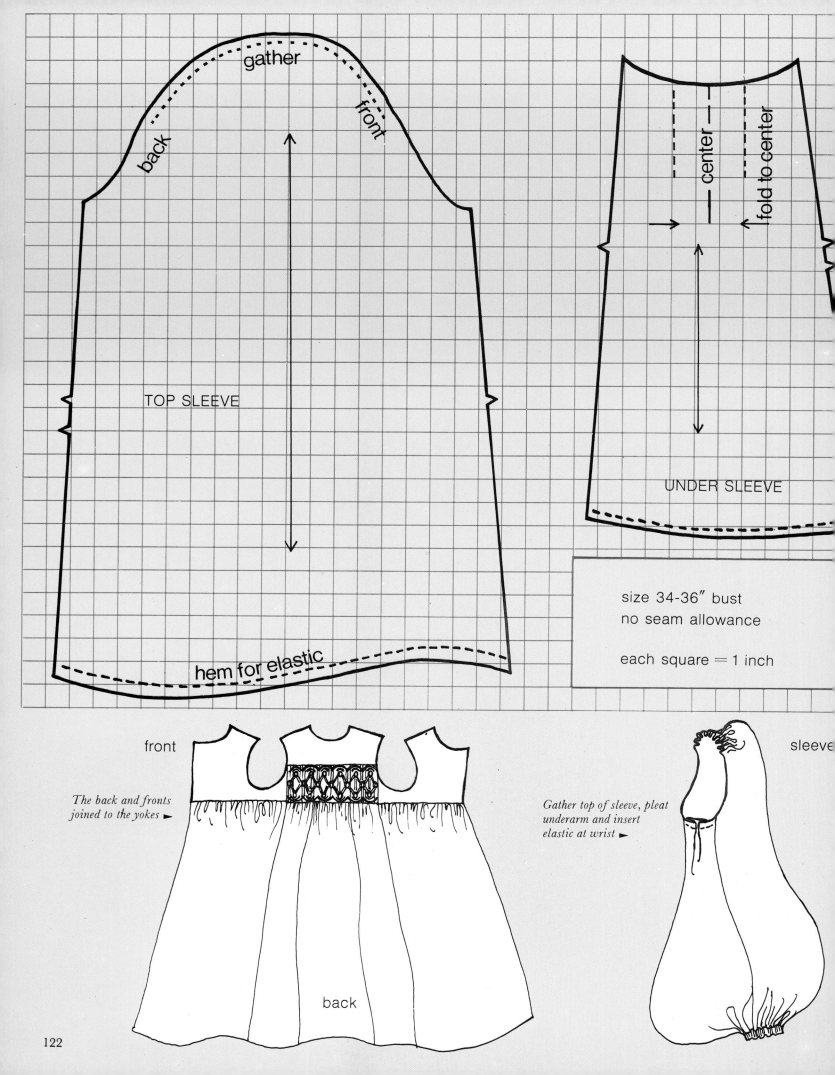

gather

back

front

TOP SLEEVE

hem for elastic

center

fold to center

UNDER SLEEVE

size 34-36″ bust
no seam allowance

each square = 1 inch

front

The back and fronts joined to the yokes ▶

back

sleeve

Gather top of sleeve, pleat underarm and insert elastic at wrist ▶

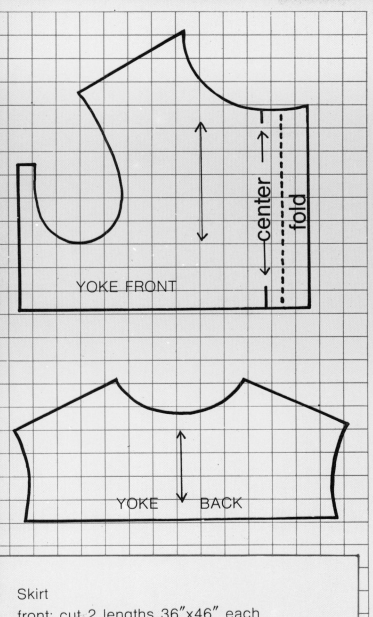

YOKE FRONT

center fold

YOKE BACK

Skirt

front: cut 2 lengths 36″x46″ each

back: cut 1 length 36″x 58½″

cut 2 lengths 18″x 58½″ each

front

◄ *Make a narrow hem along front edges and hem of skirt*

To make this negligee to fit a 34 to 36 inch bust you will need:

☐ 7¾ yds 36 inch wide lawn, pink
☐ 3½ yds double satin ribbon, white for bows
☐ Strip of transfer dots ¼ inch apart, 72 inches long by 6½ inches deep
☐ 3 snap fasteners
☐ D.M.C. Pearl cotton—1 skein each of white, green and pink
☐ Sewing thread for making garment and for gathering
☐ ½yd narrow elastic
☐ 1 inch squared paper
☐ Pencil

Size

For a smaller size, cut the pattern without a seam allowance and with about 6 inches less on the width of the area to be smocked. For a larger size, cut the seam allowance ¼ inch larger and allow about 6 inches extra on the width of the area to be smocked.

To make the pattern

Copy the pattern from the graph onto 1 inch squared paper. Cut out the pattern and lay it on the fabric according to the layout guide. Cut out allowing ⅝ inch seam allowance on all edges.

Negligee back

Seam by machine stitching the two narrow back panels to each side of the wider back panel. Work a second line of stitching ¼ inch out from the first line. Trim the fabric to this second line of stitching and finish the seam edges by zigzag machine or overcast by hand. Iron the transfer across the top of the panels onto the wrong side of the work. Pick up the smocking dots as instructed in Embroidery Chapter 26, but for this garment pick up just above the transfer dots, not right on them. When you come to a seam, pick up the dots both sides leaving the seam free. Work the smocking.

To make the garment

Gather the front skirt and join it to the yoke. Baste the smocked panel to the back yoke and sew together by hand as described under the heading "Making the top" in Embroidery Chapter 27. Join back and fronts together at side seams. Stitch the shoulder seams together. Bind the neck edge. Finish by sewing snap fasteners to close the yoke. Join top sleeve to under sleeve, matching notches as indicated on the pattern. Gather the top of the sleeve as indicated on the pattern and make a pleat at sleeve underarm as shown in the diagram. Set the sleeves into the armholes and stitch. Make a small hem at the wrist and thread with elastic. Stitch a narrow hem down front edges and along hem of negligee. Make two bows for wrists, and one with streamers 18 inches long for front neck edge. Sew in position as in diagram.

▼ *The pattern layout (reverse one front yoke pattern for one-sided fabric)*

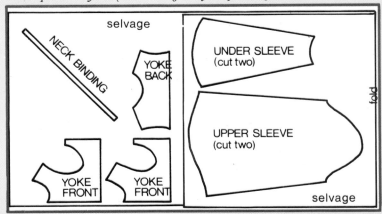

Chapter 31

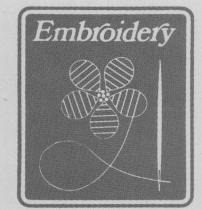

Lattice smocking

Lattice smocking is worked without a foundation of gathering and produces an effective form of pleating on the right side of the fabric.

Fabrics

Fabrics with a pile, such as velvet and corduroy, are the best to use, but any heavy quality fabric which does not crease easily, such as satin, will do. Allow approximately double the quantity of fabric to the required finished measurement.

Threads

Use strong sewing threads such as buttonhole twist, button cotton or nylon sewing thread in the needle.

Method

Commercial transfers are made for stamping the dots used in the smocking, (see Embroidery Chapter 26) but it is possible to mark your own if you prefer. The dots are spaced in rows $1\frac{1}{4}$ inches apart.

All the smocking is worked on the wrong side of the fabric. The stitches will not show on the right side after the smocking pleats are formed. After the dots are marked on the wrong side of the fabric,

start the smocking at the upper left-hand corner. Knot the end of the thread.

Pick up the dots by inserting the needle into the fabric to right of dot and out through the left side of the same dot.

The thread is carried from dot to dot on the working side of the fabric. Pick up dot 1 with the needle and make a second holding stitch as shown in figure **1**. Then pick up dot 2, go back to dot 1 and pick up again as shown in figure **2**. Pull dots 1 and 2 together and knot securely as shown in figure **3**. Pick up dot 3 then, with the thread above the needle, slip the needle under the thread between dots 1 and 2 as shown in figure **4**, pulling the thread tightly at dot 3 to form a knot. Be sure to keep the fabric flat between dots 1 and 3. Pick up dot 4, then go back and pick up dot 3 again as shown in figure **5**. Pull the dots together and knot them securely. Pick up dot 5 as shown in figure **6**, slip the needle under the thread between dots 3 and 5 and knot as in figure **4**. Continue to work down the row of dots in the same manner, starting with figure **2** and picking up dot 6 next. Secure all the ends firmly.

Far right: lattice smocking worked in velvet for the sleeves of this delightful dress ►
▼ *Tracing guide to repeat as necessary*   *Step-by-step working instructions* ►

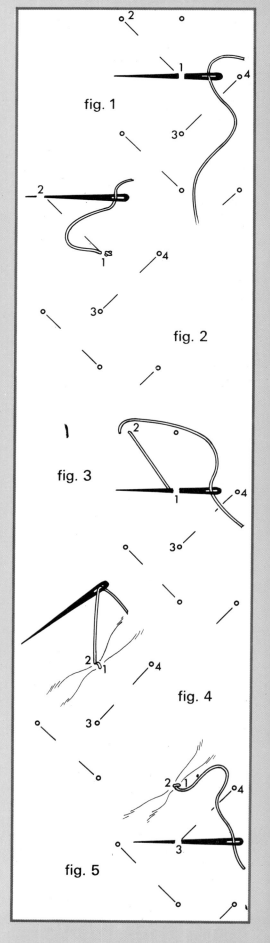

fig. 1

fig. 2

fig. 3

fig. 4

fig. 5

ROW 1	ROW 2	ROW 3

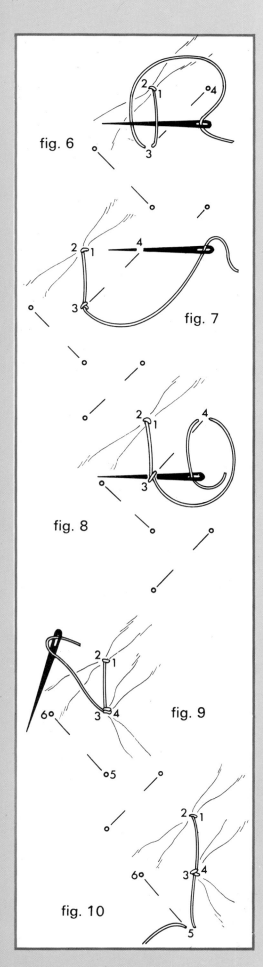

fig. 6

fig. 7

fig. 8

fig. 9

fig. 10

Collector's Piece

Fairytale smocks

These beautiful, long smocks were worked by Frances Coleman, a young dress designer, the inspiration for which was based on more traditional designs.

She started to make clothes as a result of her interest in the weight and density of fabrics. Both the smocks contain an enormous amount of material which allows them to hang heavily from the shoulders and achieves an overall balance for both the dress and the wearer. The sleeveless smock is made of homespun cotton and embroidered in plain smocking stitch. It fastens at the shoulder and falls to ankle length. The other smock is worked more closely in plain smocking stitch and honeycomb stitch. The material is fine muslin which has been cut into two layers so that the fan effect can be achieved. A porcelain bead hangs at the end of each tail, which again gives weight to the dress.

The smocking on each garment has been sewn in pale, pastel colors to achieve an almost autumnal effect.

Chapter 32

Introduction to drawn threadwork

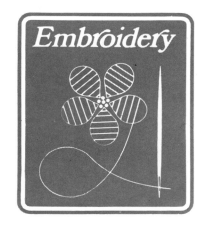

Drawn threadwork is a form of counted thread embroidery in which the threads are cut and pulled out from a loosely woven fabric and the remaining, exposed threads are stitched together in patterns. It originated as a decorative embroidery in ancient Egypt more than twenty-five hundred years ago. One of the simplest and best-known ways of using this fascinating technique is for making decorative hems on handkerchiefs and household linen, particularly sheets, pillowcases, tablecloths, napkins and traycloths.

Making a drawn thread traycloth

Although ready-hemmed traycloths can be purchased, for drawn threadwork it is better to make the cloth from a length of fabric since purchased cloths rarely follow the true grain of the fabric.

For a traycloth measuring 20in by 14in with a 1in hem all around, you will need:
- ☐ ½yd 36in wide even-weave material (such as linen or crash)
- ☐ Six-strand embroidery floss in a matching or contrasting color.

To make the traycloth
Working on a flat surface, find the center of the material by folding it in half horizontally and then basting along the crease, following the grain (see Embroidery Chapter 4). Fold the material in half vertically and baste along the crease, following the grain. The material is now divided into four sections and the center marked. Leave the basting stitches in position until the work is completed because they are essential to the placing of embroidery.

Working with a long side horizontal, measure 10 inches to the left and 10 inches to the right, from the center point, to find the length of the traycloth. Measure 7 inches up and down from the center point to find the depth of the cloth. Mark the area all around with a line of basting stitches, following the grain of the fabric.

From the line of basting, measure inward the depth of the hem on all four sides (1 inch). With a needle, lift one horizontal thread and snip it carefully with scissors. Still using the needle, carefully pick out this thread, working away from the center toward the corners, and similarly, draw a thread on all four sides until the drawn threads meet and form a square hole at each corner. Don't pick them out any farther than the corners, but leave the ends long enough to darn back into the fabric to avoid fraying. One to three threads withdrawn is sufficient; if more are pulled out, the fabric may be weakened. Measure the hem depth (1 inch) outward from the basting line all around and mark with another line of basting stitches.

Trim off the excess fabric ½in outside the second line of the basting. The cloth should now measure 23in wide by 17in deep. Fold the crease on the first line of basting and then on the second to form a 1in hem. Baste the hem to within one thread of exposed threads. Before hemstitching, miter the corners.

Mitered corners
Working on the wrong side, fold each corner point down so that the point lies where the drawn threads meet. Press each point down, open out and trim the point off diagonally, ¼ inch above the crease. Fold the ¼ inch turning back on the crease and bring points A and B together (see diagram). Slip stitch along the creases.

Handkerchief hemstitch
Embroidery threads used for drawn threadwork are usually matched to the fabric, but colored thread can be used for a pretty contrast. Six-strand floss, soft embroidery cotton, cotton and metallic yarns can be used effectively.

Choose a thread in relation to the thickness of the fabric. For coarse fabrics such as linen, three or four strands of floss or similar weight of thread is suitable. For lighter fabrics, such as organdy or lawn, one or two strands of floss would be sufficient.

Working on the wrong side and from left to right, with the end of the thread inside the hem, place the needle in from the right, picking up four of the exposed threads. Pull the needle through and pick up two threads of the turned hem. Make sure that the same two horizontal threads are picked up all along the hem.

The instructions for making the traycloth can be applied to making napkins, place mats or tablecloths.

Inset borders
Hemstitching can also be used for appliquéd inset borders with drawn threadwork. Working from the right side, three or four of the exposed threads are picked up and then two threads of the inset border fabric.

For larger cloths, cut the contrasting fabric into long, separate strips, and join with a miter at the corners before hemstitching.

▼ *Darning back drawn threads*

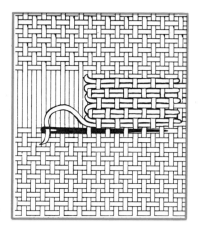

▼ *Mitering a corner*

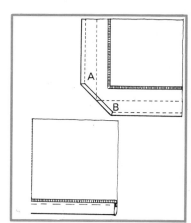

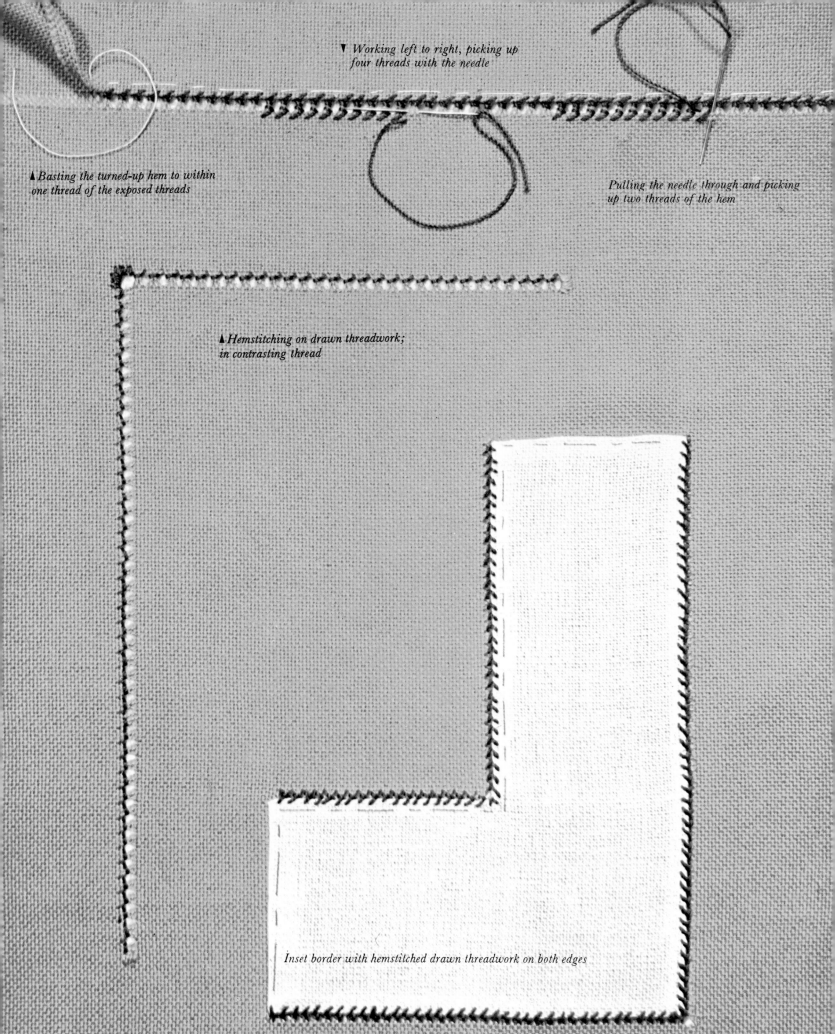

▼ *Working left to right, picking up*
four threads with the needle

▲ *Basting the turned-up hem to within*
one thread of the exposed threads

Pulling the needle through and picking up
up two threads of the hem

▲ *Hemstitching on drawn threadwork;*
in contrasting thread

Inset border with hemstitched drawn threadwork on both edges

129

Chapter 33

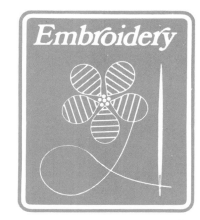

Variations in drawn threadwork

Decorative, reinforced corners are an important stage in drawn threadwork and the three pretty corner finishes described here will help you to achieve a professional look on your handmade linen.

This chapter describes several attractive variations which can be worked on the basic hemstitch described in the previous chapter—ladder hemstitch, zigzag hemstitch and one of the effects obtained by knotting groups of threads. With a little imagination, you will be able to work out your own variations by using different yarns and by grouping and twisting the threads in other ways.

Decorative, reinforced corners

When two or more rows of threads have been drawn out (as for instance on the traycloth shown in Embroidery Chapter 32), a square empty space is formed at the corners where the drawn threads met. After the ends of the threads have been darned in, the edges of the square are worked very closely with satin stitch or buttonhole stitch to prevent the hole from fraying. With fine fabrics, the hole is very small and may be left with just the edges finished off. With coarse fabrics, the hole is larger and is filled with a worked web to decorate and strengthen the corner. Both dove's eye filling and loop stitch filling are simple to do and form the basis for more complicated and decorative fillings.

Each of these fillings is based on a simple, reinforced corner— a corded or buttonhole-stitched edge is worked very closely along the edges of the square (see illustration).

Dove's eye filling

To work dove's eye filling, fasten the embroidery thread to one corner of the square and take it across diagonally to the opposite corner of the square. Return to center and work in the same way across the other two corners. Where the threads cross, work the dove's eye by stitching around and around until the eye is large enough. Take the thread across to one of the corners and fasten off.

Loop stitch filling

Loop stitch filling, which has a pretty, lacy look, is used when the corner hole is not very large. Follow the diagram (right) for the method of working this simple decorative filling.

Variations on hemstitch

Ladder hemstitch

This simple hemstitch variation is worked where four to six threads have been drawn. Work hemstitch on both sides of exposed thread area, making a series of vertical groupings. Two, three or four threads are taken up by the needle to form the groups.

Zigzag hemstitch

Begin this stitch by working a single row of hemstitch, taking up an even number of threads (two, four or six). On the opposite side of the drawn threads, take up half of the same group of threads with half of the adjacent group, making a zigzag effect.

Knotting groups of threads

The knotting of groups of threads produces more attractive variations on ladder hemstitch. Twisted chain stitch is the knot which holds the groups of threads firmly (see the illustration at the bottom of the opposite page), and is obtained by placing the needle as for chain stitch and passing it under the group of threads. The embroidery thread is left visible and forms part of the pattern. You can remove more threads, working more rows of chain stitch to form zigzag patterns.

To work dove's eye filling, fasten thread to top left corner of hole and take it across diagonally to bottom right corner. Slip the needle up through the reinforced edge stitch to come out at top right and then across diagonally to bottom left. Oversew back along the crossed thread to the top right corner and then slip the needle through the reinforced edge stitching to top left corner. Oversew the thread down to center of crossed threads and weave dove's eye to required size. Oversew the remaining diagonal thread to finish bottom right.

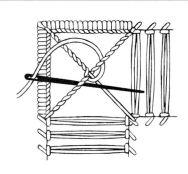

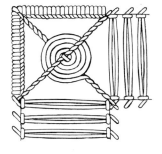

Loop stitch filling is worked by first fixing the thread to the left side of the reinforced hole and then by looping the thread to the upper edge, then to the right edge, then to the lower edge and finishing back on the left (follow the diagram given) ►

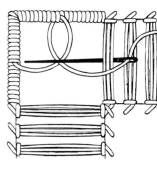

The completed loop stitch filling ►

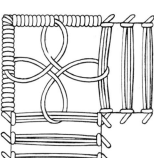

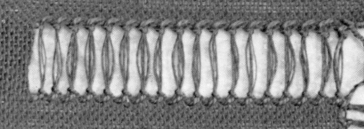

Dove's-eye filling worked on satin stitch reinforcing, in contrast color ▲

Loop stitch filling on satin stitch reinforcing in matching thread ▲

▲*Simple reinforced corner using buttonhole stitch in contrasting color*

Ladder hemstitch worked on both sides of the drawn threads ▲

Zigzag hemstitch worked over groups of four drawn threads ▼

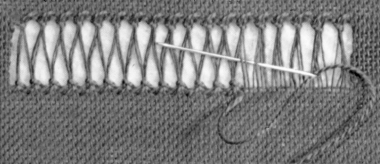

Three groups of threads knotted together with twisted-chain stitch ▼

Chapter 34

Design in drawn threadwork

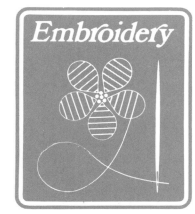

The stitches shown in this chapter can be adapted to form beautiful modern designs such as the vest, pillows and wall panels illustrated on the following pages.

Drawn threadwork is an interesting form of embroidery based on the removal of either the warp (lengthwise) or the weft (crosswise) threads from a precise even-weave fabric. The remaining threads are grouped together into patterns by knotting or interlacing, based on a foundation of ladder hemstitch (see Embroidery Chapter 33).

Each group should contain the same number of threads, usually an even number, so that the threads can be divided evenly when knotting or interlacing to form a pattern.

For an interlaced pattern a large number of threads have to be withdrawn from the fabric to allow sufficient play to form a pattern. The actual number of threads drawn depends greatly on the fabric and thickness of the weave, so it is a good idea to practice on a spare piece of the material before starting the actual work. Avoid withdrawing so many threads that the fabric is weakened.

Fabrics
The best fabrics to use for this technique are even-weave linen or furnishing fabrics of man-made fibers with a precise even weave, such as Dacron. If the fabric weft threads are of a different thickness to the warp threads, the patterns will be distorted and, depending on the thickness of the threads, this will show up in a design to different degrees.

However, if the design is of a free or abstract nature, this unevenness of weave can be turned to advantage. The more experienced embroiderer can experiment with unusual and interesting fabrics to create different effects.

For wall hangings, great effect can be achieved with even-weave woolen fabrics, burlap, sacking and the various types of canvas normally used in needlepoint. With canvas an interesting contrast of textures can be achieved by combining drawn threadwork and needlepoint stitches.

Yarns
Traditionally, linen yarns were used for drawn threadwork, but these are no longer easy to obtain. Some extremely interesting results can be achieved with modern threads, however, by using a combination of unusual fabrics and yarns such as gold, silver or copper lurex, weaving yarns or plastic raffia, as well as the more usual yarns such as pearl cotton, embroidery thread, matte embroidery cotton and 6-strand floss. Cords, braids or fine ribbon make attractive interlacings.

Stitches
There are several ways of using the basic foundation of ladder hemstitch with knotting or interlacing to create different pattern effects.

Four of them are shown here. Zigzag hemstitch (Embroidery Chapter 33) can also be used as a foundation stitch, but for some special effects a foundation stitch is not necessary. The results are looser and more open but also less hard-wearing.

Complementary stitches
In modern embroidery almost any combination of stitches is acceptable provided the finished result is attractive and does not look jumbled. Drawn threadwork and needlepoint stitches combine well because they are both worked over counted threads. Many other filling and line stitches go with drawn threadwork too. For example, rows of drawn threads separated by rows of blocked satin stitch, richly worked spider webs or detached eyelets all build up into instant designs, texture contrasting with the open, lacy look. Stitch Library gives two such complementary stitches.

Color
In drawn threadwork the decoration relies more on texture contrast than color combinations, and the best results come from a restricted use of color. Whichever color you choose for the embroidery yarn, be it a lighter or darker tone of the fabric color, an exact match or a complete contrast, use the same color tone range throughout. A combination of several contrasting colors of yarn simply detracts attention from the design.

Where to use drawn threadwork
Drawn threadwork gives an individual and expensive look to household items or clothes—pillows, curtains, wall panels, dresses, vests, blouses and children's wear. Contrasting ribbon or fabric can be placed behind the embroidery to dramatize the effect.

Stitch Library

Rosette chain stitch
This stitch gives a braid effect if worked closely, a petal shape when openly spaced. It can be used in straight or curved lines and is worked from right to left or top to bottom.

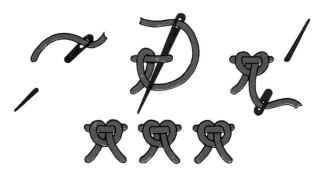

Sorbello stitch
This is a knotted stitch which looks best worked in a thick yarn. In a thinner yarn it has a completely different effect. Use it close together as a filling, in single or groups of rows as a border or as a powdering.

Needleweaving

Because the withdrawn threads are replaced by closely woven blocks of stitches, this is a hard-wearing form of the drawn thread technique.

Woven hemstitch

For the simplest form, withdraw five or six threads. Weave over the first group of threads (three, four or five, depending on the texture of the fabric—if the fabric is coarse, work over fewer), and under the second group. Work back and forth over these two groups, continuing along the upper half of the threads. The next block is then worked over the lower half of the second group and the new third group. Pull the weaving firmly so that spaces are left between the blocks. Work with a tapestry needle.

Pyramid border

The needleweaving border is worked over ten groups of threads tapering off to two groups. The number of threads withdrawn and the number in each group depend upon the texture of the fabric.

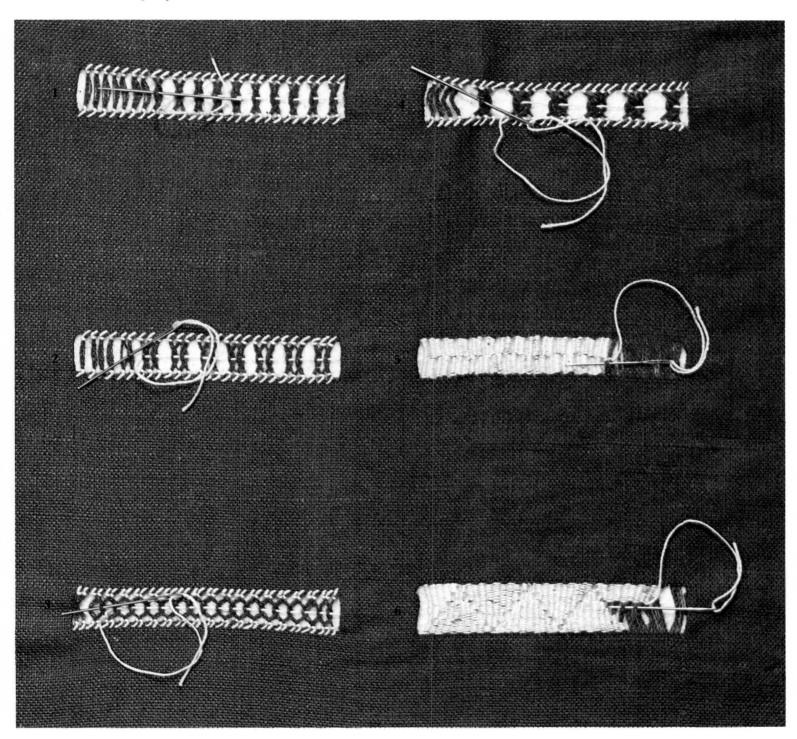

1 *The simplest form of interlacing worked over groups of four threads*
2 *Interlacing worked over groups of two and four threads*
3 *A pattern worked over groups of three threads*

4 *Interlacing worked over four groups each of four threads*
5 *Woven hemstitch*
6 *Needleweaving a pyramid border*

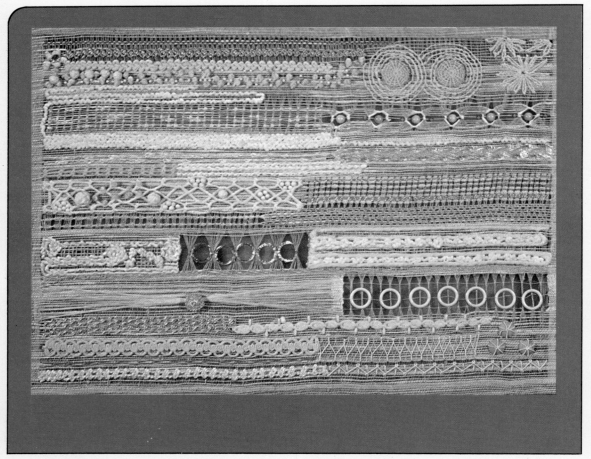

The articles shown on these pages are examples of modern drawn threadwork displaying a variety of textures and the uses to which drawn threadwork can be put.

Abstract panel

This is in the nature of a sampler worked on textured stripes of open-weave vision net curtaining. Some threads have been pulled out giving two very open areas. The rest of the design is a combination of a variety of pulled fabric stitches further decorated with surface stitches such as twisted chain, rosette chain, raised chain band, French knots and couching. Some braids and lampshade trimmings have been stitched onto the surface to give a more solid effect. Further texture has been added by using curtain rings, wooden button molds and wooden beads. The sampler is mounted on a contrasting fabric over a wooden frame and measures about 15 inches by 20 inches.

▲ *Abstract panel in the nature of a sampler worked on vision net curtaining fabric*
▼ *A dragonfly worked in a combination of Hardanger embroidery and drawn thread stitches*

Dragonfly

As the nature of drawn thread-work is to follow the grain of the fabric, the rounded shapes of the insect have been reduced to basic geometric shapes. The design uses a combination of Hardanger embroidery (see Embroidery Chapter 35) and drawn thread techniques. The design is worked on even-weave linen with threads pulled out for the body stripes which are worked in simple drawn thread stitches. Surface stitches such as raised chain band, woven spider web and couching for the body outlines give strength and texture to the design. Needle-weaving has also been incorporated using a self color yarn on the body, feelers and tail.

Blue-green pillow

The fabric used is a loosely woven synthetic furnishing tweed which lends itself well to drawn threadwork. The decoration is formed by using small blocks of satin stitch interspersed with large eyelets. The band of withdrawn threads is threaded with narrow, navy blue satin ribbon. The raised

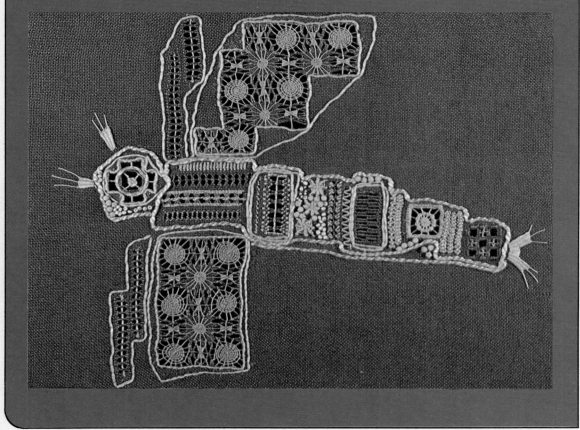

decoration and border at each end of the pillow is formed with a row of shell crochet worked in crepe-textured knitting yarn.

Cream pillow

Synthetic curtain fabric with a narrow woven stripe has been used for this pillow. Working from the center outward, the decoration has been formed as follows: The center band of withdrawn threads has been interlaced with two thicknesses of fluffy cotton yarn which has been knotted at regular intervals. Next, a row of square stitch in a broken line is worked using cream pearl cotton. A row of sorbello stitch follows worked in apricot colored pearl cotton. Close to this a row of coral stitch is worked in cream colored matte embroidery cotton.

A row of shaggy weaving cotton follows, couched down, and the next row is knotted stitch in dark cream pearl cotton. The final row of embroidery is pulled satin stitch in broken blocks using dark brown pearl cotton. The border edge is worked in sorbello stitch and pulled satin stitch blocks. The raised bands are rows of shell crochet, which also decorate each end of the pillow.

Vest

The vest is made in cream rayon curtain fabric consisting of stripes of solid and open-weave upon which the embroidery design is based.

The panels on either side of the vest are identical. The stitches used, working from the center of each panel outward, are as follows: The center row of stitching is coral knot stitch using thick cream wool worked over the open threads. The next row is raised chain band worked in alternate lengths of crunchy nylon weaving yarn and six strands of floss. The next row is formed with lengths of square stitch and French knots using pearl cotton, Nos. 5 and 8. The outer row is raised chain band worked in thick wool over the open threads of fabric.

▲ *A fashionable vest richly decorated in a variety of simple stitches*
▼ *Detail of stitches on the cream pillow*   ▼ *Detail of stitches on the blue-green pillow*

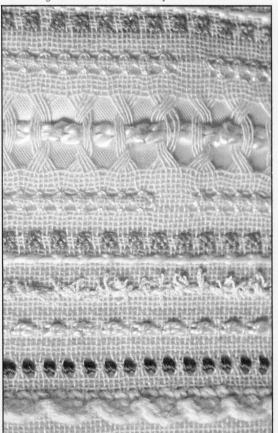

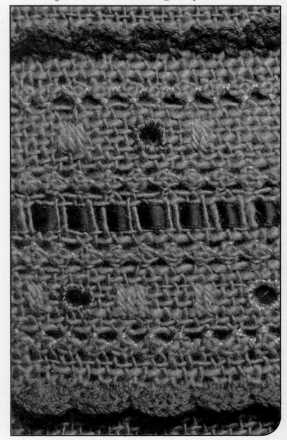

Collector's Piece

Tablecloth for a banquet

This beautiful tablecloth was made in Denmark. It is worked in a variety of styles including Scandinavian counted threadwork, and English drawn threadwork. The cream and coffee colors have been selected to achieve a modern and sophisticated effect.

The Needlewoman Shop, London.

136

Chapter 35

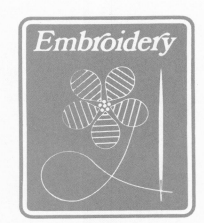

Norwegian Hardanger embroidery

Hardanger embroidery comes from the district of that name in West Norway. Traditionally the embroidery was worked in white thread on white fabric but modern designs have introduced color. It is basically a drawn thread technique and is used to decorate either household linens or items of dress.

Hardanger is worked on Hardanger fabric or fine linen with a precise even weave. Pearl cotton is the most suitable embroidery thread but it is possible to substitute matte embroidery cotton or 6-strand floss. Two different thicknesses of pearl cotton are used, No.5 for the thick satin stitch blocks and the finer No.8 for the woven bars and fillings. The satin stitch surrounds to the spaces are always worked first and this is best done in an embroidery frame. Working the spaces and drawing out the threads which is done without a frame is the second stage of working. Care must always be taken to count the fabric threads and the stitches worked with great accuracy.

The stitches used
The filled-in areas are worked in satin stitch, while needleweaving and cording is used for the bars and buttonhole stitch for edges. Four sided stitch is used for both straight and diagonal lines and as a filling stitch.

After the edges of the design have been completed the threads are then cut with very sharp scissors and drawn out, first in one direction and then in the other. The work can then be further decorated with bars with picots, or eyelets.

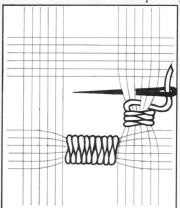

▲ *Woven bars*

▲ *Four sided filling stitch*

Hems and edges
There is a variety of ways to finish hems and edges depending on what the embroidery is to be used for. A hemstitched hem or a plain hem makes a strong edge for household linen while a buttonhole stitch (see Embroidery Chapter 11) worked around the edge and the fabric cut away makes a more delicate edge for clothing.

Traycloth

You will need
- ☐ 2 balls white pearl cotton No. 5
- ☐ 2 balls white pearl cotton No. 8
- ☐ ¾yd 22in wide even-weave linen or Hardanger fabric with 29 threads to 1 inch
- ☐ Tapestry needles sizes 20 and 24

Needles and yarn
Use No.5 pearl cotton for all satin stitch with tapestry needle size 20. For the rest of the embroidery use pearl cotton No. 8 with tapestry needle size 24.

Working the design
Mark the center of the fabric both ways with lines of basting stitches. Begin the embroidery from the point where the basting stitches cross and work the quarter of the design as given, following the chart overleaf.

The chart gives a little more than one quarter of the design and the arrows indicate the center to be marked with basting threads. The chart also shows the arrangement of the stitches on the fabric threads which are represented by the background lines.

Work all the satin stitch blocks before cutting the threads. Six threads are cut and withdrawn each way from the sections shown blank. Woven bars are then worked over the loose threads on the large areas and the fillings worked last.

Work the three other quarters of the design to correspond. Press the embroidery when completed on the wrong side. Trim the fabric to 17½ inches by 25½ inches, turn back ½ inch hem, miter the corners and sew in place.

Woven bars
These are worked over the loose threads of the fabric which remain after the other threads have been withdrawn. Weave the needle over and under three threads until the loose threads are completely covered. When passing from one bar to another be careful that the passing yarn is hidden behind the fabric.

Four sided filling stitch
Two twisted bars are worked by carrying the yarn diagonally across the space, entering the fabric and twisting the yarn over the first threads back to the starting point. The twisting of the second bar is taken only to the center. Then pass the yarn over and under the bars twice in a circular motion, then under and over twice. Finally complete the other half of the second bar.

▼ *Detail of traycloth embroidery*

▲ *A charming Hardanger cloth to grace a tray or a tea cart*

Stitch Library

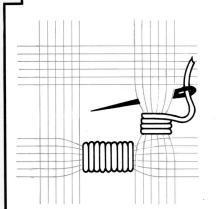

Cording
Withdraw the number of threads required from the fabric and separate the loose threads into bars by overcasting firmly over these threads as many times as required to cover the groups of threads completely.

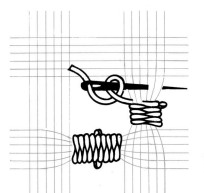

Woven bars with simple picot
Work as for woven bars but halfway along the weaving work a picot with each half of the next stitch. This is done by twisting the thread once around the needle before inserting the needle between the loose threads in the usual way. Complete the bar.

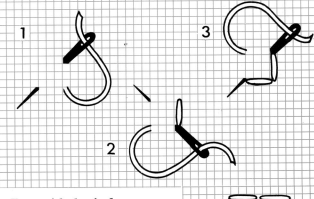

Four sided stitch
Working from right to left, form squares as shown in the diagrams, pulling the stitches firmly. For a filling stitch turn the fabric at the end of the row so that you are still working from right to left.

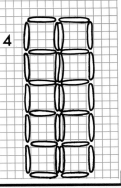

Chart giving just over a quarter of the design
Each line of the grid represents one thread of fabric

Center

Chapter 36

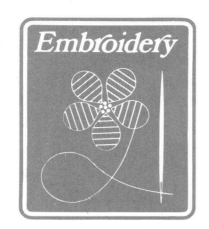

Hardanger tablecloth

To make a tablecloth measuring 34 inches square you will need:
- ☐ Cream colored Hardanger fabric—with 48 threads to 2 inches, 40in by 40in
- ☐ D.M.C. Pearl Cotton No.5, 7 skeins dark pink 893; 3 skeins light pink 894
- ☐ D.M.C. 6-cord crochet cotton No. 20, 1 ball 20gr snow-white
- ☐ Pink and cream sewing thread
- ☐ Tapestry needle No. 18

Planning the design

Use the counted thread guide to plan the outlines of the design. First trace a cross with basting thread following the grain of the fabric to find the center (shown in red on the counted thread guide). Working from the marked center, trace the outlines of the borders and squares in running stitches using matching thread. The figures on the guide represent the number of ground threads. The extreme outer line indicates the edge of the cloth after the hem has been turned. When planning the cloth, count another 30 threads all around for the hem.

To strengthen the borders

Strengthen the parts to be openworked by working a row of back-stitches inside the motifs with the pink sewing thread, six ground threads from the traced outline. Following the working charts A, B and C, embroider the triangular motifs in satin stitch using D.M.C. Pearl Cotton No. 5, so that the points of the triangles touch the traced outlines. Use chart C for the center border, chart B for outer center border, chart B for squares and chart A for the outer border. Each square on the charts represents one thread of the fabric. Each thick line represents one straight stitch. Use the light pink thread for the squares and the dark pink thread for the center and outer borders.

The openwork squares

To work the openwork squares, cut and draw 4 threads on all four sides, immediately below the pink satin stitch triangles. Then leave 8 threads, draw 8 and leave 8 alternately across and down the square. Work the cut openwork using D.M.C. 6-cord crochet cotton following the step-by-step diagrams. Work the inside border in the same way as for the square. For the openwork of the outside border, cut and draw 8 threads along each of the four sides of the tablecloth. Tie groups of 8 threads together with a blanket stitch (see Embroidery Chapter 19). In the corners make a cross of threads and tie the center of the cross with a blanket stitch. Continue the border in the same way on the remaining three sides of the cloth.

Finishing

When all the embroidery has been completed, make a handkerchief hem on the cloth, following the instructions given in Embroidery Chapter 32. Press on the wrong side.

142

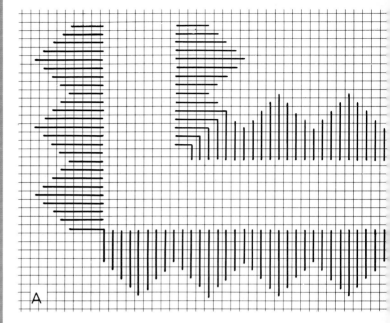

▲ Chart A for both edges of openwork border on tablecloth hem

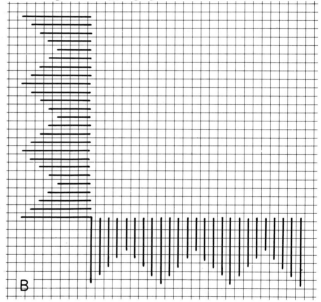

▲ Chart B for outer edge of central openwork and edges of squares

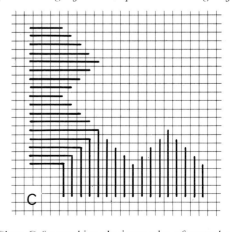

▲ Chart C for working the inner edge of central openwork

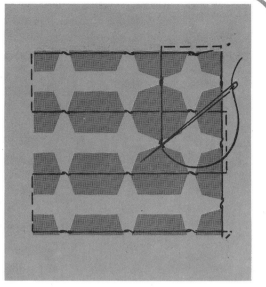

The openwork squares are edged in light pink, the central and hem areas edged in dark pink

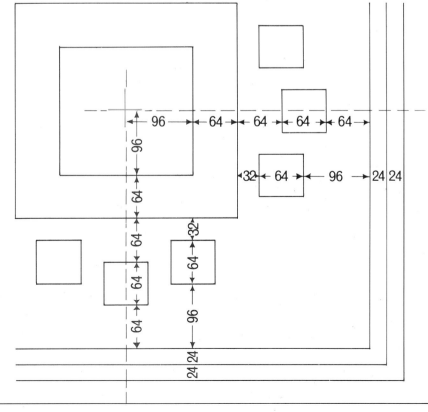

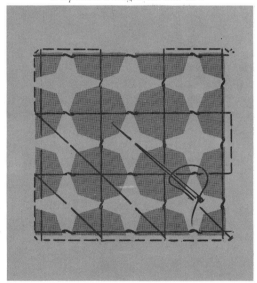

▲ *Openwork stage three*

▲ *Counted thread guide for placing openwork areas on the cloth*

▲ *Openwork stage four*

143

Chapter 37

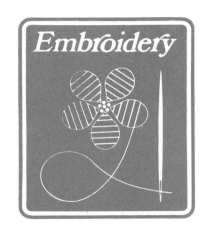

Introduction to cut work

Cut work is more correctly called Richelieu embroidery, named after the famous Cardinal who was Minister to King Louis XIII of France. Cardinal Richelieu, eager to develop industry in France, arranged for skilled Venetian lace-workers to set up schools and workshops encouraging the application of new techniques, thus helping to establish a new skilled industry in France. Cut work remained in vogue throughout the seventeenth century.

There are various forms of embroidery that come under the heading of cut work—Richelieu cut work, Renaissance cut work and reticella cut work. Richelieu is the most solid and reticella the most open. Renaissance cut work is more elaborate in design and is joined by plain buttonhole bars without the use of picots.

The nature of cut work

Cut work is a form of embroidery where the motifs such as figures, flowers and other shapes are surrounded with closely worked buttonhole stitch linked with bars, the rest of the fabric being cut away.

Stitches used in cut work

Outlines. All the outlines of the motifs in a cut work design are worked in buttonhole stitch.

Bars. Bars are buttonhole stitched or worked in cording and can be decorated with picots (for method of working bars see Embroidery Chapter 35).

Details. These can be worked in several ways: outline stitch, which can be whipped to give greater relief; backstitch, seeding, satin stitch, French knots or other simple filling stitches.

Threads and fabrics

Coton à broder is used for this form of embroidery or, alternatively, six-strand floss, using two or three strands depending on the thickness of the fabric being stitched.

It is essential to choose fine, stiff, firmly woven fabrics for cut work. Linen is the best but good quality cotton can be used as a substitute.

Preparing the work

Apply the design using a commercial transfer or dressmakers' carbon paper. Baste the fabric onto stiff, strong paper so that it is well stretched with the grain of the fabric straight. With two or three strands of floss in the needle, work small running stitches around the lines of design on the fabric only, until you come to a bar. Fasten the running thread with a tiny backstitch on the right side of the fabric without cutting off the thread, pass over the bar and pick up two or three threads of fabric, pass back to the far side and continue the running stitches (see diagram).

Bars are worked at about $\frac{3}{8}$ inch to $\frac{1}{2}$ inch intervals, following the curves of the design. Where a large area of fabric is to be cut away, branched bars are worked to fill in the space.

Working cut work design

When running stitches and foundations for the bars are completed, cover them with closely worked buttonhole stitch, keeping the stitches very neat and even. To give more strength and a raised edge, the buttonhole stitch is worked over a laid thread of one strand of coton à broder or two or three strands of 6-strand floss, in the same way as for cording (see Embroidery Chapter 21). The buttonhole stitch (see Embroidery Chapter 11) is also worked with either two or three strands of cotton depending on the thickness of fabric being embroidered. When a bar is reached, pass another thread across the two existing ones and cover all three threads with cording or buttonhole stitch, working over the passing threads only and not picking up the fabric underneath. The buttonhole stitch bars can be decorated with picots. When making the bars, great care should be taken to insure that the tension of the stitches is even—not too loose or too tight—as any unevenness will spoil the work. Fasten off the work by taking a few running stitches along the line of the design where they will be covered by buttonhole stitch. To join onto buttonhole stitch, make a few running stitches and bring the needle up through the back of the work and up through the last buttonhole loop made. Do not fasten off work when making a bar because it looks unsightly.

Branching bars

Work two basting threads between A and B. Work buttonhole stitch from B to C and from there work another two basting threads to E. Work buttonhole stitch from E to D and from there work another two basting threads across to F. Cover the length from F to D, D to C and C to A with buttonhole stitch (see diagram).

Cutting away fabric

When all the embroidery is complete, rip the basting stitches

▼ *Cut work in progress and a bar being worked*

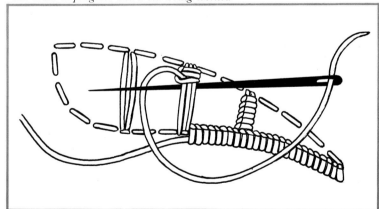

▼ *The motif completed with picots worked on each bar*

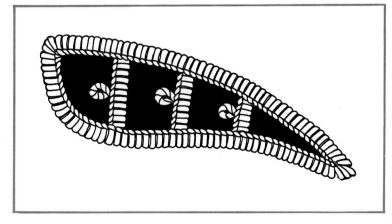

and remove the paper from the back of the work. Press the embroidery carefully on the wrong side of the work over a soft pad, using a damp cloth. Using a small pair of very sharp and pointed scissors, trim the fabric away up to the buttonhole-stitched edges of the design, cutting as close as possible to the stitching so that no rough or raw edges show. When cutting be extremely careful not to damage bars or buttonhole stitches. Work of this kind can be ruined by using blunt scissors or by careless cutting, resulting in a limp piece of work with ragged edges. After cutting is complete, press the embroidery again on the wrong side over a damp cloth.

Uses of cut work

Cut work is mainly used on table linen, but it makes an elegant decoration for sheets and pillow cases. It can also look attractive on clothes—on the collar of a dress, for instance, or on a blouse in the form of panels down sleeves and as an edging for sleeves and hems.

For an individual fashion detail, embroider a deep border of cut work on the hem of a wedding dress.

Designs

Designs can be either simple or intricate. The simpler designs generally have sections cut out of the actual motifs, but more complicated designs leave the motif or shapes solid, linked to the background with bars. Most of the designs available in transfers are traditional, very few of them show a modern feeling. Look for inspiration for designs of your own in church windows where the leading of stained glass windows suggest the bars of cut work. The intricate crispness of cut work is accentuated by using white embroidery on white, or neutral on neutral fabric. The simplicity and beauty of the work is lost by introducing a variety of colors. Texture can be added by using various line and filling stitches for details.

▼ *Method of working branching bars*

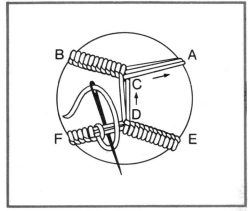

► *A 17th century Italian cap in linen with cut work and needlepoint fillings*

▼ *A detail from the cap*

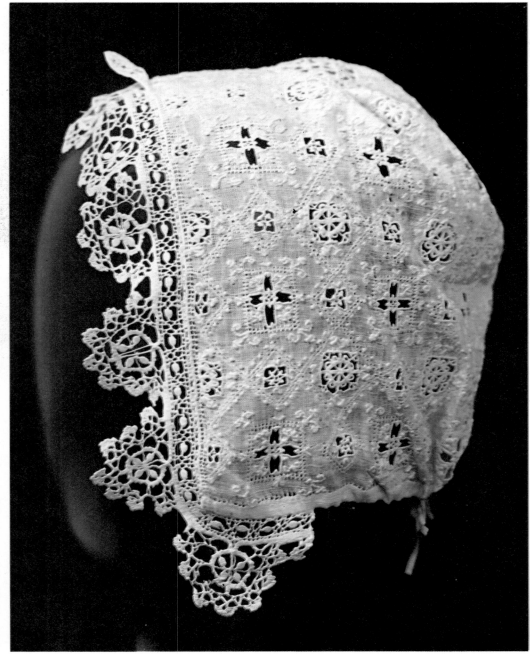

145

Chapter 38

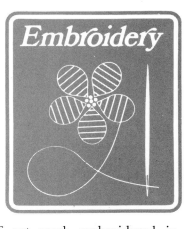

A modern interpretation of cut work

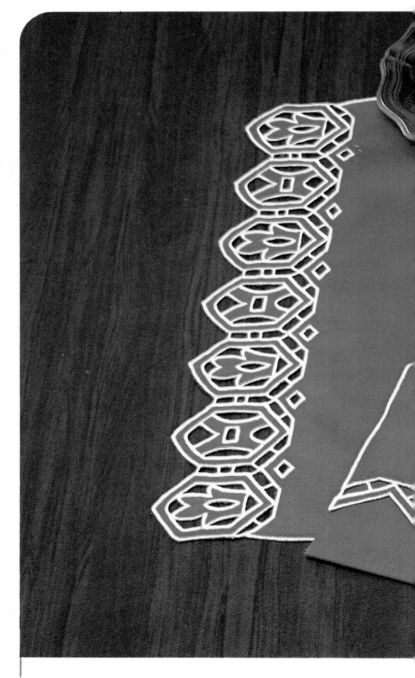

This modern interpretation of cut work embroidered in brilliant white on dark blue linen makes a striking decoration for a place mat and napkin holder. The embroidery would look equally attractive worked on any strong contrasting colored linen, or for a more traditional look work the embroidery in the same color as the fabric. The quantities for fabric and yarn are given for making one set only. For a set of six place mats and holders you will need $2\frac{3}{4}$ yards of linen and 48 skeins of yarn. Make or purchase a plain napkin to tuck into each holder. If you make the napkins, use one of the borders to decorate the edges.

To make a place mat measuring 12 inches by 18 inches and a table napkin holder measuring 5 inches by $10\frac{1}{2}$ inches.
You will need:
☐ 16 inches by 36 inches fine blue linen
☐ 8 skeins snow white D.M.C. Brilliant Embroidery Cotton No. 25
☐ Blue sewing thread to match fabric
☐ Crewel needle No. 8

Preparing the fabric
Cutting on the straight of the material, cut one rectangle measuring 14 inches by 20 inches for the place mat and another rectangle measuring $12\frac{1}{2}$ inches by 15 inches for the table napkin holder.

Transferring the design
Trace the outlines of the place mat and the napkin holder design from these pages. Transfer these designs onto the fabric using white or yellow carbon paper, placing the borders one inch in from the cut edges.
Trace a single line to mark the top and bottom borders of the place mat. Trace a single line on the side edges of the napkin holder flap; the flap should measure 4 inches deep from the pointed edge of the border.

Working the design
The cut work embroidery is worked entirely with snow white Brilliant Embroidery Cotton No. 25. Embroidery Chapter 37 gives the instructions for preparing and working the buttonhole edging and buttonhole bars.
Work the pointed edge over 2 threads of the linen material taken as cord foundation.
Once the work is complete, press with a damp cloth, placing the right side of the material downward on a thick, soft pad.
Cut away the edges of the openwork. Press a second time on the wrong side of the work over a pad.
Finish the plain edges of the napkin folder by making a hand-sewn hem about $\frac{2}{5}$ of an inch wide.
Fold the napkin holder and close the side seams with small slip stitches.

146

▲ *Crisp white cut work on dark linen makes a modern looking place mat and napkin holder to complement modern tableware.*

◄ *Actual size tracing design for half of the place mat border.*

Actual size tracing design for half of the napkin holder flap. ►

147

Chapter 39

Decorating with insertions

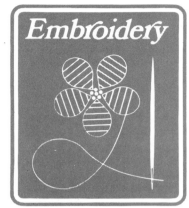

Insertion trimmings are enjoying a new popularity. It is a delightful form of decoration involving solid areas of fabric which are joined together with lace-like stitches. This chapter deals with threads, fabrics and the methods of working.

Insertion is a method of joining two edges of fabric with decorative stitches. It looks charming on table linens and linen guest towels but it can be used to particular advantage on some kinds of clothing.

Rouleau or ribbon, alternated with insertion stitches, make a more interesting decoration for inset panels or edgings. Use either narrow or deep bands of rouleau on clothing such as on yokes or midriffs. Sleeves take on a distinctive look decorated with inset bands at intervals down their length.

Insertions are also an ideal method of adding length or letting out a garment. A deep band of rouleau set in a skirt can be worked in self fabric or fabric of a similar weight.

Fabrics

Work an insertion on a firm fabric such as fine linen cotton, fine wool or silk. Plain colors make better backgrounds than prints or patterns.

Threads

Any medium weight embroidery thread, with the exception of 6-strand floss which is not strong enough, is suitable. All the insertions shown in this chapter are worked with D.M.C. pearl cotton No.5. If the piece of embroidery fabric is made of yarn-dyed linen or wool, threads drawn out from the fabric can be used for the insertion stitching.

Preparing the work

Make neat narrow hems on the edges to be joined or make lengths of rouleau by cutting 1 inch wide bias strips of the fabric. Fold in half lengthwise, right sides together, and make two rows of machine stitching either $\frac{1}{8}$ inch or $\frac{1}{4}$ inch from the folded edge, depending on how deep a rouleau is required. The extra fabric gives a padded, rounded effect to the rouleau. Thread the ends of the sewing thread left from the stitching into the eye of a bodkin and secure these ends with several backstitches. Slot the bodkin through the rouleau, pulling it through to the right side.

Baste the pieces of fabric, or rouleau, to heavy wrapping paper with the hemmed or rouleau edges $\frac{1}{8}$ to $\frac{1}{2}$ inch apart, depending on the finished effect desired. The further apart the hems are placed, the weaker the join will be. The two edges are then joined together with any of the following insertion stitches.

Bullion bar insertion

This is worked from right to left. Bring needle out on top edge. Cross over open space and insert needle directly below. Wrap thread around the bar just formed one or more times depending on the width of the open space. Insert the needle in the top exactly where the thread first emerged and slide the needle through the hem to position for next bar.

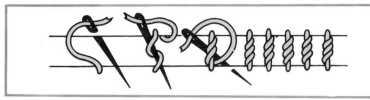

Knotted insertion

Work from left to right. Bring the thread out on the near edge and insert the needle from the front into the opposite edge. Make a loop as in buttonhole stitch, then thread the needle through as shown. Pull tight. Repeat the knot stitch on the opposite edge. Continue working a knot stitch on each edge alternately. When worked closely, this makes a firm, strong stitch.

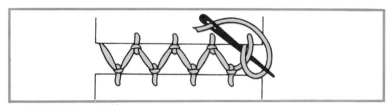

Laced insertion

Before basting the fabric to the paper work a row of plain knotted insertion stitch along each edge separately. Baste the pieces of fabric to the paper and then lace with thread in a self or contrasting color. Work the lacing in open Cretan stitch (see Embroidery Chapter 14) or merely whip the edges together.

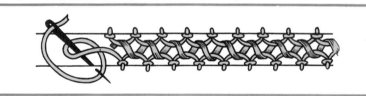

Buttonhole insertion

Working from left to right, make one or more buttonhole stitches on the top edge, then make the same number on the lower edge. The size and number of stitches can vary but should be consistent throughout one piece of work.

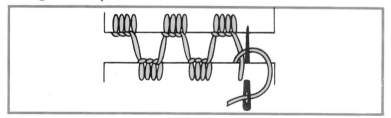

Open Cretan insertion or faggoting

This is worked in the same way as Cretan stitch (Embroidery Chapter 14), picking up a small amount of fabric from alternate edges.

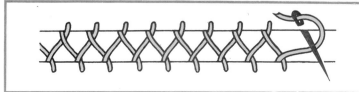

▲ *Blue linen place mat decorated with open Cretan insertion worked in white*

Half Cretan insertion

Work the stitches of this insertion very small and close together. A twist is formed only on one side compared with open Cretan insertion in which both sides are twisted.

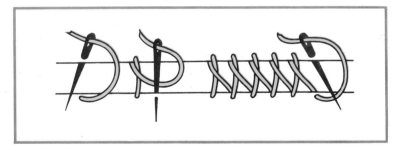

Italian buttonhole insertion

Although this stitch looks complicated it is relatively simple and rich in effect. Begin with a loop base and buttonhole in the sequence shown. The stitches are in fact worked close together, the diagram is spaced openly for clarity.

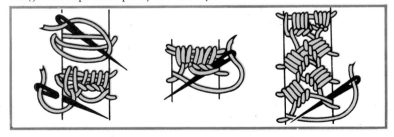

Twisted insertion

This stitch is also known as faggoting and is worked in a similar way to open Cretan insertion, but as each stitch is worked the needle takes a twist over the thread of the last stitch made.

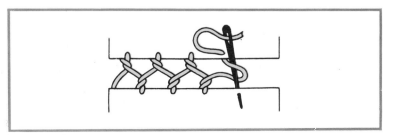

Faggot bundles insertion

The bundles are worked as shown and should be fairly close together with a firm thread otherwise the stitch is not rigid and will wear badly.

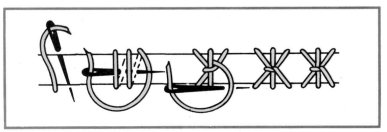

Chapter 40

How to use a decorative alphabet

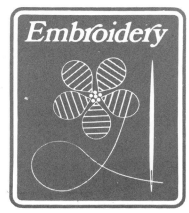

Embroidered initials, whether simply or elaborately worked, add a distinctive and individual touch to personal items or household linen. Letters can also be used as a basis for designs and pattern formations. The shape and style of the letter can suggest the stitches to use. For example, angular letters translate well into counted threadwork.

Letters, usually thought of in terms of initials and monograms for personalizing household linen and accessories, can also represent a rich source of inspiration to the embroiderer. Modern trends in embroidery design and techniques can make a letter an exciting and interesting shape on which to work.

Letters come in hundreds of different shapes, styles and sizes—Roman faces, Egyptian, seriffed, italics and scripts—and all of them can be interpreted into embroidery. Look for unfamiliar and attractive letters in newspaper and magazine titles, in advertisements and in old books. Keep a scrapbook of those that appeal to you and don't overlook the fascinating symbols and characters of other languages, such as Chinese, Japanese, Arabic and Persian.

Using letters for decoration

Letters can be depicted in almost every embroidery stitch and technique. They can be simple, applied in brightly colored fabrics, felts and leathers or intricate, worked in hand and machine embroidery. Work single letters or monograms on pockets and fashion accessories, using the basic shape as a framework for decorative flowers or other small motifs. Build up a design of letters in bold appliqué for casual skirts and pants or work a single, small letter for an unusual and attractive brooch or pendant. Letters can also be used as an integral part of wall panel designs. For instance, an educational yet attractive panel for a child's room could consist of large letters with motifs worked within the shape or groups of letters and motifs telling a simple pictorial story. Letters are also used to tell a message in church embroideries, banners and flags.

Three basic methods of working letters

Satin stitch and cording

This is a very simple and basic embroidery method for working letters. Transfer the letters onto the fabric and pad the solid areas with rows of running stitch, backstitch or chain stitch. The fine lines are padded with backstitch or outline stitch. The solid areas are then worked over in satin stitch and the fine lines in cording. The example shown in this chapter is very simple and suitable for items which receive hard wear such as towels. For a pretty effect on guest linen, the initials can be decorated with a scattering of eyelet holes or small flowers and worked on sheets and pillow cases or dainty guest towels.

Decorative letters

Classic letters take on a decorative illumination style if superimposed over simple flower motifs. One of the "N"s opposite is sewn in double backstitch. The outline of each leaf is worked in outline stitch, the inside in couching and French knots have been added to give texture to the design. The third "N" is worked in Pekinese stitch. This is easy to do. Simply work a row of backstitch (see Embroidery Chapter 5) and interface with a different colored thread, looping the stitch in and out. Pull the loops slightly so that the work becomes regular. See diagram of Pekinese stitch in Embroidery Chapter 44.

Machine embroidered letters

These can be worked on a zigzag machine, in satin stitch or running stitch using the free-motion embroidery method and decorated by hand afterwards. Some machine manufacturers supply a set of semi-automatic templates to be fitted to the sewing machine, and instructions for using these are supplied by the manufacturer. The scarf illustrated here was worked using the template method.

◄ *A fashionable scarf with machine embroidered initials*

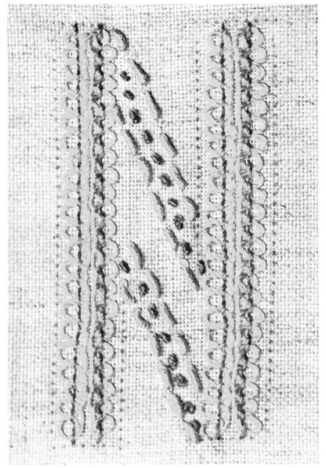

▲ *The letter "N" worked in Pekinese stitch*
▼ *The letter "N" worked in satin stitch*

▲ *Twelve types of the letter "N", all suitable for embroidery*
▼ *The letter "N" worked in double backstitch*

A B C D E F G
H I J K L M
N O P Q R S T
U V W X Y Z

*Trace and enlarge any of the letters from these alphabets
and embroider them in different colors and stitches*

A B C D E F G
H J J K L M
N O P Q R S T
U V W X Y Z

ABCDEFG
HIJKLM
NOPQRST
UVWXYZ

ABCDEFG
HIJKLM
NOPQRST
UVWXYZ

153

Collector's Piece

The sampler below was worked in the early 18th century. It is a clear piece of work embroidered in flowers and animals. The borders are typical of this period. Later samplers became much more extravagant and cluttered. The piece of work on the right shows the beginnings of this trend.

The alphabet and figures feature on the sampler opposite. Hannah Taylor has also worked her name and age on the bottom which is more typical of the late 18th century.

Towards the middle of the 19th century samplers were worked in wool, and design played a more important part than the educational factor.

Learning from samplers

Originally the sampler was worked as an exercise in different stitches. They also served to teach young girls their alphabet and figures.

Chapter 41

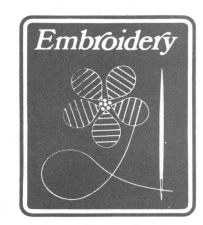

Introduction to cross-stitch

Cross-stitch is one of the oldest and most international embroidery stitches, frequently found in the national costumes of Europe and the Orient where it is often worked in gay, bright colors. It lends itself to fillings and building up traditional geometric patterns, as in Assisi designs, and is also used for interpreting realistic and precisely detailed pictures in the modern Danish manner.

Ideally, cross-stitch should be worked on an even-weave fabric because this makes it easier to count threads, and the whole effect of the stitch depends on its regularity. Each cross-stitch should make a perfect square, since it is worked down and across over an equal number of threads on an even-weave fabric.

The main point to remember is that in whichever direction you work the stitch, the upper stitches must always lie in the same direction (usually from bottom left to top right). If they do not, they will reflect the light differently from the other stitches and will stand out clearly as mistakes.

Methods of working

The most even finish for filling in large areas of color is obtained by working a row of diagonal stitches (half cross-stitches) in one direction and then completing the stitches by working another row in the opposite direction. If you are working an entire design in cross-stitch, keep the texture even by first working the whole design in half cross-stitch and then completing it in the other direction. This also helps you see results very rapidly. If there is only a small area to cover, it is permissible to use the method where one stitch is completed at a time, although this will look less even. To embroider very fine or uneven fabrics, use the canvas method to keep the stitches even. Place a piece of soft cotton canvas

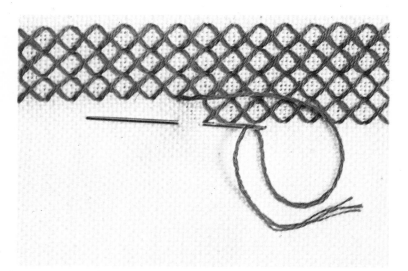

When filling small areas, complete one stitch at a time. Be careful to count the threads, using the weave of the fabric as a guide so that the stitches line up evenly. Work from either left to right or right to left

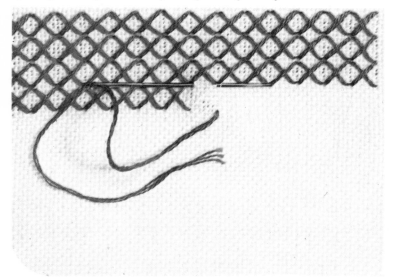

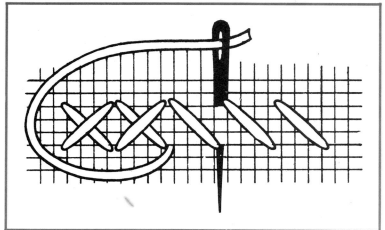

▲ *For large areas it is best to work the cross-stitch in two operations*
▼ *Double cross-stitch steps should be worked in the same order throughout*

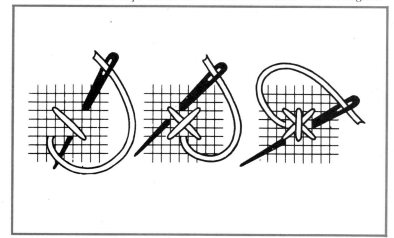

on top of the fabric, matching the warp and weft of the canvas to that of the fabric. Baste it in place. Work the stitches over the threads of the canvas and through the material underneath, being careful not to catch the canvas or pull the stitches too tight. When the embroidery is completely finished, gently pull out from under it the canvas threads one by one.

Home is where the heart is

This gay picture brings a fresh modern approach to the old sampler idea. It was designed to be a very special birthday greeting for the designer's husband, but it could equally well be mounted on a small tray and covered with heatproof glass.
Working charts and full instructions are given on the following two pages, together with color suggestions.

These charts are planned in such a way that you can either use the motifs individually or group them to add up to the complete composition. Each motif has its own color coding which is indicated by the key at the side of each chart. One of the best features of charted designs is that they provide a permanent reference which you can use again and again.

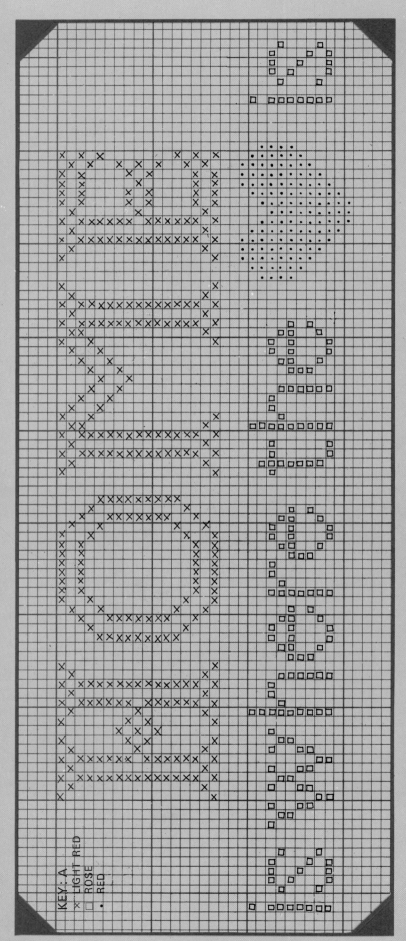

KEY: A
× LIGHT RED
□ ROSE
• RED

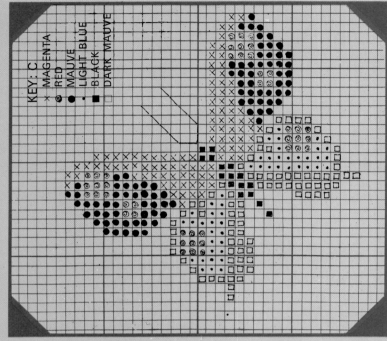

KEY: C
× MAGENTA
⊘ RED
● MAUVE
□ LIGHT BLUE
• BLACK
■ DARK MAUVE

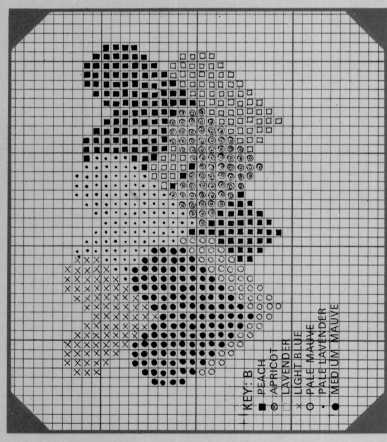

KEY: B
■ PEACH
⊘ APRICOT
□ LAVENDER
× LIGHT BLUE
○ PALE MAUVE
• PALE LAVENDER
● MEDIUM MAUVE

Materials

To make the picture shown (finished size 9in by 8½in) you will need:

- □ ⅔yd of even-weave linen (39 threads to the inch)
- □ 1 skein each of 6-strand embroidery floss in the colors given on the charts, but the leaf green needs 2 skeins
- □ Crewel needle size 8 or 9

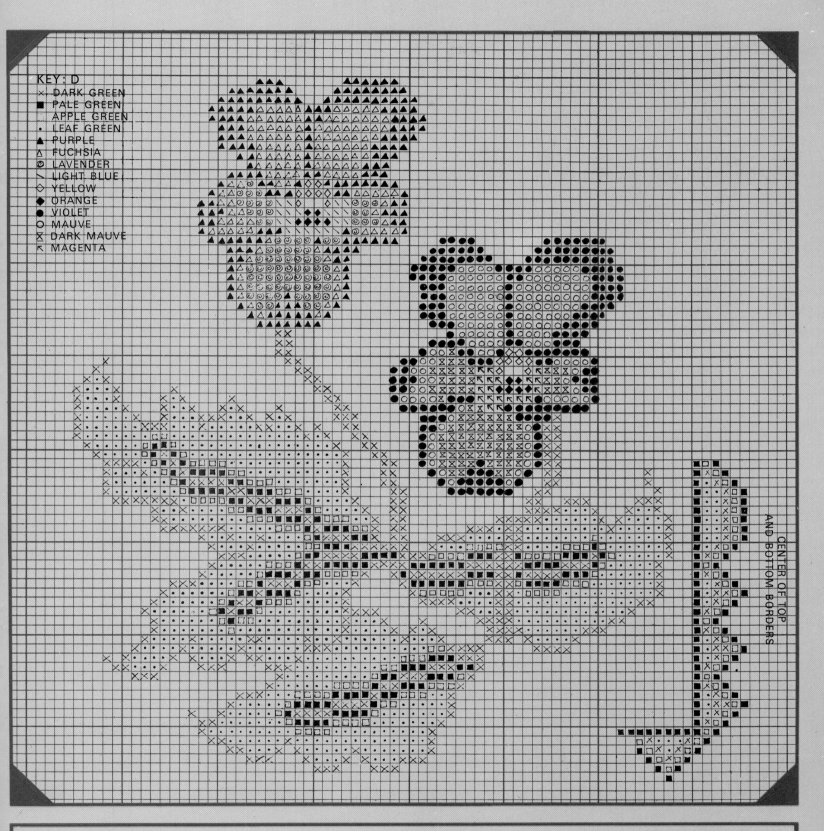

KEY: D
× DARK GREEN
■ PALE GREEN
  APPLE GREEN
· LEAF GREEN
▲ PURPLE
△ FUCHSIA
⊘ LAVENDER
╲ LIGHT BLUE
◇ YELLOW
◆ ORANGE
● VIOLET
○ MAUVE
✕ DARK MAUVE
✂ MAGENTA

CENTER OF TOP AND BOTTOM BORDERS

How to work the sampler

Mark a center line on the fabric with basting stitches. This applies whether you are going to use a single motif or the complete composition. Always start at the center of the design and work outward because this makes the counting easier.

Each square of the chart represents 2 threads of fabric, so work the stitches accordingly, using 3 strands of floss throughout.

When completed, block the embroidery by dampening and pinning to shape. If you are going to use the embroidery for a tray, stretch it on firm cardboard cut to the right size. Fasten excess fabric on the back of the cardboard with masking tape. Cover with glass. If you are making a picture, take the embroidery to an expert for mounting and framing, unless you feel able to do it yourself. Instructions for mounting and framing follow in Embroidery Chapter 21.

Collector's Piece

The Hastings Embroidery

This embroidery was commissioned by the Borough of Hastings from the Royal School of Needlework to celebrate the 900th anniversary of the Battle of Hastings. A team of 18 embroiderers took just over a year to complete the embroidery which consists of 27 panels, each measuring nine feet by three feet, 243 feet in all. They depict important events in British history, from the arrival of William the Conqueror to the present day. Shown here are panels nos. 7, 14, 16 and 17.

14th–15th century

At the Battle of Bannockburn in 1314, Robert the Bruce of Scotland defeats Edward II of England.

Relations between England and France become hostile, and the year 1337 witnesses the start of the Hundred Years' War.

The French are defeated in 1346 at the Battle of Crécy by the English army under the leadership of Edward III and the Black Prince.

16th–17th century

Queen Elizabeth I commissions Sir Walter Raleigh to found the first colony in America, Virginia. Mary Queen of Scots, accused of originating a plot to assassinate Queen Elizabeth, is found guilty and condemned to death in 1586. The Spanish Armada sails into battle with the English fleet in an attempt to overthrow Elizabeth I's campaign of Protestantism.

17th–18th century

In late summer of 1620, the *Mayflower*, with Pilgrims aboard, sets sail for America, landing on December 11. Civil war rages in England, the monarchy against Parliament. The crowd rejoices at the restoration of the monarch in 1660.

17th–19th century

The Great Plague of 1665 ravages London, killing thousands of people. A year later, London is hit by the Great Fire which started in a baker's shop and burned for three days. Many of London's buildings and churches were destroyed, including St. Paul's Cathedral which was rebuilt by Christopher Wren.

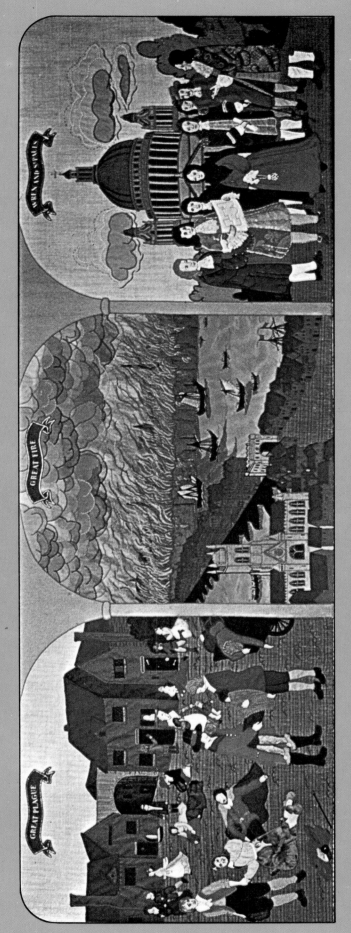

Chapter 42

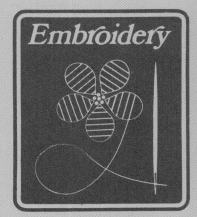

Decorative table mats in cross~stitch

These delightful butterfly motifs, worked in cross-stitch on a medium weave fabric, are typical of the freshness associated with Scandinavian table linen designs. Worked to the size of the charts on pages 164 and 165, the motifs will make table mats measuring about 6 inches square. Worked on coarser weaves, so that the motifs are enlarged, the butterflies can be used for a square tablecloth, worked in the corners or in the center. A single motif would also make a charming pillow design or, mounted in a small frame, a pretty picture.

To make the set of six mats, each measuring 6 inches by 6 inches, you will need:
- □ ½yd 60 inch wide ecru colored linen with 25 threads to 1 inch
- □ Tapestry needle No.24
- □ D.M.C. 6-strand floss in the following colors and amounts:
  One skein each of—
  brown 975, light orange 973, medium orange 972, light mauve 210, dark pink 600, pink 602, light pink 604, light mustard 834, dark mustard 832, dark orange 971, dark mauve 552, light blue 996, dark blue 995.
  Two skeins each of—
  dark green 470, light green 471

Use D.M.C. 6-strand floss in the following colors for each mat

Mat No. 1—975, 973, 972, 210, 600, 470, 834, 832.
Mat No. 2—975, 971, 972, 973, 471, 470, 834, 832.
Mat No. 3—210, 552, 996, 995, 471, 470, 834, 832.
Mat No. 4—600, 996, 995, 972, 971, 470, 834, 832, 471.
Mat No. 5—975, 604, 602, 600, 210, 552, 470, 834, 832.
Mat No. 6—975, 973, 972, 971, 604, 602, 600, 471, 470, 834, 832.

Working the mats

For each mat, cut a square of fabric measuring 10 inches by 10 inches on the straight grain of the fabric. Prepare the work by drawing out two threads on all four sides, 2¼ inches from the edge. Overcast the edges to prevent fraying. Refer to the photographs as a guide to the placing of each design and work, following the graphs. Work cross-stitches (see Embroidery Chapter 41) over two threads of fabric each way using two strands of floss. The solid areas are worked in cross-stitch and the single lines, such as those for the butterflies' antennae and legs, in double running stitch.

Making the mats

When the embroidery is completed, press on the wrong side over a damp cloth. Cut away the surplus fabric to within 1¼ inches from drawn threads on each edge. Make a hem all around each mat ¼ inch deep, miter the corners and turn up the hem to the very edge of the drawn threads and baste. Secure the hem with hand-kerchief hemstitch (see Embroidery Chapter 32), picking up two drawn threads at a time and pulling the working thread firmly to bunch each group.

1

4

2

3

5

6

1

2

4

5

Chapter 43

Introduction to blackwork

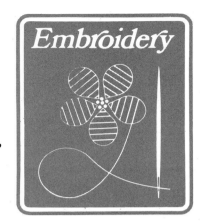

Embroidery

Blackwork embroidery was probably of African origin and introduced to Spain by the Moors. Although blackwork was not entirely unknown in England, Henry VIII's Spanish wife Katharine of Aragon increased its popularity, and throughout Tudor and Elizabethan times the embroidery was used extensively on clothes and gradually came to be used on household linens such as bed hangings.

The delightful panel of fishes in this chapter has been specially designed for us as a modern interpretation of blackwork, and though it may at first sight appear complicated, the design can be easily copied from the tracing outline on page 168, where instructions for making the panel can also be found.

In simple terms, blackwork is a monochrome method of embroidery. It relies for effect on the relationships of tone values and consists of a variety of light fillings in well-planned shapes with neatly defined outlines. Traditionally worked in black on white with additional touches of gold and silver threads, the dramatic tone contrast has always been the main attraction of this method.

In modern embroidery design, however, color has been introduced. The choice of color or colors needs considerable care and the stronger the contrast the more dramatic the effect. Experiment with color contrasts and combinations of colors such as white embroidery on black, red on pink, brown on cream or beige, until you achieve the desired effect and your own individual style.

Blackwork can be used to great effect on all types of clothing such as blouses, dresses and skirts, or on household linens such as runners, tablecloths, place mats, curtains, pillows and wall panels. Stitches in blackwork are worked over counted threads of even-weave fabric and as a result designs tend to be angular. However, areas of filling can be tapered off to produce more rounded or pointed shapes which do not have to be enclosed in an outline stitch. Alternatively, flowing lines of stitching can be incorporated as an integral part of a design to give a freer feeling. Certain pattern lines and shapes can be strengthened by using a thicker yarn or by working over fewer threads of fabric, whereas lighter areas are created by working with finer yarn or by working over more threads of fabric.

Fabrics

Suitable fabrics include embroidery linen, or synthetic dress or home furnishing fabrics with a precise even weave of between thirteen to thirty-nine threads to the inch, provided the threads are clear enough to count.

Yarns

Generally speaking, the thickness of the yarns should correspond to the threads of the fabric, but this can vary depending on the final effect required.

Six-strand floss, pearl cotton, sewing thread, machine embroidery thread, matte embroidery cotton and various kinds of metal threads (see Embroidery Chapters 45 and 46) can all be used in blackwork. To keep the effect precise, it is best to use single thread in the needle, but for a softer effect use two or three strands of six-strand floss.

Stitches

Blackwork outlines can be worked in a variety of stitches such as outline stitch, backstitch, whipped backstitch, coral stitch and couching.

Filling stitches, which are used to form the patterns, are based on straight stitches—running stitch, backstitch and double running or Holbein stitch. Cross-stitch and its variations are also used as filling stitches, and darning, which is one of the simplest forms of embroidery, makes an interesting filling.

Stitch Library

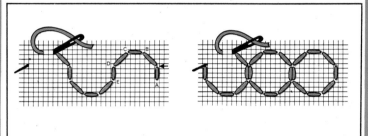

Ringed backstitch
Alternate halves of the circles are worked in backstitch and completed on the return journey. This stitch can be used as a filling or border stitch.

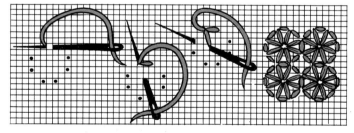

Eyelet filling stitch
A pretty filling stitch of eyelets with a backstitch worked over two threads of fabric between the spokes of the stitch.

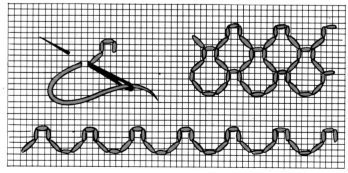

Festoon
This filling stitch is worked in backstitch. It can also be used in horizontal lines.

Double running stitch (Holbein stitch). This stitch is worked in two stages by working running stitch over the counted threads and then a second row filling the spaces left by the first.

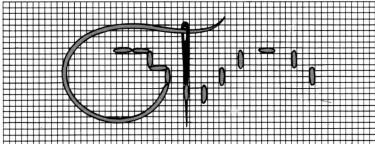

▲ *The two stages of working double running stitch*

Eye stitch. Worked with eight stitches of equal length radiating from a central point.

Coral stitch. Working from right to left, bring thread up through the fabric and hold with the thumb of the left hand. Take a small stitch at right angles to the thread, going under and over it. Pull up to form a small knot.

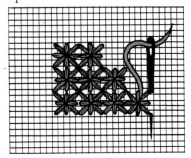 

▲ *Method of working eye stitch*   ▲ *Method of working coral stitch*

Transferring designs
Use the trace and baste method for transferring designs, described in Embroidery Chapter 4.

Using a frame
It is advisable to use a frame for this type of embroidery. A hoop is suitable for small pieces of work and a square frame for larger pieces.

A blackwork panel of fishes for you to copy shown life size ►
▼ *One of the fishes in the panel enlarged to show stitch detail*

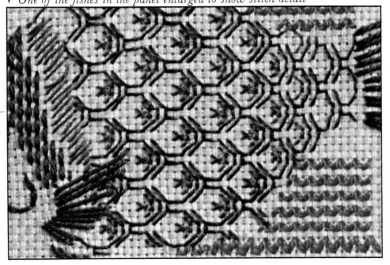

Blackwork fish panel

Add sophistication and style to your home. Make this fish panel in blackwork and try out different stitch patterns to create your own exciting effects. The diagrams on the opposite page give you an idea of the basic pattern and stitch forms you can incorporate into your work.

Materials you will need
- [ ] Hardanger cotton 22 threads to the inch
- [ ] Tapestry needle No. 24
- [ ] Crewel needle No. 7 or 8
- [ ] Embroidery threads

Fish A
tail	Coton à Broder
fins	Coton à Broder
face	Pearl Cotton No. 8: one skein
body	Six-strand floss: one skein

Fish B
face	Coton à Broder
tail	Coton à Broder
fins (below face)	Coton à Broder
body	Six-strand floss: one skein
main fins	Pearl Cotton No. 8: one skein

Fish C
outline	Coton à Broder
eye	Coton à Broder
lower shape	Coton à Broder
tail	Coton à Broder
fins	Coton à Broder
body	Six-strand floss: one skein

How to transfer the pattern and design
Trace the outline drawing onto tissue paper and baste to background fabric (see Embroidery Chapter 4) making sure the sides are parallel with the grain. Tear away tissue paper carefully and stretch the background material in a frame, or pin it to a rectangular one, keeping the fabric perfectly square. Start with a line of the stitching down the center of an area and work outward, stopping wherever it touches the basted outline.

How to enlarge the design
A heavier fabric can be used to enlarge the design. However, if the stitches are copied direct from the photograph on page 167 they will automatically be more open, but by using a thicker thread a closer texture will be achieved. Alternatively, see what additional pattern you can add to a stitch in the way of diagonal, horizontal or cross-stitches.

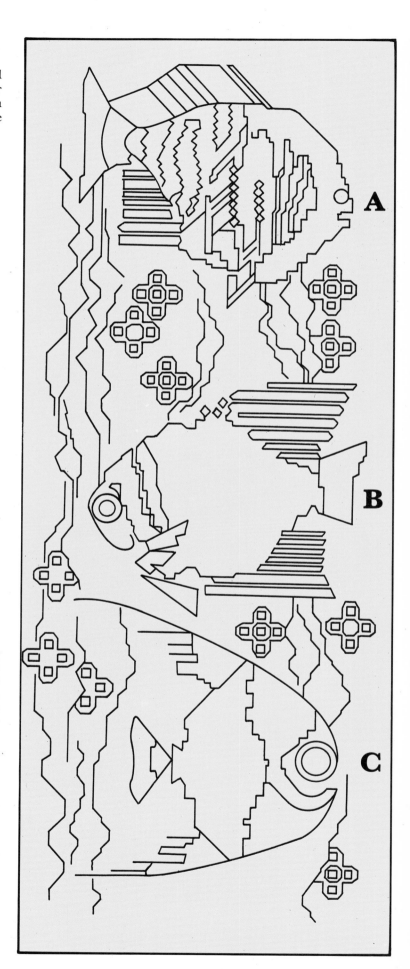

Try out different stitch patterns

Have plenty of material so that stitches can be tried out on the side. This is important in order that you can see what thickness of thread gives the weight and achieves the effect you want in the design. The same stitch worked using a thick thread and then a thin thread gives a very good idea of the total values you can achieve. Look, for instance, at the zigzag stitches on the fins of Fish A and then at those on its back.

Remember, stitches normally go over one thread or square at a time, so if you want a long line or longer stitch it must be divided and worked as a backstitch. This can be illustrated by the working on the head and body of Fish A. The exception to this can be seen in the tails and some of the fins. You can always break a rule providing the effect achieved is correct.

Designing your own stitches

Start with a simple, basic stitch and add to it in different ways, so building them up to make your own designs. Remember to leave the original stitch open in order to make room for additions.

The pattern on the back of Fish C is achieved by filling in the basic pattern with crosses of different weights so that an even texture is formed. Basic patterns for you to start working from are shown below.

Basic patterns to start working from

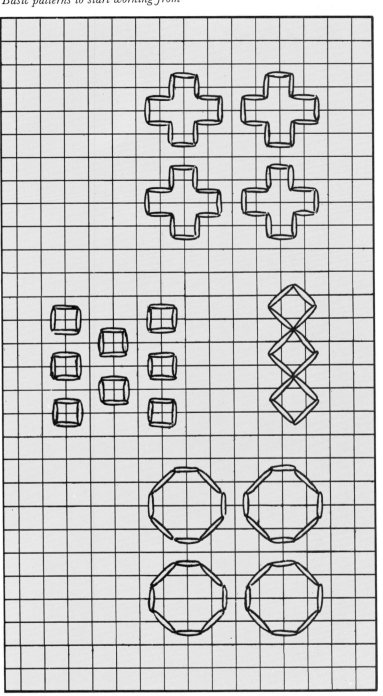

Cross-stitch forms the basis of each stitch pattern

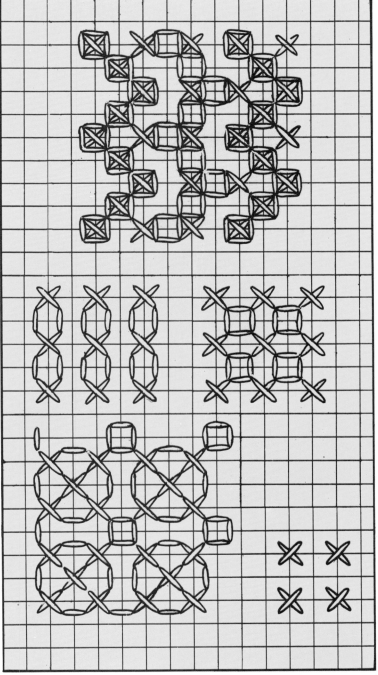

Chapter 44

Eastern fantasy panel in blackwork

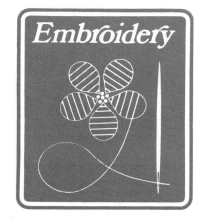

This intriguing Eastern fantasy panel uses a modern interpretation of the ancient form of embroidery known as blackwork. The completed effect is simply a build-up of straight and simple stitches. Each individual building on the panel is a complete design in itself and can be used on its own.

On the following pages is an almost life-size reproduction of the Eastern panel with a scale below indicating the number of threads. The panel can be used as a chart from which to work.

Materials you will need
- ☐ ½yd 59 inch wide even-weave linen with 21 threads to the inch (finished size of panel 23½ inches by 13½ inches)
- ☐ 6 skeins black six-strand floss
- ☐ 1 spool Penelope metallic gold cord
- ☐ 3 cards Penelope gold lurex
- ☐ 1 card Penelope silver lurex
- ☐ Tapestry needle size 22 (for working gold and silver threads)
- ☐ Tapestry needle size 26 (for working six-strand floss)
- ☐ Hardboard 23½ inches by 13½ inches
- ☐ Embroidery frame

Working from the picture overleaf

This is a counted thread design and the stitches are worked over the counted threads of the fabric. The almost life-size picture of the panel on the following pages can therefore

170

be used as a working chart. The diagrams show how some of the more complicated filling patterns are built up, and these are numbered to identify them with the areas to be worked in the patterns on the outline diagram. Each grid line of the filling pattern diagrams represents one thread of the fabric.

Using the threads
Six-strand floss. Use two strands for the filling patterns and outlines, one strand for the paving, and four strands on the towers of the left-hand building.

Gold and silver lurex. Use single for stitching, double for couching.

Metallic gold cord. Use double throughout.

Stitches in the design

Outlines
In blackwork, the outline is worked before the filling patterns. The main outline stitch in this design is whipped back-stitch worked in 6-strand floss. Other outline effects are as follows:

Couched gold. Two lengths of couched gold lurex thread are caught down with one thread of 6-strand floss on the large towers of the left-hand building and on the outline of the center front roof of the right-hand building.

Whipped backstitch. This is worked entirely in gold lurex on the base of the large towers of the left-hand building, around the diamond shape on the center roof of the same building, on the side turrets and the

top center dome of the center building, and around the large dome of the right-hand building.

A row of backstitch is worked over as shown in the diagram, using either a self color or a contrasting color.

Double whipped backstitch. Black backstitch with gold lurex whipping on the side domes of the right-hand building.

This is worked in the same way as whipped backstitch, and a second row of whip stitches is worked back along the line of backstitches in the opposite direction.

Backstitch. This is worked on the edge of the section immediately below the domes on the right-hand building.

Pekinese stitch. This is worked with black backstitch and gold lurex interlacing on the center section of the large dome on the center building. A foundation line of small backstitches has a second thread looped through. Do not carry second thread to back of work except at beginning and end of row.

Filling stitches
Pattern fillings are worked after the outline has been completed and consist of straight stitches worked over counted threads. The two smaller rounded towers and the doors of the large building are worked in double cross-stitch. The filling pattern on the large central dome consists of satin stitch blocks worked and interlaced with metallic gold cord.

Threaded satin stitch. The blocks of satin stitch are threaded through in zigzag fashion using self or contrasting color thread.

Mounting the panel

When the embroidery is completed, remove it from the frame and press lightly on the back of the work using a dry cloth to protect the metal threads from heat. Mount the panel on a piece of hardboard, as described in Embroidery Chapter 21.

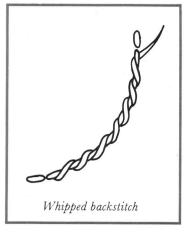

Whipped backstitch

Double whipped backstitch

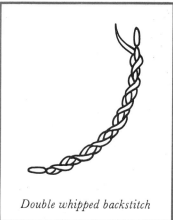

Pekinese stitch

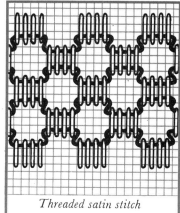

Threaded satin stitch

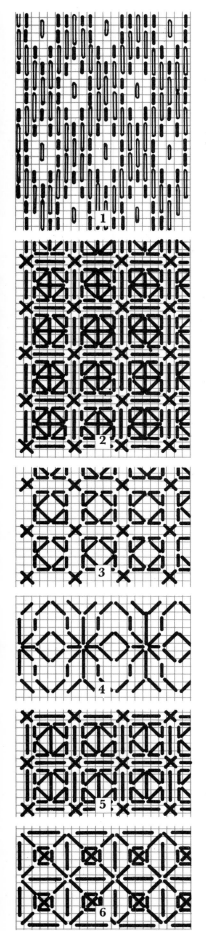

▲ *An Eastern fantasy wall panel* ▼ *The numbered areas in the diagram refer to the filling patterns on this page*

171

10   20   30   40   50   60   70   80   90   100   110   120   130   140   150   160   170   180   190   200   210   220   230

Each mark on the scale indicates every tenth thread on the fabric

260 270 280 290 300 310 320 330 340 350 360 370 380 390 400 410 420 430 440 450 460 470 480

173

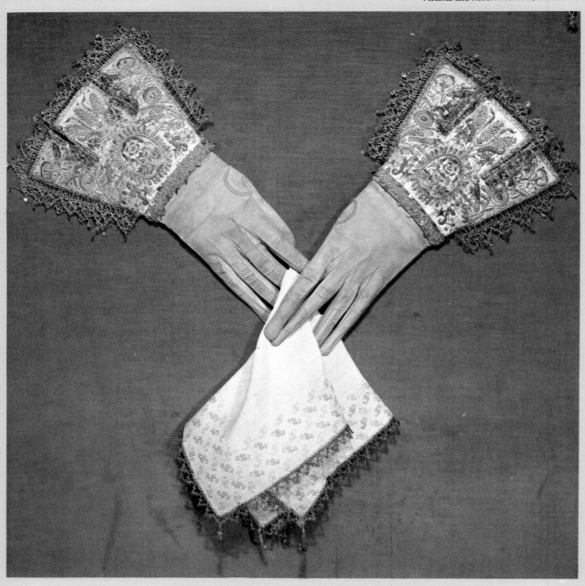

Collector's Piece

Gloves fit for a Queen

At the court of Queen Elizabeth 1, the practice of giving presents at New Year was an important part of court life, and embroidery was considered a valuable gift, worthy of being presented to the Queen. Elizabeth received presents from all her high-ranking officials—embroidered gowns, petticoats, doublets and other articles of clothing—and embroidered gloves featured high on the list. The Queen was presented with costly embroidered gloves on other occasions also; she received a pair from both Oxford and Cambridge Universities when she visited them. The embroidered gloves of this period were so ornate and heavy that they were no longer regarded as useful articles but purely as ornamentation. They were rarely worn, and subsequently examples of the beautiful work have survived, the colors only slightly faded. The gloves illustrated are made of pale colored doeskin with gauntlets of silk cut into six scallops or tabs. The crimson velvet "mittens" have their gauntlets cut into eight tabs. The designs worked on both gloves are typically Elizabethan, consisting of flowers, fruits, insects and entwined stems, with each of the tabs containing a different flower or plant motif. Colored silks, gold threads and small jewels were used for the embroidery, and the doeskin gloves are trimmed with gold lace.

Chapter 45

Introduction to metal thread embroidery

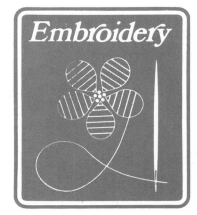

Embroidery

The character of metal thread embroidery is completely different from that of other kinds of embroidery. Gold or silver threads are couched onto the surface of fabric, while beads, pieces of kid, gold purl and colored yarns add contrast, richness and texture to the design.

Everyone who becomes interested in gold work experiences a thrill in working with the precious metal threads. The shimmer and glitter of the embroidery evoke images of rich tapestries and fabulous jewels, and even the simplest designs have a satisfying splendor about them.

The success of gold work lies in a thorough understanding of the materials used, careful planning and skillful manipulation of the metal threads.

This chapter deals with the basic materials and equipment needed for this fascinating craft.

Tools and equipment

The various pieces of equipment needed for metal thread embroidery, or gold work as it is generally known, may seem at first to be somewhat numerous. However, there are different techniques in gold work and all the items here are important to the success of the work.

Embroidery frame

It is essential to use a frame for metal thread embroidery. The fabric must be held taut in order to support the threads in smooth lines and to avoid puckering.

Needles

Three sizes of crewel needle are required: No.5 for framing; No.8 for general use and No.10 for couching and applying purl gold. A chenille needle size No.20 is used for finishing off ends of metal threads and a heavy embroidery needle is used for string.

String in gold work

A strong string or twine is used for framing. You will also need two balls of good quality string of different thicknesses for padding purposes.

Felt sausage

Pure gold threads are kept wound on a roll of felt to prevent kinking. Make a "sausage" by rolling a 9in by 9in piece of felt and slip stitch along the edge to hold the roll in shape.

Purl cutting board

Prepare a cutting board by gluing a rectangle of felt or velvet measuring 3 inches by 4 inches to a piece of cardboard. Purl gold pieces are cut above the board so that the pieces fall onto the

fabric. The pile prevents the springy coils from jumping away.

Gold thread storage

Gold threads are fairly costly, particularly the pure gold qualities, and care should be taken to prevent the unused threads from becoming damaged. Keep threads wound on rolls of felt and stored in an air-tight container. A can with a press-on lid would be suitable, or an opaque plastic container with a fitted top.

Acid-free tissue paper

This is essential for covering gold work while it is in progress, for protection and to help prevent tarnishing. Acid-free tissue paper is the most common variety and is available in most stationers. As an extra precaution, check the variety with the assistant.

Varieties of metal threads

There are several qualities of metal embroidery thread (see Yarn Chart on pages 12 and 13), ranging from pure gold and silver to the synthetic types. Some of the threads are inclined to tarnish but they are still worth including in a design for the contrast which slightly discolored threads can lend to gold work.

Japanese gold

Japanese gold is pure gold thread. Because it does not tarnish, it is often used for the main lines of a design. Japanese gold consists of a core of fine silk floss thread over which finely beaten and cut gold is coiled. The silk core varies in color and if the coiled gold unwinds, the core shows through, spoiling the look of the work. It is sometimes necessary to twist the metal thread between thumb and forefinger before and after each couching stitch is made. Japanese gold should be kept wound in double threads around a felt roll.

Passing gold

Passing gold thread contains a high proportion of gold and has a soft, smooth appearance. This thread is easier for beginners to use because the gold is coiled more tightly than Japanese gold and the core doesn't show through when corners are turned.

Admiralty quality

These threads contain a high proportion of gold but are less expensive than the pure gold quality. Admiralty quality is inclined to tarnish, but so slowly that it is often unnoticeable.

Synthetic gold thread

Synthetic metal thread will not tarnish, but the surface is even and the shine almost hard compared with pure gold, which has a much warmer appearance. Contrast is, however, an essential part of embroidery design and, combined with real gold threads, synthetic gold supports and enriches the overall effect of gold work.

Silver thread

Silver threads are available in the same range of qualities and types as gold threads.

Braids, string and cords

There are a number of braids, novelty gift wrapping strings and cords which can be used in metal thread embroidery. These are mostly synthetic. Braids and strings can either be used as they are or unraveled. Used in their wrinkled state, unraveled threads can give a three dimensional quality to a design.

Types of gold purl

Purl looks like a fine metal spring coil and is usually made from

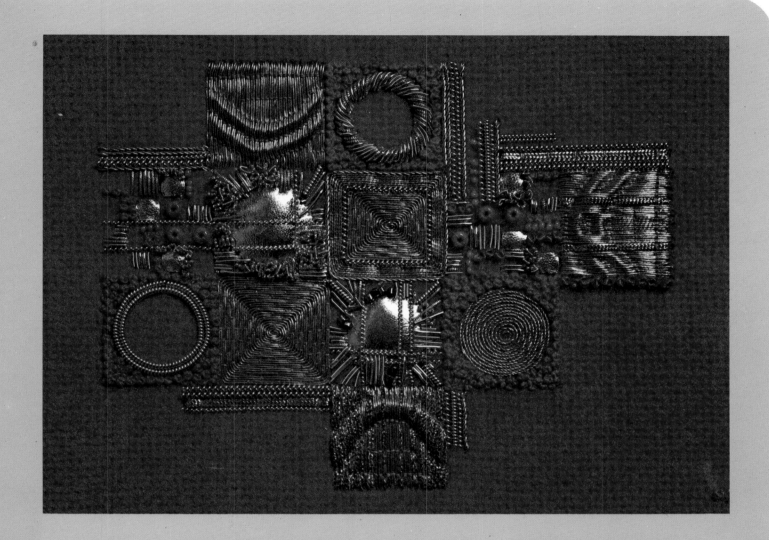

▲ *This modern design in metal thread embroidery shows examples of many of the threads mentioned here. Working techniques are given in the next chapter*

Admiralty quality metal. Purl is purchased in lengths, and various surfaces and thicknesses are available.

Pearl purl This is a coarse and slightly inflexible purl and is usually couched in lengths rather than cut into small pieces.

Check purl A fine metal thread which has been bent into angles before being coiled, check purl has a sparkling, checkered appearance.

Smooth purl Smooth purl is a flexible plain coil with a highly polished surface.

Rough purl Rather misnamed, rough purl does not have a rough surface but it does have a softer effect than smooth purl.

Threads and yarns

In gold work designs, colored embroidery threads can be used for contrast and for breaking down the glare from flat, highly reflective areas.

Maltese silk

This is recommended for couching. Several shades of yellow are available for working on gold thread and gray is used when working on silver thread.

Materials for padding

Pieces of non-woven material, such as kid, leather, vinyl and felt are used in gold work designs, either applied flat to the surface or padded out.

Fabrics and backings

Almost any material can be used for metal thread work providing it isn't too loosely woven. Dress-weight fabrics made from man-made fibers should be avoided because they are likely to split when the metal threads are pulled through.

In metal thread embroidery, as with other forms of embroidery, contrast of texture is an important part of design. Tweed, soft wool, and home furnishing linen, as well as pure silk and velvet, can be used very effectively.

It is advisable to line background fabrics before starting gold work, choosing a material of approximately the same weight. Linen, muslin or other cotton can be used, but lining material should be pre-shrunk before being used.

The next gold work chapter deals with design and methods of working the materials used in gold work.

Chapter 46

How to work metal thread embroidery

Beautiful metal thread work depends largely on the manipulation of the precious metal or synthetic threads. The techniques are simple, but the results exotic.

Preparing to work. Once you have collected the various pieces of equipment (Embroidery Chapter 45) choose a suitable background fabric and back it for extra strength. Trace the design onto the right side of the fabric (Embroidery Chapter 4) using the basting method and a thread matched to the background fabric.

Mount the backed fabric on a frame (see Embroidery Chapter 18).

Couching with metal threads. Work with two lengths of fine gold thread for both single lines and solid areas. Drag a length of Maltese silk once through a block of beeswax to strengthen it against the friction of the metal threads. Using a No.1 crewel needle, first make a knot at the end of the silk and then work one small backstitch on the design line. Hold the two gold threads together in position, leaving free about one inch from the beginning, to be worked through the fabric later. Work two couching stitches over the gold thread, stitching through the same hole in the fabric, and continue along the length of the metal thread, working single couching stitches about $\frac{1}{4}$ inch apart. Pull the gold threads slightly taut as you work.

Stop about $\frac{1}{4}$ inch from the end of the design line being worked and make two couching stitches as you did at the beginning,

178

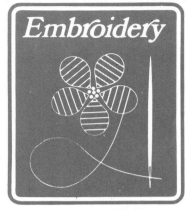

finishing with two backstitches. Cut off excess gold thread, leaving about one inch to be worked through later.

Finishing off ends. Ends of gold thread should be left on the right side of the fabric until work is completed. If the ends are taken through while work is in progress, they are likely to tangle or unravel.

Using a No.18 chenille needle, insert the point into the fabric where the metal thread is to go through. Thread the inch of metal through the eye of the needle (diagram **2**). Supporting the work with the left hand underneath, quickly and firmly pull the needle and thread through the fabric. Some threads may be too thick to go through all at once. These should be divided and each strand taken through separately. Once the metal threads are at the back of the work, cut to $\frac{1}{2}$ inch and overcast them to the backing fabric with two or three stitches.

Couching over string. An interesting effect is achieved by couching several lengths of gold thread close together over a "ladder" of string (see sample). The string must be stitched firmly to the background before the metal threads are couched down.

Cut off lengths of string. Hold one piece of string in position, leaving an inch free, and at the beginning of the line make two stitches, working through the same hole to secure the string to the background fabric. The stitches should go through the core of the string and not over the surface. Work stitches each side of the string (diagram **3**) and finish off with double stitches at the end. Cut off excess string, as close to the double end stitches as possible. When all the pieces of string required for the padded area have been couched down, work the gold threads over the string "ladder" (see sample). The gold threads should be worked lying close together so that the string is completely covered.

Turning corners and angles. Sometimes a design demands that the metal threads turn at angles on the surface of the fabric (see sample). To work corners and angles, make normal couching stitches along the two metal threads to within $\frac{1}{4}$ inch of the corner or angle. Each single thread is taken around separately, the outer one first. Make a sharply defined angle in the metal thread, using a pair of tweezers, and then make two diagonal couching stitches into the corner, one on each thread, first stitching the outside thread and then the inner one.

Solid areas of couching. When a large area of gold thread couching is worked, instead of cutting both ends of the threads on each row, one of the two threads is brought back on the second row with a new single thread (see sample). A double stitch is required on the turn and a hidden double stitch is worked to hold the new thread in place.

For circular or irregular shapes made up entirely of metal threads, start at the outer edge to establish the shape and work toward the center. Pure gold thread is generally used for outlining a design because this thread does not tarnish and the outline stays clearly defined. Make sure that the metal threads lie close together in

solid areas. If the needle is angled toward the metal thread when the couching stitches are being made, this will help to achieve the effect (diagram **1**).

Using purl. The sample shows several different ways of using pieces of purl. They can be built up into geometric patterns, formed into loops on the surface and used for powdering or seeding on the background. Purl gold cut into short pieces, up to $\frac{3}{8}$ inch long, can be stitched like beads onto the background.

Purl can be used over padded areas to give a raised, purl area or stitched around the edges of applied gold kid. It can also be couched in rows over string, either at right angles or diagonally across it. Purl can be used in short pieces or couched in lengths.

To make purl loops, bring the needle through to the right side and thread on a small length of purl. Put the needle back into the work a shorter distance than the length of the piece of purl, and pull the thread tight until the loops stand up.

Bring thread through to the right side and repeat.

Always cut purl on a cutting board (see Embroidery Chapter 45).

Padded Areas.

Any material which does not fray can be used in metal thread work—kid, suede, leather, vinyl or felt.

To pad fabrics, draw the shape to be padded onto felt and then cut out the shape fractionally smaller all around. For more raised padding, consecutively smaller layers of felt are cut out. The smallest piece of padding is stitched to the background fabric first and then each larger layer in turn, the stitches going right through to the background fabric (see diagram). The surface fabric of the shape is then pinned over the padding and secured with three or four stitches around the edge, or in the corners. Complete the stitching all around, using stab stitch and working the stitches at right angles to the cut edge.

To make a pendant

Materials
- [ ] Piece of silk measuring 7in by 7in
- [ ] Piece of cardboard 2⅛in by 2⅛in
- [ ] Small scrap of gold kid
- [ ] Metal threads of various types
- [ ] Metal link: gold and green beads
- [ ] ½yd velvet ribbon
- [ ] Hooks and eyes

Trace, enlarge and transfer the design from this page onto the background fabric using the basting method described in Embroidery Chapter 4. Work the design using the metal threads as shown, stitching beads and purl loops into position. Mount the piece of work over the cardboard and secure firmly by lacing as if mounting a panel (Embroidery Chapter 21). Cover the back of the pendant with a piece of the fabric or a small piece of fine Japanese silk to match the background color and stitch neatly in place. Sew the metal link securely to one of the corners of the pendant and then onto the ribbon. Hem raw ends of ribbon and sew on two sets of hooks and eyes.

This sample illustrates the methods of working and some of the effects that can be achieved in metal thread embroidery. Read from the top.

1. *Top row, left to right:*
Simple couching effects. The method of couching down metal threads, the needle angled to insure that the stitches lie closely together; double stitches worked at the beginning and end of a row and bricked couching; couching stitches evenly distributed; two ways of couching down flat braids using large couching stitches or small diagonal backstitches; flat plaited braid couched down with tiny backstitches down the center of the braid; a method for couching down twisted metal thread, the stitches made at an angle to the twist and into the middle of the thread; a method of couching pearl purl, small angled stitches being made between the twists of purl.

2. The method used for pulling metal threads through to the wrong side of the work.

3. Couching over string. Stitched down string, the ends cut close to the double stitches; three effects of couching over string, (left to right), passing gold thread with two double couched stitches between; flat lurex braid with one double couching stitch between the pieces of string and uneven bricking; using several different types of gold thread.

4. Couched threads turned at an angle on the background fabric.

5. Four different effects when working couched threads over a large area (read downward). For a round or irregular shape, start on the outside of the shape and work inward toward the center; turning alternate threads back and introducing new threads, the couching worked in a bricking effect; simple even couching stitches, alternate threads turned back and new threads introduced; small pieces of cardboard stitched to the background fabric first and metal threads couched down over the cardboard.

6. Progressive stages of making a raised padded area. The smallest piece of felt is stitched down first and each larger layer is stitched over the smaller layer in turn. Four stab stitches are made at equidistant intervals around the edge of each piece of felt to insure even spread of fullness, then the rest of the stitches are filled in. The piece of gold kid is stitched down over the felt padding, using the same method.

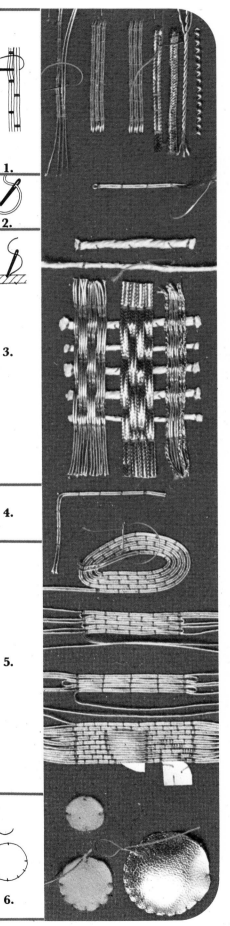

Chapter 47

Experiments in metal thread embroidery

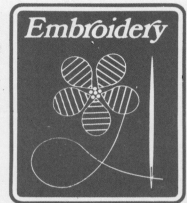

This chapter on metal thread embroidery illustrates some of the different effects which can be achieved by varying the threads and the techniques of applying them.

Although gold threads are rich and exciting to work with, silver and silver lurex threads produce embroidery with a cool and exquisite look.

Uses

Metal thread embroidery is traditionally associated with ecclesiastical work as a decoration for copes, miters, altar frontals, pulpit falls and prayer book covers, but in modern embroidery it is used for wall panels and as a decoration for lids of fabric jewelry boxes.

On fashion garments metal thread embroidery adds luxurious richness, and need not cause cleaning problems as a variety of washable lurex yarns are available.

Fir cone

The background fabric is a cotton/synthetic mixture in dark brown. The applied fabrics are Japanese silk in bronze, gold kid in a variety of tones, and gloving leathers in browns. The metal threads used are Japanese gold, pearl purl, lurex in antique gold and gold fingering knitting yarn. The Japanese silk was applied first, couched down with Japanese gold and lurex. Shapes cut from leather and gold kid form the cone seeds detail. Couched gold threads and gold fingering knitting yarn are used for the finer design lines.

Tree bark

The background fabric used here is natural colored burlap, and the applied fabric is gold orion cloth which resembles kid. The raised, padded sections were worked first. Several layers of felt in varying sizes were stitched in place beginning with the smallest and finishing with the largest, giving a smooth, rounded padding. The orion cloth was then stitched down over the padding. The textured stitchery is a combination of gold and lurex threads couched down in vertical flowing lines to form rhythm in the design.

Silver on blue

This sampler is worked on a slub textured home furnishing fabric, using a variety of materials in tones of silver. Narrow silver ribbon was bunched in a random fashion and tiny matte silver beads were stitched into the folds. Silver checkered purl, cut in lengths, was applied in small loops. Finer silver and lurex threads and pure silk scatter the background in the form of small star stitches and random crossed threads to contrast with the heavier textures. The circles of silver kid make interesting focal highlights.

▼ *The design entitled "fir cone" worked in gold kid and leather*

"Tree bark" which uses padded areas▼   *Silver on blue, cool and lovely*▼

COLLECTOR'S PIECE

An embroidered pachyderm

This sophisticated animal motif illustrates how versatile embroidery can be. An ingenious idea is the addition of shells, sequins and silver kid on the rhino giving it a glamour quite unknown in the real animal! The rhino's tough, heavy skin has been translated into an intricate pattern without losing the impression of weight. Coarseness of texture has been emphasized by using shells and small padded areas. Plain fabric shapes form a balanced contrast. The stitchery is restrained, so that the fabric and padding dominate the composition.

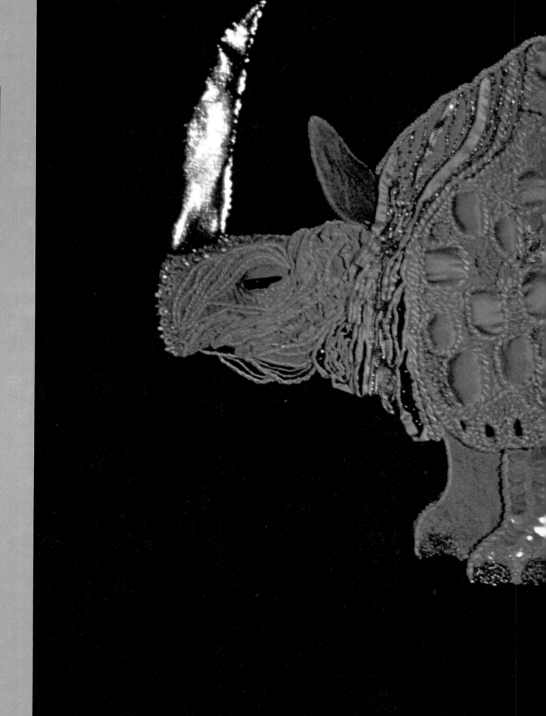

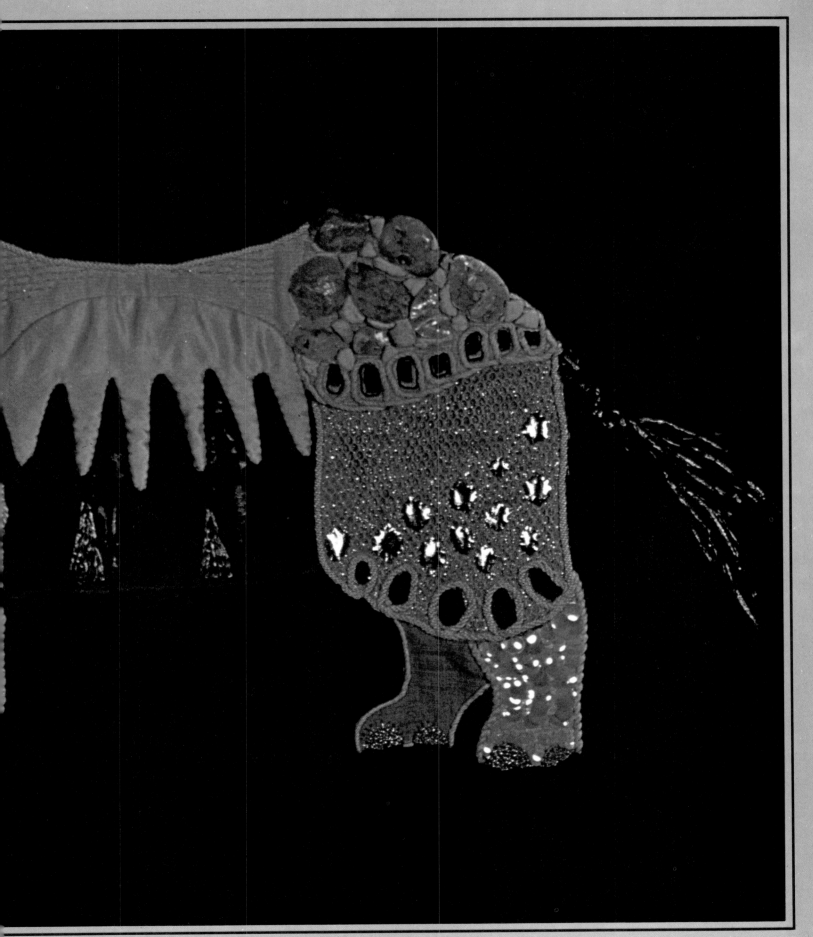

Chapter 48

Introduction to beading

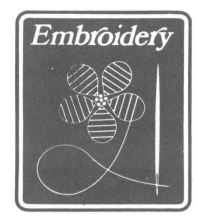

Methods and materials used for modern bead embroidery.

Materials and equipment

Thread
Cotton or silk thread is used for bead embroidery, and should be of the finest and strongest quality available. Before use, the thread is drawn once across beeswax and is used double thickness. Generally, in beadwork, the thread should not show on the right side of the work and a color suited to both the background fabric and the beads should be chosen.

Needles
Beading needles are long and fine and are available in sizes 10 to 13.

Frame
A hoop is generally advisable for working beading and is essential for tambour beading, both hands being left free for working—one hand using the hook and the other setting the beads.

Beads and sequins
There are many different types of beads and sequins available, each in a wide range of colors and sizes. Sequin material, which can be cut into pieces and various shapes, is obtainable in sheets of 12ft 6in lengths, about 2 feet wide. Sequin waste, the material left over after sequins have been cut out, is useful; it is about 3 inches wide and is available in lengths.

Applying beadwork designs

Designs are marked out on the background fabric in the same way as for embroidery. Mark designs on the right side for hand stitched beading and on the wrong side for tambour beading. Beading should always be worked on the pieces of a garment before they are joined. For perfectly worked seams, work the beading up to the seamline. Stitch the garment seam by hand, and if there are any gaps showing in the beading, fill the odd beads in.

Methods of beading

Six methods of attaching beads and sequins to the background fabric are given. The illustrations and diagrams show beads and sequins applied in straight lines, but design lines can of course curve, and can be broken or added to. The tension of the stitches used for beading should be firm but not too tight or the effect is spoiled. Make sure that the thread is fastened off securely at both ends of a row of beads.

Method 1
Bring the needle through to the front of the work and pick up one bead. Slide it along the needle and just onto the thread. Pick up one thread of the background fabric, the length of the bead along the design line. Draw the needle through the fabric to place the bead on the fabric and pick up the second bead.

Method 2
This method requires two needles and thread in use at the same time. Needle No.1, the beading needle, picks up two or more beads and stitches them to the fabric (following the technique in method 1). Needle No.2 then works the second stage, making a small slanting stitch between each bead, catching down the linking thread.

Method 3
Bring the needle up through the hole of the sequin, set the sequin on the fabric and take a tiny stitch to the side of it on the line of design. Bring the needle up through the next sequin and continue to the end of the line. This results in a scale-like effect.

Method 4
Bring the needle up through the hole in the first sequin. Set the next sequin on the fabric and insert the needle. Set the third sequin on the fabric and bring the needle up through the hole and then, making a backstitch, into the hole of the previous sequin. Continue applying further sequins using a backstitch each time.

Method 5
Each sequin is sewn to the fabric with a single backstitch, and again a contrasting thread can be used.

Method 6
Each sequin is held in place by a small bead which must be larger than the hole in the sequin. Bring the needle up through the hole, pick up a bead on the needle and insert the needle back through the hole in the sequin. Bring the needle up through the hole of the next sequin and continue.

Tambour beading

This is a method of attaching beads and sequins by means of a small, sharp hook in a holder. The same method is used as that described for tambour work in Embroidery Chapter 13. Set the fabric in the frame with the wrong side uppermost. Thread the beads onto a spool of cotton—they can be threaded in a pattern sequence if required. Hold the hook in the right hand above the frame, the left hand holding the thread, and flick up a bead beyond the hook as each stitch is made. For a "speckled" effect, flick up a bead for every second stitch only. Tambour beading is an especially good method for attaching small beads, bugles and sequins if the pattern is linear. Combine tambour beading with hand stitched beading for even more unusual effects.

Beaded cuffs

To bead two cuffs you will need:
- [ ] Sheet of sequin material measuring 2ft 6ins by 2ft
- [ ] 2½mm gold pearls
- [ ] 5mm cup sequins in coral shade
- [ ] Yellow chalk beads
- [ ] 5mm flat sequins in blue-green shade
- [ ] White chalk beads
- [ ] Gold beads
- [ ] Small size pale blue chalk beads
- [ ] Sewing thread (cotton or silk)
- [ ] Beading needle

Working the cuffs
Prepare the thread by dragging it through a block of beeswax. Thread the needle with double thread. Mark the oblong shapes on the sequin material, using a fine ball point pen and a ruler. The size of the shapes can be adjusted to fit the depth of the cuff and the measurement around the wrist. Cut the shapes out with a sharp pair of scissors and pierce the holes with a pin, holding the sequin shape over a soft felt pad. All the beads, sequins and sequin shapes are sewn on by passing the thread through a small bead on top (method 6). Complete all the beadwork before making the cuff and attaching it to the sleeve.

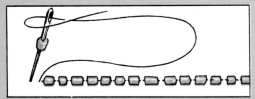

▲ *Method 1. Each bead stitched down separately*

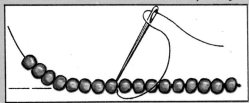

▲ *Method 2. Working two or more beads*

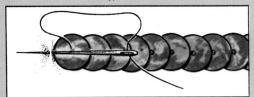

▲ *Method 3. Scale effect with sequins*

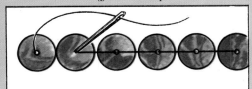

▲ *Method 4. Applying sequins with backstitch*

▲ *Method 5. Sequins sewn with single backstitch*

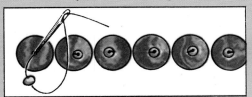

▲ *Method 6. Sequin held with a small bead*

◄ *Shimmering effect of toned beads and sequins*

▼ *Diagram for working the beaded cuff*

Gold oblong shape cut from large sheet attached by 2½mm gold pearls.

Coral 5mm cup sequin – yellow chalk bead. Blue/green 5mm flat sequin – white chalk bead.

Gold beads attached with small pale blue chalk bead — sewn on foldline.

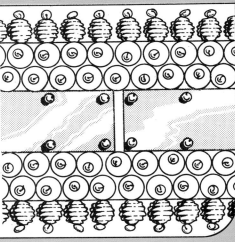

Chapter 49

Beading in fashion

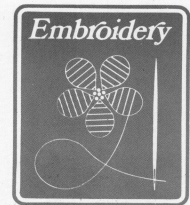

This second chapter on beading deals with uses of beading for fashion garments and accessories, how to work out beading designs, and gives methods for applying designs and working out the quantities of beads and sequins required.

Beading in fashion

Beading should be planned as an integral part of the garment design, enhancing the line, and giving the garment an added richness and an exclusive quality.

Beading for fashion must be bold enough to show well at a distance and yet have sufficient detail for close-up interest. The arrangement of the embroidery on a garment is particularly important. Use perhaps two or three patterns on one garment. For example, a rich small scale pattern on the yoke; a small spaced spot motif over the main part of the garment, and a narrow border for edges. Dress accessories of all types can be beaded to form luxurious and exclusive fashion highlights to simple garments. One plain, well-cut dress, for example, can gain new life with a set of different beaded belts, collars or cuffs. A set of beaded buttons can completely transform an otherwise ordinary garment, though beaded buttons are rather impractical and should only be used for decoration. Beaded buckles for belts or shoes are fun to embroider, quick to make, and are ideal items for the beginner to experiment upon. Hats, headdresses, evening bags and gloves are also ideal for bead embroidery, but particular care must be taken when attaching beads to ready-made items to insure that the tension of the stitching is firm and even.

Designs for beading

Generally it is the least complicated designs which are the most effective for bead embroidery. Select designs with bold shapes and avoid those formed of small shapes and thin lines as these give little scope for creating the rich, clustered textures which are possible with beading. As with all forms of embroidery, texture plays an important part and beads should be chosen in various sizes and shapes, complementing both each other and the background fabric. Many of the embroidery designs already given in this book can be adapted to bead embroidery or can be enhanced by the addition of beads. For solid effect all-over designs, such as those used on evening bags and belts, charted geometric designs can be used. These are worked on fine double-mesh canvas, each bead being stitched separately using a tent stitch over one set of double threads each time. For added texture, larger beads can be applied over the grounding design.

Designing directly onto fabrics

Beads lend themselves to free designing without the use of a pattern or a chart. Select beads in a color scheme to complement the fabric and mount the fabric in an embroidery frame.

Scatter the beads onto the mounted fabric and arrange them in patterns, anchoring the beads in position by pushing a pin through the hole, as the pattern develops.

Combining beading with embroidery

Beading can be combined with other forms of embroidery to great effect. Machine or hand embroidery can be used as the basis of the design, which is then highlighted and enriched with beading. For a rich and interesting effect on velvet, for example, using machine embroidery, use a thick thread, such as chenille, in the bobbin. This gives a lively texture on which to base beading. Metallic threads can also be used in the same way, or couched on by hand or zigzag machine stitch. For further texture interest, apply

◄ *Machine embroidery and rich beading on hand-printed fabric combine to lift a simply cut evening dress into the haute couture class*

shapes of silver or gold kid. Beads can also be combined with smocking designs which look marvelous for evening or bridal dresses. For a peasant look, combine hand embroidery with wood and china or chalk beads. Padded appliqué and quilting also take on a new richness when combined with beading.

Printed fabric and beading

Printed fabrics can provide inspiration for the basis of a beaded embroidery design. On the elegant evening dress shown in this chapter, for instance, the beading is worked over a hand-printed design combined with free-motion embroidery. When working on printed fabrics, choose bold prints and select focal areas of the pattern to highlight. Small, complicated prints should be avoided as the beading will only complicate the design. Avoid over-beading a pattern or the result will be a confused mess. If you are not sure whether you have done enough, hang the beaded section somewhere where it can be viewed easily and leave it for a day or so. When you return to it, you will find it easier to be critical and be able to decide whether to add more beads or to leave it as it is.

Transferring designs

Method 1. Pricking and pouncing. Draw the design onto tracing paper and lay the paper face downward over a soft pad, such as a folded blanket or a sheet of felt. Perforate the lines of the design with a pin (or a sewing machine needle may be easier to handle), keeping the holes closely spaced. Baste the pricked design rough side uppermost (the right side up) to the fabric and, using a small round pad made from a piece of tightly rolled-up felt 2 inches square, dab powdered chalk through the holes. Use powdered chalk on dark colors and powdered charcoal mixed with a little chalk on light colors. This method is especially suitable for complex designs and designs which need to be repeated two or more times. Fix the pounced design by painting over the dotted lines with watercolor paint, using a very fine brush. Because the design is thus permanently marked onto the fabric, the lines of the design must be strictly followed during beading.

Method 2. Tracing. For beading on semi-transparent fabrics, place the design under the fabric and very carefully trace through using a hard lead pencil with a very fine point. Alternatively, trace the design onto tracing paper using a felt-tipped pen. Pin the design securely in position underneath the fabric, and with small running stitches follow the line of the design without working through the paper.

Method 3. Basting. Place the traced design onto the right side of the fabric and baste the outlines, using small stitches, through to the fabric. To remove the paper without damaging the fabric perforate it with a needle between and under each stitch, then tear the paper away carefully.

Calculating quantities

If the area to be beaded is large or includes a number of repeats, it is essential to work a sample of any design first to calculate how many beads are required.

Measure the length and depth of the worked sample and then work out how many repeats of the sample are required to cover the area to be beaded. Count the number of beads used on the sample and multiply this by the number of repeats required to find the total number of beads of each kind required.

Stretching beadwork

When planning a design, bear in mind the weight of the beads and their "pull" on the fabric. If the beading is likely to be heavy, use the fabric double, particularly when working with sheer fabrics, or for added strength mount each piece of the garment on unbleached muslin before beading.

Sometimes, a completed piece of beading may show signs of puckering, and if this happens the work will require stretching. Place two or three sheets of damp blotting paper over a wooden surface larger than the area of the finished work, such as a drawing board. Place the beading right side uppermost over the paper and, making sure that at least one edge of the work is straight, pin it out with gold-headed thumbtacks (which do not rust so easily) at about 2 inch intervals. Work around the embroidery, easing it into shape as you pin. Continue pinning until the pins are touching each other. Leave the work to dry for at least 24 hours.

If sequins have been used in the embroidery, extra care is needed. Some sequins are made on a basis of gelatine and curl up and melt when they come into contact with water. To prevent this, dampen the first sheet of paper only, and place a layer of dry paper over it before pinning out the work.

Ways with beads

Piling beads. Beads and sequins can be sewn piled on top of each other, and it is great fun to experiment with combinations of different shapes and surface qualities. For example, pile six sequins decreasing in size, some cup shaped, some flat and of different colors, topped with a small chalk bead to secure. The examples given in this chapter show eight permutations on the "round shape". Several beads sewn on at a time can give a lovely raised, loopy effect, two bugles sewn on at a time result in a spiky texture.

▲ *Top row: swing motifs for exotic fringes. Center and bottom row: eight variations of piling beads and sequins for encrusted designs*

Swing motifs. Sewing swing motifs can be fun, too, and these can be extended to fringes which can be as light and fragile or as heavy and chunky as desired. Some examples are shown in this chapter but the permutations are unlimited. Any of the swing motifs shown can be continued along the edge of fabric to make a fringe. For picot edgings, sew beads along the edge of the fabric, securing each bead with a tiny chalk bead. Different effects can be achieved depending on the shapes of the beads used.

Collector's Piece

The Age of treasured books

Throughout Tudor times, the covers of precious manuscripts and treasured religious books, usually the Bible, were enriched by embroidery and beadwork. This charming custom had, alas, come to an end by the time Charles II came to the throne in 1661, but many beautiful examples of early embroidered bookcovers still survive. Although the original rich colorings are now somewhat faded, the striking designs in colored silks and gold and silver gilt threads

still have much of their original beauty. One of the most exquisite examples, dating from the reign of Elizabeth I, is a Bible, made by a famous printer, Charles Barker, as his New Year present to the Queen in 1584. In crimson velvet, decorated with seed pearls and gold thread embroidery, the design incorporates the Royal insignia, bordered by a symmetrical arrangement of stems and flowers. Professional embroidery of this kind would probably have been done by men. Three types of fabric were used for book and manuscript covers, the texture of the fabric dictating the design and the embroidery stitches. Early covers were made of canvas, the entire surface of the fabric being covered with tent-stitched designs. Queen Elizabeth, when still a small child, embroidered two canvas covers, one of which she gave to her stepmother, Anne of Cleves, in 1544.

Later, velvet was used and beautiful effects were achieved with decorative embroidery contrasting with the texture of the velvet, together with a great deal of laid and couched work in gold thread.
As the craft developed, silk was used, usually white, allowing much finer work. Thick raised gilt borders protected the surface of the silk and embroidery and bags or satchels were provided for greater protection.
The bags were as carefully and lovingly worked as the bookcovers themselves, usually in silver thread on canvas, but were more durable. Some of the bags carried tassels on drawcord and silken carrying cords.
The books illustrated are in the Bodleian Library, Oxford, England and include all the types of book covers which are mentioned here.

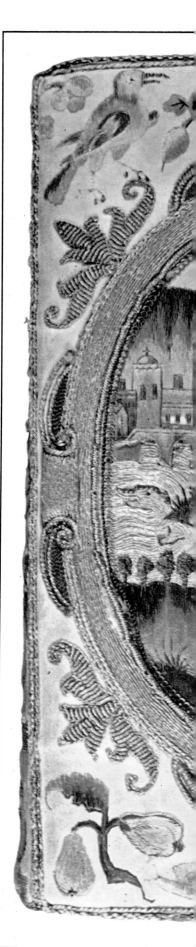

Chapter 50

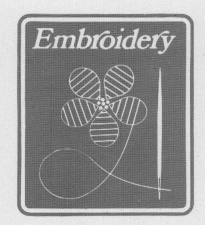

Experiments with beads and sequins

Bead embroidery, rather more than any other form of the craft, lends itself to experimentation with unusual materials. All kinds of objects can be used as an embroidery decoration for clothes and furnishings, and this chapter gives some ideas for working with unusual things and combining them with beads and stitches.

Unusual materials

Besides beads and sequins, all kinds of things can be used to decorate fabrics, and many modern' embroidery designers have produced quite striking pieces of work utilizing unlikely materials. Faucet washers, curtain rings and pants buttons, for instance, provide interesting round shapes, and there are dozens more to be found on hardware and notions counters. Hooks and eyes, snaps, pants fastenings, used in groups and rows, look exciting and original. Bits of clock mechanism provide some unusually shaped pieces too, and lengths of plastic-covered wire have been used with effective results.

Treatment of metal shapes

It may be necessary to varnish some metal objects before using them to prevent their rusting. Clear varnish is best for a protective covering but there is no reason why colored nail polish shouldn't be used for effect. Finish off with a coat of clear polish to harden the nail polish off.

Beads combined with shapes

Many objects, such as faucet washers, curtain rings and paper clips can be used individually to build up a design, but combined with beads they can look even more interesting. The pants fastenings design illustrated in this chapter has been used in conjunction with beads, the beads used to secure the pants fastening to the background fabric.

Sequin material

Sequin material can be cut with a pair of scissors into almost any shape and size to form giant sequin shapes. This is very useful because the large shapes provide a bold contrast to the smaller beads and sequins.

Sequin waste

This is the material from which the sequins have been cut, and it is full of sequin size holes. This sequin waste can be cut into lengths or an endless variety of shapes that can be caught to the background fabric with embroidery stitches making use of the holes.
Rich borders can be formed with sequin waste by working rows of herringbone stitch or chain stitch in crewel yarn. Lazy daisy stitch worked into six holes and either left as it is or finished off with a tiny bead in the center looks interesting and is simple to do. Spider web, also worked into six holes, gives a lovely contrast of texture.

Paillettes and mirrors

Paillettes have an attractive dull glow and combine well with bead embroidery. Mirrors have a brighter glitter and are cut by holding the mirror under water in a bowl, cutting it with a pair of old kitchen scissors. One-sided handbag mirrors are ideal for this.

Beads combined with embroidery stitches

This is a most interesting technique with endless possibilities. Stitches such as herringbone, wheatear, outline, fly, feather and buttonhole look completely different when beads are actually worked into the stitches. Herringbone stitch, for example, looks interesting worked with large, oval, wooden beads or glass bugles, which in turn can be caught down at top and bottom with two or three small beads worked in a double backstitch. Lines of the design can be worked in beading broken up with intermittent areas of beading.

Below: pants fastenings and beads arranged in rows to make a striking border design
Top right: contoured beads and sequins
Bottom right: beads and sequins in a hexagon
Far right: ways of using beads and stitches

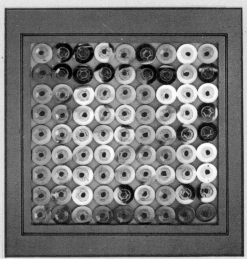

Above: formal arrangement of sequins

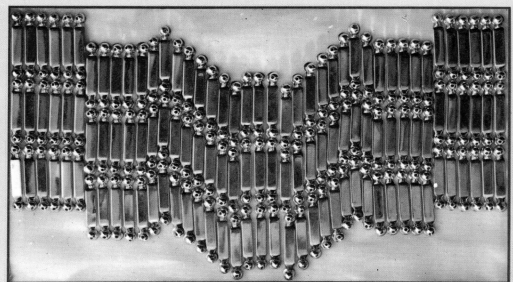

Top: a variety of embroidery stitches worked on sequin waste

Bottom: beads combined with embroidery stitches such as herringbone, Rumanian and coral knot

Chapter 51

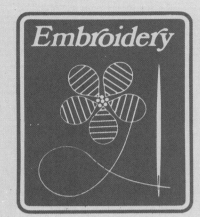

Panel in crewel work

Crewel embroidery, named after the yarn used, is a very early form of English embroidery. It reached the height of its popularity during the 17th century in the reign of James I, and is also known as Jacobean work.

The house and garden panel featured in this chapter, especially designed for us, is a modern interpretation of this type of embroidery. The basically simple stitches and encrusted areas of beads create lively texture.

Yarns
Crewel embroidery is worked in crewel wool, a thin worsted yarn of two strands. Other yarns can be introduced as desired to add highlights and texture to a design. Six-strand floss, pearl cotton, matte embroidery cotton and metal threads are all suitable.

Fabrics
The embroidery is generally worked on a background fabric of linen, but any fabric similar in weave can be used. Dress and home furnishing fabrics in man-made fibers are suitable, and those with a slight texture make an interesting background to complement the embroidery.

Stitches
Long and short stitches and couching in its various forms (see Embroidery Chapters 5 and 21) are the stitches most commonly associated with crewel embroidery, but any embroidery stitch or combination of stitches can be used in a design.

House and garden panel

Use the ideas shown in this picture of a charming house and garden to design a panel depicting your own house and garden. To make this panel you will need:
- ☐ Fine even-weave fabric measuring 24 inches by 18 inches
- ☐ Large wooden beads in assorted colors
- ☐ Small wooden beads in assorted colors
- ☐ Glass beads in assorted colors
- ☐ Tapestry needle size 22 for double strands of yarn
- ☐ Tapestry needle size 18 for several strands of yarn
- ☐ Crewel needle size 7 for single strands of yarn
- ☐ Appletons Crewel yarns in the following colors:
    1 skein each of burgundy 148; terra cotta 223; dark grass green 256; sea green 405; scarlet 501; bright yellow 554; pale fuchsia 801; fuchsia 803; dark fuchsia 805; dark rose pink 948; iron gray 967; light elephant gray 971; elephant gray 972; medium elephant gray 976
    Two skeins each of bright grass green 253; grass green 254 and medium grass green 255
- ☐ Embroidery frame

Stitches and colors
Use two strands of crewel yarn in the needle unless otherwise stated.

Landscape in foreground. Chain stitch in 253, 254 and 256.

Path. Top rectangle—cross couching, two strands of 971 couched down in one strand of 972. Lower path—two strands of 971 couched down with one strand of 971.

Steps in path. Double knot stitch using four strands of 971.

Roof. Fly stitches in 976. Horizontal lines of couching, two strands of 976 couched down with one strand of the same color.

Balcony. Cable chain stitch, worked as small as possible, using one strand of 148. Horizontal lines of couching edging to balcony worked in two strands and couched down with one strand of 976.

Front door. Rumanian stitch worked to the full width of the door shaping into the curve at top, 803.

Door frame. Raised chain band in 971.

Grass. Top patches—worked in rows of backstitch positioned alternately, each stitch taken over two threads of the fabric and in rows spaced three threads apart, using one strand of 254. The rows of backstitches are then threaded diagonally with one strand of 253. Lower patches—simple couching with the stitches matching in vertical lines. Use two strands of 253, couched down with one strand of 254.

Outlines. Outline stitch, using two strands of 967 around paths and wrought iron gate. Use one strand of same shade around house and upper curve of paths.

Wall. Couching and Rumanian stitch; Rumanian stitch is worked in 223. The couching is worked in continuous bands in the gaps between the pillars, the couching stitches forming vertical lines. Use two strands of 223 couched down with one strand of 948.

Weeping willow trees. Cretan stitch worked with 253, 254, 255 and 256.

Flowers. French knots and bullion knots in 148, 801, 803, 805, 501 and 554 together with wooden and glass beads sewn on with one strand. Stitch the larger beads on with six stitches in the form of a star.

Windows and plant plots. Rumanian stitch in 976 for windows and 223 for plant plots.

Shrubs in pots. Bullion knots in 405. Work a line of bullion knots with three twists around the needle on the outline of each shrub. With four twists around the needle, fill in the centers leaving some gaps.

Around windows and outside of house. Twisted chain in 223.

▼ Detail of the bead flowers   *Crewel embroidery in rich texture ▶*

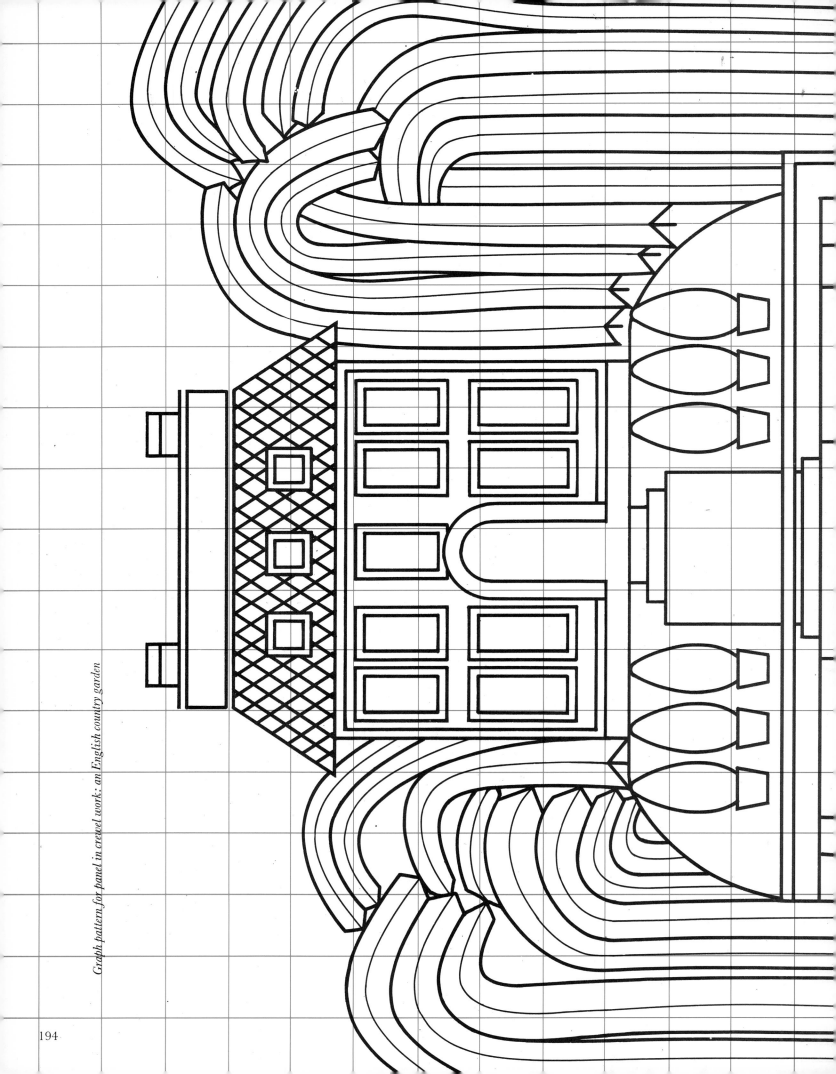

Graph pattern for panel in crewel work: an English country garden

194

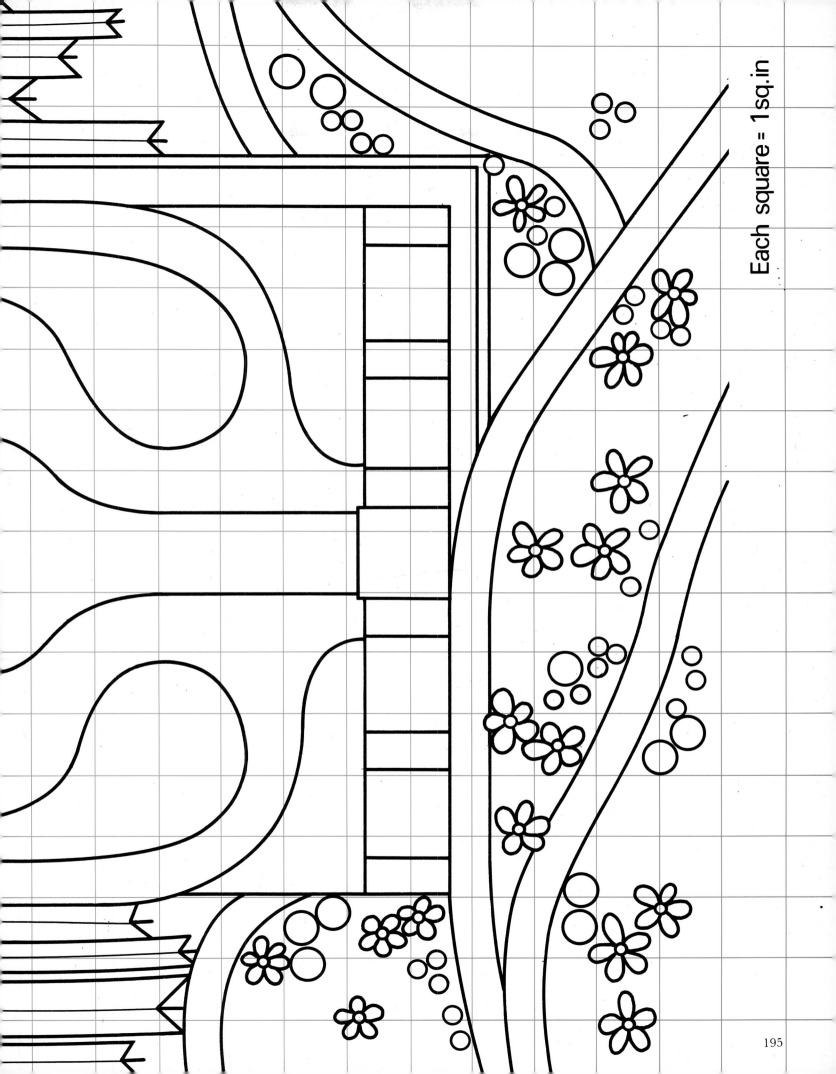

Each square = 1 sq.in

Chapter 52

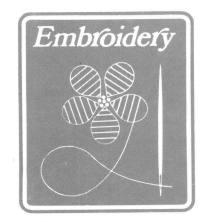

Introduction to quilting

This chapter deals with the basic quilting techniques and how to make an evening bag. Fine examples of modern and traditional quilting can be seen over the page.

Materials

The materials for quilting consist of backing, a layer of wadding and a top fabric. The backing can be either of the same fabric as the top layer or a contrast in both color and texture. A dull-surfaced fabric is better for backing if used for a bed or crib cover because it prevents the quilt from slipping. Light to medium weight fabrics such as cotton, linen, satin or silk can be used for quilting. Originally, quilts were padded with carded sheep's wool, and later with cotton batting. Today, muslin-backed nylon wadding, available by the yard, is ideal; it is easy to handle, washes well and retains its "spring". Surgical cotton should never be used. It is treated to make it absorbent and tends to take in dampness from the atmosphere.

Setting up work in a frame

It is possible to quilt very small pieces in the hand, but it is generally advisable to quilt with the work stretched on a frame. Apply the design onto the right side of the top fabric to be quilted. The bottom layer is then set up first in the frame as instructed in Embroidery Chapter 18. Stretch the bottom layer taut ready for working and place the wadding smoothly over it. The top fabric is then placed in position and all three layers are basted together firmly ready for the design to be stitched. All the work is carried out from one side of the frame, and the work should not be turned as this can cause twisting in the quilting.

Stitches and working method

The traditional wadded quilt is sewn with an evenly spaced running stitch. One hand is held under the work to receive the needle as it is stabbed through the layers of fabric, and the same hand passes it back to the right side of the work on the line of the design. Several needles are used at once, each one following a line of the design, and each needle worked a little way forward at a time to maintain tension and smoothness of work. The stitches and the spaces between them must look the same on both sides of the quilt, for reversibility is a characteristic feature of wadded quilting.

Transfer and tracing method

There are several methods of marking designs onto fabric to be quilted. A commercial transfer, or the dressmaker's carbon paper method, can be used, but as the design is usually applied to the right side of the fabric and worked in running stitch the design lines are not completely covered, and will remain visible until the quilting is washed.

Needle marking method

Marking designs for quilting with a needle gives a more clearly defined line on which to work. Tailor's chalk can be used but tends to smudge unless it is kept very sharp during use. With the needle marking method, the design can be applied to the fabric before it is set up in the frame, or bit by bit as the work is in progress. It depends on the worker's preference as to which method is chosen. For the needle marking method, the pattern shapes of the design are cut as templates of stiff paper or cardboard. Or, simple patterns can be marked directly onto the fabric using a ruler, coins, drinking glasses or saucepan lids as templates. The main outlines of the shapes are drawn around the template using the point of a large, thick needle such as a tapestry needle. If the design is to be marked out before framing, lay the top fabric over a piece of thick fabric, such as felt, on the kitchen table and mark the outlines by drawing firmly around the templates, holding the needle at a slant so that it does not catch or tear the fabric. It is better, however, to mark the design in sections while working.

Quilted evening handbag

Materials you will need:
- □ ½yd heavy quality satin and ½yd lining to match
- □ 2 pieces of Dacron wadding 9in by 9in
- □ 2 pieces of muslin 9in by 9in
- □ 2 spools of buttonhole twist thread to match satin
- □ 1 Crewel needle No. 7
- □ Small quantity of tiny gilt beads
- □ 1 spool of invisible sewing thread and 1 beading needle
- □ 1 spool of sewing silk to match satin
- □ 2yds fine piping cord
- □ 1 gilt bag frame, 6in between hinges

Preparing for quilting

Cut two pieces of satin 9 inches square. Cut two bias strips from the satin 27 inches long and 1 inch wide for piping and cut another 2 inches wide by 20 inches long for the gusset. Trace the design from the diagram and transfer it onto the right side of the satin for each side of the bag, including outline and dotted line.

Prepare the muslin backing and the wadding in the frame for quilting, and then place one of the satin pieces on top.

The quilting is worked in backstitch using buttonhole twist in the needle, and the stitching should be worked so that the stitches are as even as possible. Tighten the work in the frame if it becomes slack while quilting.

When all the stitchery has been completed, sew the beads in position at the intersection of the lines.

Repeat for the second side.

To make the bag

Trim the wadding and muslin. Outline the shape of the bag on both back and front, following the dotted line on the diagram, in small running stitches using a contrasting thread. This is the piping line. Trim quilting along the outer line on the diagram. Cut the piping cord in half so that you have two pieces each measuring 36 inches long. Baste the piping cord into the bias strips. Baste the covered cord into position on the dotted outline on both the back and front of the bag. Backstitch firmly in position.

Place the completed bag on the bag frame, and hold it in position with tie tacks through the holes on both sides of the frame, at the corners. Sew in position using sewing silk and hiding the stitches in the seam of the piping. Backstitches will make a strong and firm fitting. Cut and make a lining to fit the finished bag.

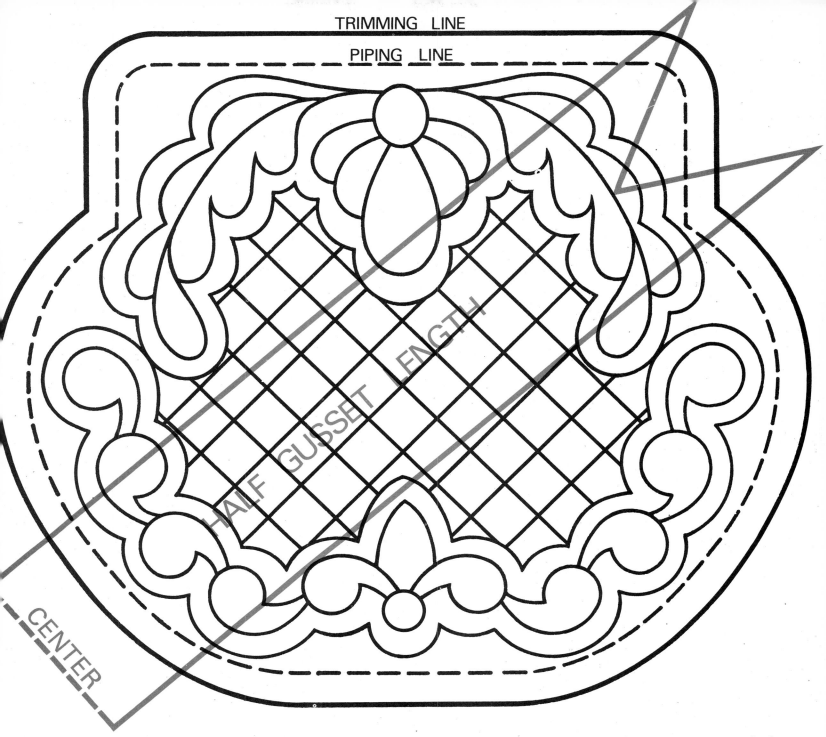

TRIMMING LINE

PIPING LINE

HALF GUSSET LENGTH

CENTER

▼ *Inserted gusset with edges trimmed* ▼ *Bag stitched to frame*　　　　▲ *Tracing pattern for cutting fabric and quilting pattern* ▼ *The evening bag*

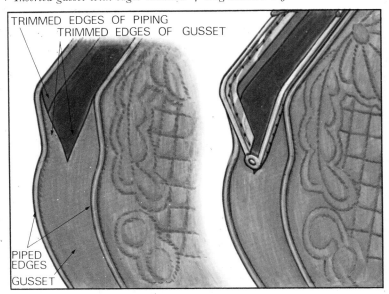

TRIMMED EDGES OF PIPING
TRIMMED EDGES OF GUSSET

PIPED
EDGES
GUSSET

Traditional quilting

Quilting is a centuries old technique. It has served many other purposes over the years besides that of providing warmth. In the 16th century it was in high fashion as it padded out the clothing to the desired shape, and combined with surface stitching and drawn fabric made up into a very beautiful garment. The quilting at this time was composed of three layers of fabric in contrast to the flat quilting of the 18th century, which consisted of only two layers.

18th century coverlet
The coverlet illustrated opposite has two layers, which is typical of this century. They are sewn together with fine backstitching in yellow silk and worked in a trellis pattern which covers the whole of the background.

Trellis and other simple geometric patterns were popular as a background to silk embroidery. These and a vermicular pattern of continuous curving lines were an easy way out for the less skilled embroiderer, as it is much easier to work in a curving line than evenly in a straight one. The embroidery on the coverlet is sewn in many colored silks. The work conjures up the 18th century image of Chinese design, which was fashionable at this time.

The center motif is that of a bird with wings outspread, all curves and movement. The birds are repeated at the corners and face in towards the center of the quilt, surrounded by the trailing leaf circle which again forms the same pattern in the center. The embroidery is worked in long and short stitch, split stitch and satin stitch.

The coverlet can be seen in the Victoria and Albert Museum, London, together with many other beautiful quilts in different colors and designs. Quilting was also worked on pillow cases, headdresses and bags and served as a padding for wartime armor in the 16th century.

Modern quilting

Quilting is as popular today as it was in the 16th and 18th century. Dresses, coats, bags and many other fashion accessories are made up of quilting and modern embroiderers work them in panels for decoration in the home, and for exhibition purposes.

The work itself is freer than it was originally, the lines curving and falling in irregular patterns, which is well illustrated by the piece shown below.

Quilted exhibition piece
The exciting quilted panel below updates traditional methods to complement the flowing, clear-cut lines of modern furnishings. The design is reminiscent of wood grain with its rough texture and uneven, rugged pattern, while the use of white on white in both stitch and fabric provides sophistication and subtlety. The light of the larger padded areas is emphasized by the slight sheen of the fabric and the corded areas contrast in narrow bands of light and shade. Trapunto quilting is used for the large padded areas and the corded quilting for the flowing lines. We give instructions for both these methods of machine quilting in Embroidery Chapter 54. This particular piece of quilting can be seen at the Embroiderers' Guild, London, where it is available for viewing and study purposes.

Chapter 53

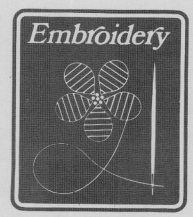

Quilted vest for a man

Quilting, like many other craft forms, lends itself beautifully to being interpreted in contemporary designs and color schemes. The luxurious man's vest shown in this chapter, designed especially for this book, shows an interesting use of quilting for a fashion garment.

To make a man's quilted reversible vest to fit size 38 chest you will need:

☐ ¾yd velveteen
☐ 1½yds wool flannel or Viyella fabric
☐ ¾yd loosely woven, lightweight, fleece filler (cotton or wool)
☐ 1 spool sewing silk in color matching the velvet
☐ 12 ¾in button molds for covered buttons
☐ 1 skein embroidery silk matching the flannel
☐ Tracing paper

Instructions

Set up the fabrics in a frame for quilting as described in Embroidery Chapter 52. Frame the wool flannel first, then reverse the frame and place the fleece filler onto the wrong side of the flannel. Place the velvet in position on the fleece.
Baste the three layers of fabric together, working through the fabric from one side to the other.
Turn the frame to the right side, wool flannel uppermost.
Enlarge and trace the design onto tracing paper. Make another tracing and reverse it for the second front.
Place the two tracings onto the flannel side of the framed fabrics, making sure that the straight grain lines match the grain of the fabric. Leave sufficient space around the two fronts for seam allowance. The velvet pile should run down the body. Baste the pattern onto the wool flannel around the outside edge. Follow the instructions in Embroidery Chapter 52 for working the design in running stitch, working through the tracing paper. When the evenly spaced running stitches have been completed, gently tear away the tissue and remove the work from the frame.

Making the vest

Cut and join bias strips of wool flannel, one inch wide. Fold the strips in half and place the raw edges together around the armholes, down the fronts and along the lower edges. Stitch ¼ inch away from the raw edge. Fold binding over the edge and hem invisibly on the wrong side, along the line of machine stitching.
Cut out two backs for the vest in wool flannel. Stitch one back to the front joining at shoulder and underarm seams. Turn up lower raw edge to wrong side. Take the second back and fold and baste all turnings to the wrong side. Placing wrong sides together, baste and slip stitch the second back over the first back. Press back and seams but not the quilting.
Cover button molds with wool flannel and sew 6 buttons on the inside of the left front and 6 buttons, exactly in line, on the outside

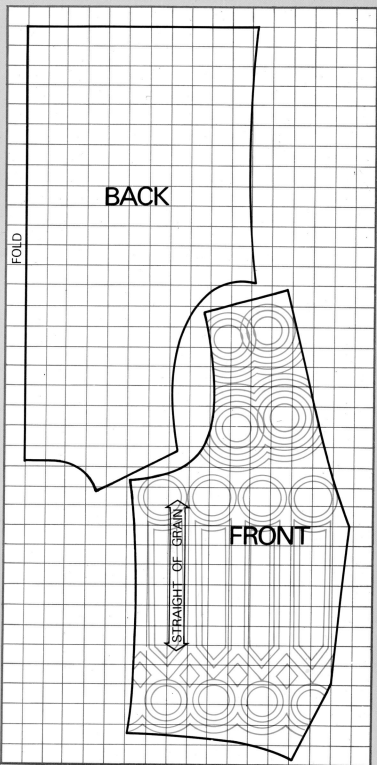

▲ *The tracing pattern and design. Each square represents one inch. No seam allowances are given*

Quilting makes a rich decoration for a reversible vest▶

of the right front. The buttons should be 1½ inches apart and ½ inch in from the bound edge. Make sure that no stitching shows through to the right side.
To make buttonhole loops, crochet a length in chain stitch with embroidery silk or linen sufficient to make button loops for both sides. Stitch the length of crochet chain along both edges of the vest, making a buttonhole loop opposite each button.

Chapter 54

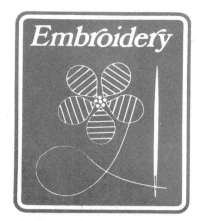

Quilting by machine

The beauty of machine quilting is that it is extremely quick to do, and is ideal for large pieces of work and fashion garments when quick results are desired. This chapter gives three types of machine quilting and an alternative hand method of Italian quilting.

The main types of quilting can be worked using the machine in the normal way with the presser foot on the machine. Straight stitch and zigzag stitch are used, with the machine threaded with machine embroidery thread No.30, or a mercerized sewing thread.

▼ Detail of machine quilting design on a skirt

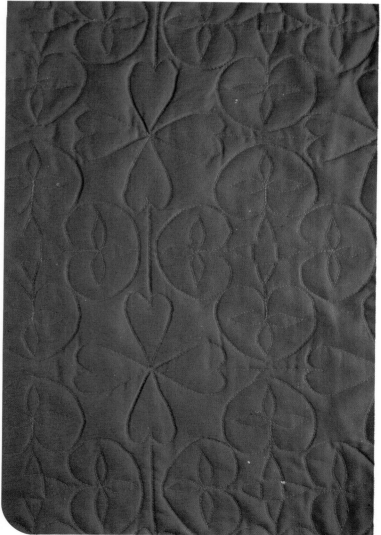

It is often desirable to add portions of applied fabric to a design as these quickly make a solid shape which otherwise would take ages to cover completely with machine stitches.

Straight lines or simple curves, which can easily be followed with the presser foot on the machine, must be used for the designs. The work should be mounted on greaseproof paper before machine stitching to prevent puckering and stretching.

Quilting

There are three kinds of quilting that can be easily worked on a sewing machine. They can be used separately or combined to create more complex designs.

English quilting. Also called wadded quilting, this is the most commonly known and simplest form of quilting where the complete surface is padded. Dacron wadding is placed between the top fabric and the backing fabric and all three layers are stitched together. The stitching is usually worked with a running stitch and the conventional motif is a diamond shape, but other geometric forms or gently curving forms can be used. The work can be stitched on the wrong side if the design needs to be marked on paper, as for a quilt for example, but work is usually carried out on the right side, in the normal way.

Trapunto quilting. The two fabrics (the top fabric and backing) are stitched together with a running stitch, the backing is slit and the shape is filled with lamb's wool (obtainable from drug stores), or kapok, and the slit sewn together again by hand. The shapes must be enclosed with stitching and should be of a shape easily stitched with the presser foot on the machine. Use lamb's wool for small shapes, and kapok for large shapes. Use a strong, firmly woven fabric, such as cotton sateen, on the back of the work to support the padding, and to keep the padded effect on the front of the work. Use these small padded areas in conjunction with appliqué and embroidery for evening bags, pillows, quilts and wall panels.

Italian quilting. The padding is formed by threading yarn, usually an 8 ply yarn such as rug yarn, through the backing fabric between channels of stitching from about $\frac{1}{8}$in to $\frac{1}{4}$in wide. Two layers of fabric are used and the channels are most easily made using a double needle on a zigzag sewing machine. They can also be worked with a straight stitch machine making the second line of stitching parallel to the first. Thread a tapestry needle with thick yarn and insert it between the lines of stitching. The backing fabric must be open weave, such as muslin, so that the needle carrying the padding thread can come out through it and be inserted again following the curve of the design. Leave a small loop each time the needle is inserted into the fabric. This makes a practical and pretty decoration on dresses, pillows, bed and crib quilts. If the top fabric is semi-sheer, an interesting effect can be achieved by using a contrasting color yarn. Some zigzag stitch and automatic sewing machines will automatically sew in cord or yarn as you work. All three methods mentioned above are quick and simple to do and can easily be worked by beginners.

Italian quilting by hand

The main difference between Italian quilting and other forms of quilting is that no warmth is added by the quilting, and instead of being padded all over, only the outlines of the design are padded to give a raised or corded effect. The transfer or design used must be one especially designed for this type of quilting, or bold appliqué designs can be used by drawing a double outline $\frac{1}{4}$ inch or less inside the original design line. The design can be applied to either the top fabric or the lining, but generally to the top fabric. Stitch the lines of the design by hand using either small backstitches or a running stitch, using sewing thread or pure silk. Pad the double lines of stitching in the same way as described for the machine method.

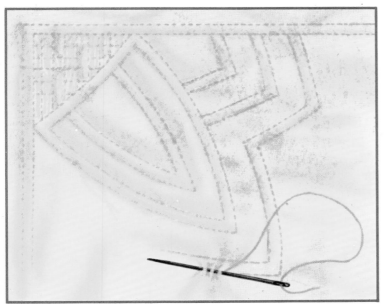

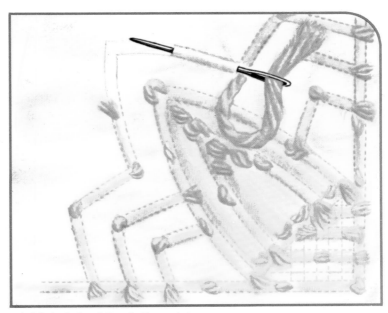

▲ *Method of working Italian quilting by hand*
▼ *A carriage cover worked in Italian quilting by hand*

▲ *Method of padding Italian quilting by hand*

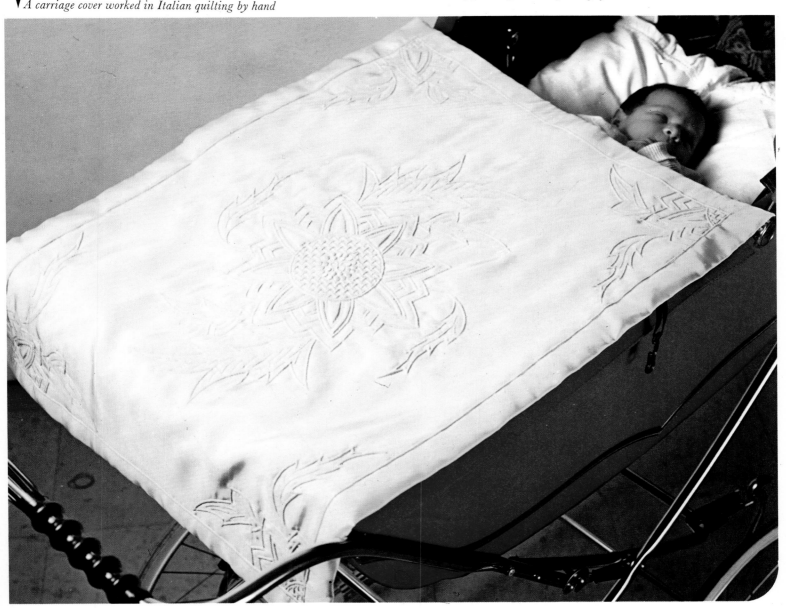

COLLECTOR'S PIECE

Quilted pictures

By the use of quilting or padding an interesting three-dimensional effect can be achieved on embroidered appliqué wall panels and pictures. These two car pictures have been worked using fabrics carefully chosen for contrasting textures— cotton velvet, rayon velvet, velour and toweling as well as plain and printed georgette. The padding is laid on the background fabric first and then the top fabrics are machine stitched to the background. As each shape is applied the excess fabric is trimmed back to the machine-stitched outline.

The surface embroidery in these pictures is worked in free machine stitch, using the straight stitch, and for this kind of work a fairly loose upper and lower tension is needed to avoid puckering.

Chapter 55

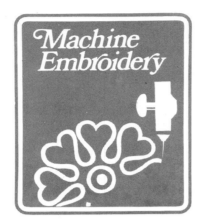

Introduction to machine embroidery

In recent years, embroidery designers have become more fully aware of the tremendous design potential of machine embroidery—not only for adding an individual touch to clothes and household linen, but also for creating unusual pictures and wall hangings.

Whether you have an up-to-date deluxe zigzag machine or are still using your grandmother's old treadle, you can produce beautiful effects and patterns yourself. In the next four chapters we describe the different types of machine and explain their various stitch and technique capabilities. The sampler opposite illustrates the many stitch formations that can be achieved by working with a machine.

The main advantage of machine embroidery over hand embroidery is the obvious one of speed. Then, how much you can achieve is related to the level of sophistication of your machine; for example, although it is possible to do some machine embroidery using a fairly old-fashioned machine, there will be limits.

There are three types of machine embroidery: straight stitching with the foot on the machine, using varying threads for decorative effects; free-motion embroidery with the foot off the machine; zigzag pattern embroidery. (Interesting effects can be achieved using the straight-stitch method by winding thicker thread onto the spool.)

Free-motion embroidery

For free-motion embroidery, the presser foot of the machine is removed and the teeth which feed the material under the needle lowered. Once this has been done, the fabric itself can be moved in every direction while the machine is running.

Uses of machine embroidery

The adaptability of machine embroidery is, of course, similar to that of hand embroidery. It helps to make clothes look more individual, adds interest to household items like towels and table-cloths, or becomes an art form if used for making appliqué pictures. Once you have followed the machine embroidery chapters and mastered the basic technique, you will then be able to experiment and work out new and original ideas.

What your machine can do

The old treadle machine was foot operated, strong and could be relied upon to do a running line of stitching on almost any fabric, however thick. It was used for dressmaking and household sewing. There are very few treadles left, but if you have one, it is possible, with the machine foot still in place, to do several simple, thicker stitches with thicker than normal threads in the spool. With the foot off, you will be able to experiment with a basic running stitch

of varying thicknesses and with different tensions.

The hand-operated models came next and these were smaller, portable and more convenient except that they were only straight-stitch machines and slow to work, as they left only one hand free to guide the fabric. Hand-operated machines are usually only to be found in museums today.

The simple electric model enabled the operator to use both hands to guide the fabric and to sew faster in a straight stitch.

Again, with the foot on, this machine will work simple stitches in thicker yarns. Once you have taken off the foot, you will be able to experiment with yarns, stitch sizes and tension variations.

The electric zigzag machine which was introduced after World War II was more versatile. This machine made zigzag as well as straight stitches available to the public and made it easier to sew a stitch with a width as well as a length.

With the foot still on this model you can experiment with thicker stitches, zigzag and satin stitches. On some models there is a shuttle design for twin needles to work tucking, appliqué, eyelet holes and hemstitching. In free-motion embroidery you will have a choice of basic running stitch plus zigzag stitch and variations.

Deluxe zigzag machines with built-in patterns set in motion with the flick of a lever or turn of a dial were the next advance.

There are obvious advantages in having this kind of machine to do embroidery. With the foot still on the machine you can try thicker stitches plus zigzag and satin stitch patterns, using the twin needles for double patterns and tucking, appliqué, eyelet holes and hem-stitching. In free-motion embroidery the basic running stitch plus the zigzag stitch can be used.

Free arm machines are not very suitable for machine embroidery unless they adapt to an ordinary flat-bed style.

Preparing to work

Needles for machine embroidery

With machine embroidery, needles should be carefully selected because the eye will have to accommodate a thread which normally might not be used with the particular fabric.

As with straightforward sewing, care should be taken with the choice of needle used in the machine. A thin fabric requires a thin needle, for example, No.11 American or 70 Continental, and fine thread. A medium fabric requires a No.12 to 14 American needle, 80 Continental and medium thread. A thick fabric should be worked with a No.16 American needle or 90 Continental and a slightly thicker thread.

Threads for machine embroidery

Embroidery and decorative stitches can be worked in machine embroidery cotton No.50 or No.30 as well as in varying thicknesses of normal sewing thread. Since these are generally imported, they are hard to find. Thicker embroidery threads can be wound onto the spool.

Stitch length and tension

Experiment with altering tensions and length of stitch. In most cases tensions must be adjusted for the top thread and are marked in numbers on a disk or indicated by a plus or minus sign. Spool cases have either one or two screws. When there are two, the one on the left is a set screw which holds the tension bar in place and the one on the right is the tension screw. When the spool case has only one screw, then that is the tension screw.

Turn the tension screw clockwise with a small screwdriver to tighten the thread and anti-clockwise to loosen it. Embroidery generally requires a tension slightly looser than normal.

The stitch length, if adjustable, is usually indicated by a numbered dial or lever.

Machine embroidery, raised areas ▲
Hand-winding a spool ▼

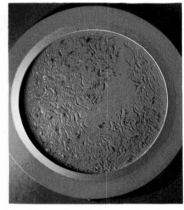

Machine embroidery on velvet ▲
Machine with the foot off ▼

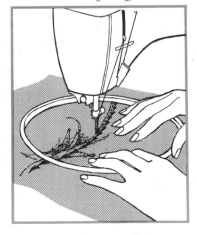

Treadle and simple electric
1. *Stitching with loose tension, thick yarn in spool*
2. *Vermicelli effect in a free pattern using a small stitch*
3–6. *Straight stitch with a thick yarn in the spool*
7. *Free pattern in straight stitch, hand applied beads*
8–13. *Different yarns on the spool*
14. *Applied ribbons using a straight stitch down each edge*
15–20. *As for rows 8–13*

Zigzag machine
21. *Satin stitch*
22. *Pattern built up using varying widths of satin stitch which are linked with lines of straight stitching using a thicker thread in the spool*
23. *Satin stitch*
24–28. *Satin stitch and zigzag worked in varying widths, spacings and tensions*
29. *Satin stitch worked in varying widths by moving the stitch width lever by hand*
30. *Decoration worked in free embroidery using zigzag stitch. Hand stitched beads*
31. *A simple geometric pattern worked around felt diamonds and decorated with square wooden beads. The second row out from the diamonds is a length of wool couched to the fabric with a small zigzag stitch*
32. *Narrow tuck stitched with two rows of straight machine stitching, one row simple, the other using a thicker yarn in the spool and a loose spool tension*
33. *A deeper tuck stitched with a wide satin stitch and a thick yarn on the spool*

Deluxe zigzag machine
34 & 35. *Programmed patterns*
36 & 37. *Satin stitch holding narrow velvet ribbon in place*
38 & 39. *Programmed patterns*
40. *As for 33*
41. *As for 32*
42–48. *Variations of tucking. Rows 42 and 48 are decorated with glass beads sewn on by hand*

(The numbers identify the row)

Chapter 56
Straight stitch and programmed patterns

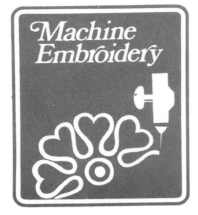
Machine Embroidery

This chapter deals with decoration and embroidery worked with the presser foot on the machine and the use of programmed patterns. The effects are different from free-motion embroidery which is worked with the presser foot removed and the feed teeth lowered.

The machine is used in the same way as for dressmaking, but sometimes threads, tensions and needles differ according to the desired result.

Decoration of this kind can be applied to clothes and accessories, and to household items such as pillow covers, curtains and pictures or wall hangings. Stitches worked with the foot on the machine are neat and practical, lie flat on the surface of the fabric and are easily washed and cleaned.

Both the pretty dresses illustrated are decorated using techniques described in this chapter.

Designing

Long straight lines or simple curves are better than short lines, because if the lines of the design are not continuous, the ends of the thread will have to be darned through to the back of the work.

Applying design to fabric

Guide lines of the design, which have to be followed by the machine needle, can be marked on the fabric with dressmaker's chalk. (Never use a pencil on the right side unless it has a very soft lead and then use it lightly, otherwise the lead will mark both the fabric and the thread.)

Sometimes it is possible to trace the design onto thin paper such as tracing paper or onionskin. Baste this onto the back of the work and stitch or baste the main guide lines from the back. Turn the work to the right side to stitch the embroidery.

N.B. Hard, unpliable, closely woven fabrics with a shiny finish are difficult to use as they pucker badly.

Method of embroidery

For all work stitched with the foot on the machine (except eyelet holes and tucking), the fabric is placed on thin paper. This paper prevents puckering, especially when the zigzag or satin stitch is used. The paper does not have to be basted to the fabric and is pulled away after all the embroidery is completed.

Thicker threads

No.30 sewing cotton is used on top of the machine and the work is stitched on the wrong side. Paper is still used on the back of the work and the design guide lines can be drawn on it.

Thicker threads, such as pearl cotton No.5 and No.8, 6-strand

floss and thin wool, are wound onto the bobbin by hand. The tension screw in the bobbin case is loosened or completely removed so that the thread runs very loosely. The top tension should be reasonably tight. This technique can be used on a straight-stitch machine or a zigzag machine. The length of stitch should be adjusted and also the width of stitch on a zigzag machine to get varied results.

Metallic threads

When using metallic threads it is not possible to wind the thread onto the bobbin on the machine in the usual way. This kind of thread is so brittle that running it through all the thread guides would only damage or snap it. Instead, slot a pencil through the spool and feed it directly from this to the bobbin winder. Keep the thread untwisted if it is a flat-sided lurex thread (see Embroidery Chapter 55). The bobbin tension must be loose and the top tension fairly tight so that only the metallic thread shows on the right side of the work. This technique is worked face downward and can be used on straight-stitch and zigzag machines and for the patterns on deluxe zigzag machines. Fine metallic threads are now available which can be worked from the top with a slightly looser top tension.

Stitches, patterns and techniques

Zigzag, satin stitch and deluxe zigzag patterns

Machine embroidery cotton No.30 and sewing cottons are used for these stitches. The bobbin and top of the machine are threaded with the same kind of thread.

Experiment by altering the length and width of the zigzag stitch—when the zigzag stitch is closed up, it becomes satin stitch. The zigzag stitch and satin stitch should look smooth with the stitches locked together at the back of the work, which means a slightly looser top tension than bottom tension. If the tension is too tight, the embroidery will not lie smoothly and the fabric will pucker.

The deluxe zigzag patterns can look very effective when worked with double needles and different colored threads. This kind of work is always embroidered right side up.

Hemstitching, tucking and eyelet holes

Hemstitching can be worked with single or double hemstitching needles. Embroidery cotton is used and this form of decoration is usually done on organdy or organza.

Tucking is worked with twin needles and a matching pin tucking foot. These come in different widths. Some machines insert a cord automatically as you sew, making the tucks broader and more durable. Backing paper is not used for this decoration, since the top threads have to be pulled together by the bottom thread to make a raised tuck. Although this technique is based on the simple straight stitch, it can be achieved only on a zigzag or deluxe zigzag machine with twin needles.

Eyelet holes

These may require a special eyelet embroidery plate and foot. Pierce a hole in the fabric with an embroidery stiletto and then place the fabric in an embroidery frame. The feed is lowered so that the frame can be swung freely around in a circle to make the satin stitch around the hole.

All these fascinating techniques are quick to do, which is the main advantage of machine embroidery. They are easy to learn, but as some machines differ from others, any extra information can be found in the instruction booklet of your particular machine. If you bought one secondhand without a manual, the manufacturers are usually able to supply one.

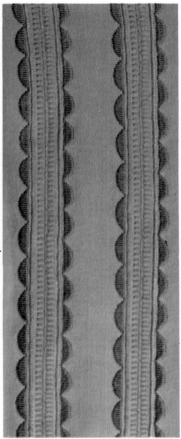

▲*Stitch detail of pale blue dress*
Automatic patterns—instant charm ►
▼*Stitch detail of pink/gray dress*

209

Collector's Piece

Machine embroidery at its most exquisite

This machine embroidered mat was worked by Rebecca Crompton in 1938. It is made of a fine, off-white fabric with a translucent quality, which adds a delicacy to the figures. The stitches include crazy stitch, cording with lace fillings, eyelet holes and zigzag stitch and has been worked on a swing-needle machine. The zigzag stitching has been worked freely with the teeth dropped and the needle straight to allow the embroiderer to draw out the patterns. It has been used for the filled-in areas on the mat, such as the ladies' bodices. Silver thread is embroidered onto the design which serves as a contrast to the all-white effect and adds textural interest to the work.

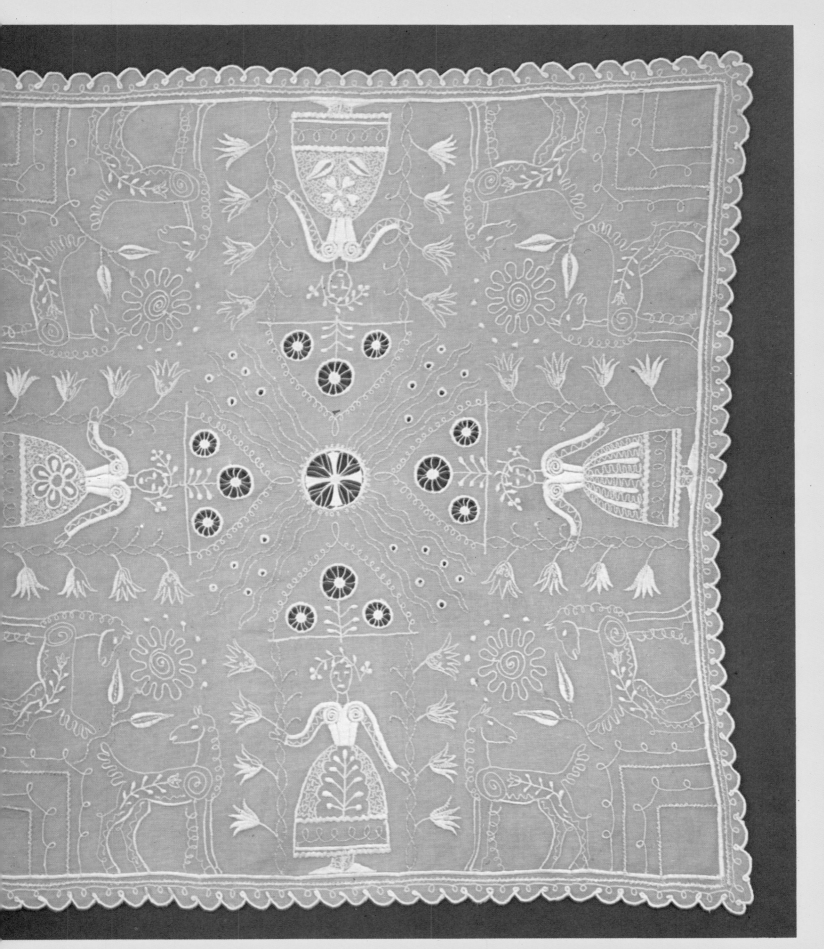

Chapter 57

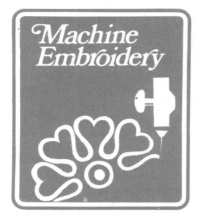

Free-motion embroidery

These two charming dresses are worked using the free-motion embroidery

The term "free-motion embroidery" is used when the machine is released from the control of the presser foot and feed teeth so that you can stitch in any direction quite freely. Although designs are usually worked to a pattern, machine embroidery has a degree of spontaneity about it and you will develop a style that is all your own.

Free-motion embroidery

This is an exciting technique because the designs which can be achieved are infinitely more interesting than those obtained with the foot on the machine or with programmed patterns.

A limited amount of free-motion embroidery is possible on a treadle machine or an ordinary home-type electric machine, but the greatest variety of effects is achieved on swing-needle models.

Embroidery hoops

In free-motion embroidery, the work itself is guided under the needle, the fabric held taut in a hoop. Special machine embroidery hoops which have a screw fitment are available and these hoops are made of either wood or metal. Choose a size suitable for the work—a 4 inch, 6 inch or an 8 inch diameter is used with home machines. Hoops which are only $\frac{1}{4}$ inch to $\frac{1}{2}$ inch deep are desirable.

It is advisable to bind the embroidery hoop with bias strips of material if you are working with very fine or light-colored fabric to prevent your work from becoming snagged or soiled.

Materials

Machine embroidery thread may be available in two thicknesses—No.30 and No.50. Many embroiderers prefer No.30 because it is thicker and less likely to break. Sewing thread can also be used and is available in a much wider variety of colors than the machine embroidery thread.

A No.11 American or No.70 or No.80 Continental size needle is recommended for machine embroidery, but make sure that the needle is sharp. Damaged or bent needles will cause stitches to be missed and make snags in the material.

Refer to the previous chapter before choosing your fabric.

Setting up the machine

First, remove the presser foot and then lower the feed which lies immediately below the presser foot. Some modern machines have a lever for lowering the feed, but if your machine has not got this lever, the feed will have to be covered with a special plate for working free-motion embroidery. The manufacturer of your machine or the local service center will help you to obtain the plate.

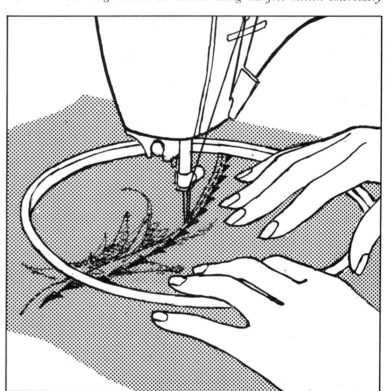

Keep fingers just inside the hoop, well clear of the needle

Thread the machine in the normal way, using machine embroidery thread. While you are practicing stitches and effects, use a colored thread in the bobbin to contrast with that used on the top of the machine so that tension mistakes can be spotted easily. Tension is difficult to check when both threads are the same color.

Both top and bottom stitch tensions should be equal and not too tight—a tight stitch will pucker the fabric. The thread from the bobbin affects the look of the stitch on the top of the work, so learn to adjust the tension screw in the bobbin case. For instance, if the bobbin thread is too loose, the result will be a beady, rough stitch on the surface of your embroidery.

To work machine embroidery on a zigzag machine, using the zigzag stitch, set up the machine in exactly the same way, but use the stitch width lever. This will give a much thicker free embroidery style, either as zigzag or as satin stitch.

A close-up of the embroidery shows how the use of simple whip stitch (see next Machine Embroidery chapter) can transform a plain dress

The close-up shows how spots have been used as a base on which to plan a most attractive design to follow the yoke shaping of the dress

Interesting stitches and effects can be achieved by altering tension and by using thicker yarns or metallic yarns. These are explained more fully in the next chapter on machine embroidery.

Preparing the fabric for embroidery

Stretch the fabric to be embroidered tightly across the hoop and then tighten the screw as far as it will go, so that there is no possibility of the material slipping while it is being worked. This is important because without the presser foot on the machine, stitches will be skipped if the fabric is at all slack.

The method of working

After mounting the fabric in the hoop, place the fabric under the needle and bring the bobbin thread to the top of the work so that both threads are on the surface of the fabric. Lower the lever which would normally lower the foot because this lever also controls the top tension.

Hold both threads in the left hand and start the machine, moving the fabric until two or three stitches have been worked. The threads become locked together and the loose ends can be cut off. You can now move the hoop and fabric under the needle and stitch in every direction quite freely.

Keep the elbows down and hold the hoop with the thumb and little finger of each hand, with the remaining fingers lying just inside the hoop (see diagram opposite). Be very careful not to let the fingers slip under the needle. Finger protectors, which can be fitted to any make of machine, are available.

After completing the embroidery, remove the hoop, with the threads, very carefully from the machine, remembering that the needle is unprotected.

Chapter 58

Experiments in free-motion embroidery

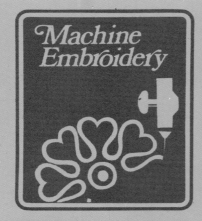

A striking example of the use of machine embroidery for fashion

There is a great variety of stitches and techniques used to obtain effects in free-motion embroidery, and this chapter gives detailed instructions on how to set up the sewing machine to achieve these effects. The illustrations opposite show the results of using these methods of free-motion work and give an idea of the different textural patterns involved.

The dress and bolero shown in this chapter are an exclusive design, but you could adapt the idea to make a perfect going-away outfit. Choose commercial paper patterns for the dress and bolero which you can adapt and use the chart given overleaf as a guide to the embroidery.

Once the basic running and zigzag stitches are mastered, more advanced free-motion embroidery stitches can be tried. These are made by altering machine tension, using thicker or metallic threads on the bobbin, or by catching threads too thick to use on the machine to the background fabric.

Whip Stitch
Tightly stretch the fabric to be embroidered into a hoop. Remove the presser foot, lower the feed teeth, and set the machine for running stitch. Loosen the bobbin tension from normal and tighten the top tension. This brings the bottom thread to the top of the work, making a beady

corded stitch much thicker than the basic running stitch. To produce a good neat stitch, move the hoop smoothly and slowly so that the little loops are close to one another. The top thread should not be seen. If the tensions are altered even more (by loosening the bobbin and tightening the top tension still further), a very exaggerated, spiky stitch results because the top thread is so tight. This stitch is best worked into circular shapes because it can then lie flat on the background fabric. A slightly thicker thread used on the bobbin gives an even more pronounced effect.

The choice of thread must be determined by the weave of the background fabric because thick threads will not pull easily through a tightly woven cloth.

When altering tensions, either on top of the machine or in the bobbin, make the alteration gradually, trying out the effect between each change.

Working in thicker threads
Begin by setting the machine for running stitch.

Thicker threads such as pearl cotton No.5 and 8, 6-strand floss, thin yarn and metallic threads are wound onto the bobbin by hand as described in Embroidery Chapter 56.

Machine embroidery thread or mercerized sewing thread is used on top of the machine. The work is stitched face downward because the interesting thread is in the bobbin. Bobbin tension should be loose and top tension either normal or slightly tight for working

with these types of thread. If the speed of the needle is kept steady and the fabric moved smoothly, a cording effect will result. For really thick threads, keep the bobbin tension quite loose or it will pull too much on the background cloth.

Toweling stitch
With pearl cotton, 6-strand floss or thin wool on the bobbin, a more loopy effect can be obtained by loosening the bobbin tension even more and tightening the top tension. By pushing the hoop slowly under the needle, the loops have time to build up.

For a greater looped effect using a thick yarn, such as sports yarn, completely remove

the tension screw on the bobbin case. The free or darning foot is used so that larger areas of fabric can be covered at any one time without using a hoop. Always remember to lower the presser foot lever whether the foot is on the machine or not, as this engages the top tension.

Metal threads
Only metal threads which are specifically made for machine embroidery will stitch through fabric. Other kinds break and should be wound onto the bobbin by hand and worked from the wrong side.

Providing the fabric is not too tightly woven, lurex thread can be used for whip stitch. In this case, the thread on

214

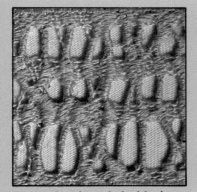

Drawn threads worked with zigzag

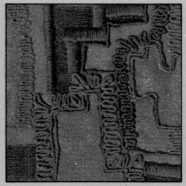

Embroidery on a printed organza

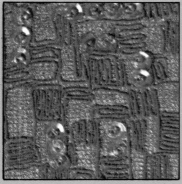

Whip stitch decorated with sequins

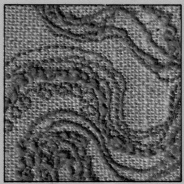

Toweling stitch with thick wool

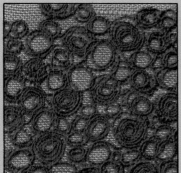

Whip stitch worked in fine circles

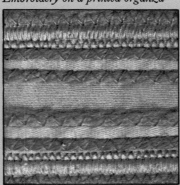

Thicker threads couched with zigzag

Flower design in fine whip stitch

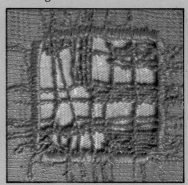

Whip stitch decorated square hole

Satin stitch with metal thread

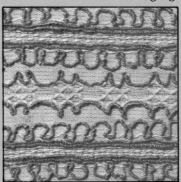

Design worked around fabric weave

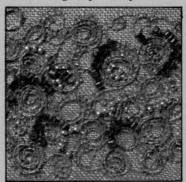

Whip stitch in gold with beads

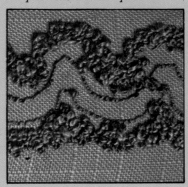

Toweling stitch with pearl cotton

top must not show. When using metal threads, work very smoothly and at a slightly slower speed than with other kinds of threads. This is because a sudden jerk will snap the metal thread.

If you are working zigzag or straight stitch, the tension of the metal thread needs to be slightly looser than the top thread. The top thread remains on the wrong side of the work, the metal thread is smooth and the work completely metallic on the right side. If the metal thread is of a type which can be used on top of the machine, a larger needle should be used. Metallic threads look especially rich and decorative when used in zigzag stitch.

Fabric with unusual weaves
Zigzag stitch can be used most successfully on soft and open-weave fabrics. A pulled fabric effect results on open-weave fabrics, such as linen scrim, open home furnishing nets etc., by working with machine embroidery thread with both tensions slightly tighter than normal. The zigzag stitch pulls the open-weave threads together and small motifs can be worked leaving large areas of the background fabric unworked. Alternatively, cover the fabric completely with hundreds of zigzag stitches touching each other so that the finished result is rich and textured. The best results with this technique are obtained with the fabric held

in a hoop.
For drawn threadwork and machine embroidery, choose loose-weave fabrics such as scrim, burlap or linen, and pull out the warp or weft threads (or both) using different widths of zigzag stitches. The effect is particularly interesting where the fabric is made of two colors and the threads pulled out in either direction so that one color remains.

Embroidering holes
Lacy effects are worked by using zigzag stitches around a shape in the design and then cutting the inside fabric away, leaving a hole. For a spider web effect, for example, work

running stitch across the hole and then strengthen the stitches with a small zigzag stitch. To achieve this, the fabric must be in a hoop and the tension of top and bottom threads exactly equal so that they twist around each other when worked across the space.

Very thick textured threads
Any thread which is too thick to be wound onto the bobbin, or too textured to pull through, can be caught to the fabric with a running or zigzag stitch. This method of couching by machine using the ordinary or free foot can be worked using knitting yarn, weaving yarn, string, raffia, ribbons, tapes or braids.

Free fashion embroidery

To make a bolero like the one illustrated, which was made up in a washable synthetic fabric, first choose a commercial paper pattern and mark the outline of the garment onto the fabric. Some of the stitches described in this chapter have been incorporated into the bolero. The embroidery design is not repetitive but we give guide lines to trace for one front plus a large flower motif, which the more experienced embroiderer could adapt for the left front of the garment. Use a hoop and either follow the guide accurately or improvise with your own ideas.

Do not cut out the pattern pieces until the embroidered design has been worked. Once the embroidery is finished, make the bolero according to the pattern instructions.

Trace the outline of the design on these pages and use as a guide for free-motion embroidery

Collector's Piece

Rear window

This appliqué and needle-point wall panel is a good example of the brilliant effect which can be achieved when a designer breaks the conventions of embroidery. The background stripes are worked in various textured needlepoint stitches using

tones of purple and pink
yarns and then the blue shape,
representing the mirror
frame, has been cut out of
matte wool fabric and applied
to the needlepoint with
invisible stitches. The
dullness of the blue enhances
the mass of needlepoint in
the central circular shape and
forms a barrier between that

and the striped stitching of
the outer background.
The central panel, which
represents the view seen in
the driving mirror through the
rear window of a car, has
been freely worked; the
stitches are not confined to
separate shapes but run into
each other and overlap. The
art lies in keeping the free

effect without a jumbled mess
resulting. Many of the
stitches in the central panel
vary within themselves as a
result of the embroideress
using differently textured
threads of similar colors, by
her changing the direction of
a line of stitches or by the
varying angles of the stitches
themselves.

Chapter 59

Introduction to needlepoint

From the time that someone called the famous Bayeux panel a tapestry, people have been confused about what is embroidery, what is tapestry and what is needlepoint.

In fact, the Bayeux panel is an example of early English embroidery, worked in wools on a linen fabric. Tapestry is always woven, in patterns and pictures, on a loom, with small sections woven individually, then stitched together by hand. The next time you visit a museum, look carefully at the tapestries and you'll see how small some sections are.

Needlepoint is embroidery on canvas. It was very popular in England and Europe from the early sixteenth century until the mid-eighteenth century, but then it marked time, until it was recently revived.

Now the lovely variety of traditional needlepoint stitches, which have for so long been neglected, are enjoying a new importance. They are being used in fabulous modern designs, often with unusual new yarns which were not formerly associated with embroidery.

Today, needlepoint is an adventure in the use of stitches, yarns, and abstract designs which lend themselves to the square formation of the stitches.

Colorful, textured and tough

The attraction of needlepoint today, apart from the fact that it is handmade and not mass produced, is that all-over embroidery on canvas makes objects and decorations which are really tough and hard-wearing.

It is simple to do, and you have only to visit the yarn counter of any shop to be inspired. Brilliant wools, metallic threads, stranded shiny cottons, soft matte cottons, new nubbly-textured wools and bright plastic raffia all come in a myriad of beautiful colors.

As well as the color, the success of all needlepoint depends upon the texture of the stitches and the threads.

Canvas size

The canvas must be firm, supple, and evenly woven, and the number of threads to an inch can vary from 24 per inch for fine work, to $3\frac{1}{2}$ per inch for very coarse work.

There are two types, single thread canvas and double thread canvas. You can also use evenly woven fabrics such as Aida cloth, or Hardanger, and even-weave linens or woolen fabrics.

Single thread canvas is measured by the number of threads to the inch and double thread canvas is measured by the number of double threads to the inch. Single weave canvas is the best to use since it is possible to embroider a wide variety of stitches on it, whereas double weave is restricted to four or five only.

Needles

Use tapestry needles with large eyes and blunt points. They are available in a variety of sizes, of which sizes 18-22 are the most popular, but size 14 is better for very coarse material.

Frames

Needlepoint should be worked in a frame. This helps you to maintain the correct shape of the work while it is being embroidered. Small items which you can easily hold in your hand need not be framed. See Embroidery Chapter 18.

Yarns

In needlepoint the stitches must completely cover the canvas. Yarns are available in differing thicknesses and some are made up of several individual strands which are twisted together but can be separated as required. To cover the canvas you need to use the correct thickness of yarn. If, however, the yarn coverage looks thin, you should pad it out with the technique known as tramming to fill the space. Never use too long a yarn, as it will wear thin and your work will look uneven and tired. If you find the yarn becoming thin or fluffy, start a new length of yarn at once. It is usually quicker to use a short length—which is a yarn about 12 to 14 inches long.

A modern cushion designed by Joan Nicholson, with abstract pattern repeats, and clear bright colors which blend well together

The right yarn for the canvas

1. Double thread canvas (6 through 15 available)
6 double threads to 1in shown.
Yarns: tapestry yarn, crewel yarn, 4-ply knitting yarns, pearl cotton, 6-strand floss, metallic yarns, stranded pure silk.
2. Double thread canvas (7 through 15 available)
10 double threads to 1in shown.
Yarns as for No. 1 plus knitting worsted, plastic raffia.
3. Petit point canvas (18 and 24 available)
24 threads to 1in shown.
Yarns as for No.1.
4. Single weave canvas (10, 12, 14, 16, 18 available)
18 threads to 1in shown.
Yarns as for No.1 and No.2 plus knitting yarns in a variety of textures such as mohair, tweed, metallic and wool mixtures, soft embroidery cotton, carpet thrums, rug yarn, applied braids and cords, spinning yarns.
5. Single weave (10, 12, 14, 16, 18 available)
10 threads to 1in shown.
Yarns as for No.1 and No.2 and No.4, using more than one thickness of yarn where necessary, plus fine ribbons, strings.

Check off your canvas information against the picture on the right ▶

1

2

3

4

5

Chapter 60

Introduction to half cross-stitch

Half cross-stitch is hard-wearing—smooth, flat and ideal for things which need to be tough, like stool and chair seats. But because it is so simple to do, it is one of the best stitches to use for any small scale patterns. In this chapter we explain how to work half cross-stitch and also tramming, which serves as a padding stitch. Incorporate both these methods of stitching into making the buttons illustrated on the opposite page.

Half cross-stitch

This stitch is worked as shown, from left to right. Up through the canvas from bottom left, down through the next "hole" on top right. This makes a diagonal stitch on the front and a short straight stitch on the back.

Fasten off at end of each patch of color and begin again so that you do not carry long lengths of thread at the back.

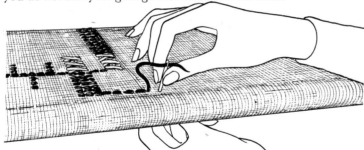

The drawing shows the method used when working in a frame.

Tramming

Tramming is a padding stitch which is used when the yarn is not thick enough to cover the canvas completely.

The tramming yarn runs along each horizontal single canvas thread, or pair of threads (called "tramlines") as shown in the illustration at the right. Bring the yarn up through these tramlines, leaving a short tail at the back. Work in overlapping tramming stitches, not more than five inches long, for the length of your working area. Then take the yarn down through the tramlines again. Work the stitch over the tramming yarn, binding in the tramming tails as you go.

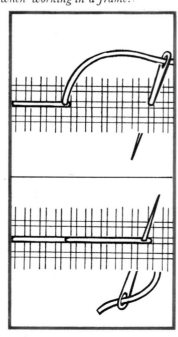

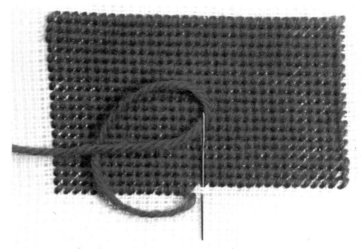

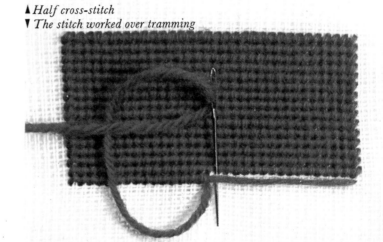

▲ *Half cross-stitch*
▼ *The stitch worked over tramming*

How to make the buttons

Use do-it-yourself buttons which come in many sizes from most notions departments. Here are three designs to start with, plus a chart to show you the right fabric and thread to use for each size of button. Always use either a very fine canvas, Aida cloth (which is softer than canvas), or an even-weave cloth.

The chart gives the turning allowance which will take the worked material safely over the edge to the back of the button. Simply draw a circle around the button, allowing enough for the turnings as well, and you are ready to start, but do not cut out until the needlepoint is finished.

N.B. The buttons are simple to assemble and come with easy-to-follow instructions on the package. Use half cross-stitch, trammed, or untrammed, as you find it necessary. (The background could be worked in long-legged cross-stitch for a more exciting textural effect.) Follow the exact number of stitches shown in the picture. To work out your own patterns, plot them out first on squared graph paper with colored pencils.

Trim button size + turning	Fabric threads to the inch	Suggested threads
$\frac{3}{4}$in + $\frac{1}{8}$in turning	28	3 strands of 6-strand floss 2 strands of crewel wool pearl cotton
$\frac{7}{8}$in + $\frac{1}{8}$in turning	25	4 strands of 6-strand floss
$1\frac{1}{8}$in + $\frac{1}{4}$in turning	18	6 strands of 6-strand floss
$1\frac{1}{2}$in + $\frac{1}{4}$in turning	14 Aida cloth (14 blocks of thread to the inch)	6 strands of 6-strand floss tapestry wool raffia 4-ply knitting

How to start

1. Find the center of the piece of canvas by folding it in half twice; mark the center lightly with a colored crayon or thread. Start in the center, but instead of using a knot, draw the needle up through the canvas, leaving a tail about half-an-inch long at the back.

2. Hold this yarn close to the canvas and work over it, binding it in with the first few stitches (which are seen here from the back).

To finish off

Darn the yarn into the stitches at the back of your work to secure it. To continue with a new yarn, darn its tail into back of the previous row.

Never allow any of these yarns to accumulate in one place as this results in unsightly bumps.

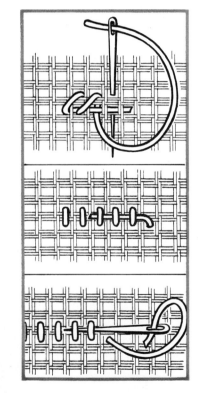

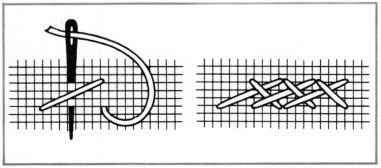

▲ *Long-legged cross-stitch, a simple but effective variation*

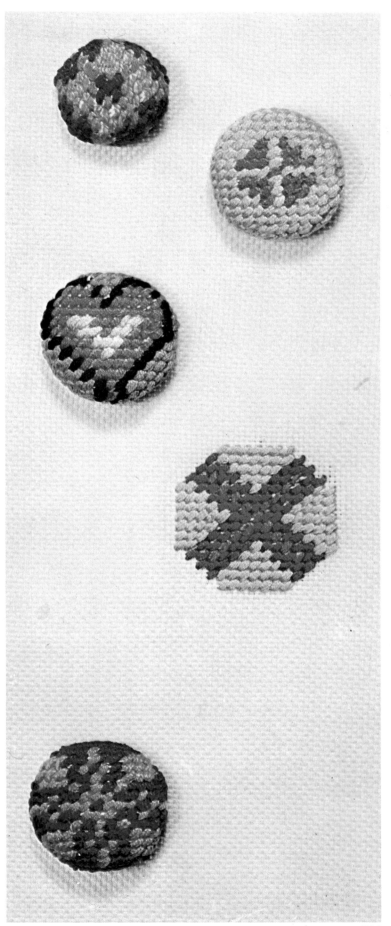

Chapter 61

Designs in half cross-stitch

Adapted from a tile-patterned wallpaper, this striking design in chunky yarns is quick to work. The stitch used here is half cross-stitch (see Needlepoint Chapter 60) but other stitches can be used to create more textured effects. Several exciting ideas for using the design are illustrated, and similar designs can be lifted from pottery tiles.

To work the panel measuring 18 inches square you will need:
- ☐ Piece of single-weave canvas 24 inches square with 21 threads to 2 inches
- ☐ Piece of lining fabric measuring 20 inches square
- ☐ Piece of ¼in plywood cut to measure 18 inches square for mounting
- ☐ Tapestry needle size 18
- ☐ D.M.C. Art 313 Embroidery Yarn in the following colors and amounts: 7 skeins blue 7317; 6 skeins blue 7313; 5 skeins blue 7314; 1 skein blue 7307; 4 skeins green 7351; 2 skeins green 7346; 1 skein green 7428; 5 skeins white

To work the panel
Work the panel in half cross-stitch over one thread of the canvas. Block completed work and mount the panel over the wood. Finish the edges with a finger knotted cord and four large tassels. Make a further length of finger knotted cord to hang the panel.

▼ *This chart shows ¼ of the design. Each square = 1 stitch*

Chapter 62

A bolero in half cross-stitch

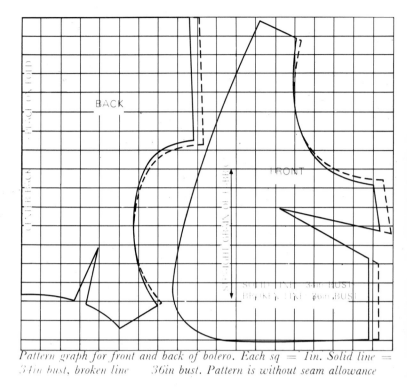

Pattern graph for front and back of bolero. Each sq = 1in. Solid line = 34in bust, broken line 36in bust. Pattern is without seam allowance

This beautiful bolero is specially designed for this book, with two color schemes to choose from. On this page is the graph for the pattern—turn over for the embroidery chart.

What you will need to make the bolero:

- ⅜yd double-weave canvas with 10 double threads to 1in
- ⅜yd corduroy or velvet 36in wide for back of bolero
- 1¼yd lining 36in wide
- 2yds folded braid
- Sewing thread
- D.M.C. Tapestry yarn
- Soft lead pencil
- Large sheet of paper

The pattern

Simply copy the pattern for your size from the graph on this page onto paper drawn with 1in squares. Cut out the pattern. The graph pattern is given in 34in and 36in bust sizes only; but you can use a commercial bolero pattern in a larger size if you need to. Simply extend background stitching over the extra canvas. For larger sizes remember to check yardage and background yarn amounts.

Transfer the outline for the bolero fronts onto the canvas by basting the pattern in place, then drawing around the edge and into the darts accurately with a soft pencil. Now work the design onto both sections (full design details on next page). Complete the needlepoint before cutting out the fronts, as you need the rectangle of canvas to enable you to set the work up in a frame. (It is essential to work a piece this size on a frame to keep it in shape.)

Working the design

The original design was worked in half cross-stitch with the centers of some of the flowers in slanting Gobelin stitch (see Needlepoint Chapter 68) and cross-stitch. You can add more texture stitches if you wish, but be careful not to use too many or you may detract from the design itself. Or, if you prefer, you can use tent stitch throughout (see Needlepoint Chapter 68). Work the stitches right up to the traced edges and just over the dart line, so that no canvas shows when the darts are closed.

Cutting out

When the design is completed, block and trim the canvas as described in Needlepoint Chapter 74, leaving ⅝in allowances on shoulder and side seams only. Trim the canvas as close to all other edges as possible without cutting into the stitching. Cut out the back of the bolero from the corduroy and then cut out lining to match both the back and the fronts, adding ⅝in seam allowances on the side and shoulder seams.

Making the bolero

Sew the darts on the bolero fronts either by machine or with a firm backstitch. Slash up the center of the dart and press it open with a slightly damp cloth and a medium hot iron. Trim away canvas to ⅝in, tapering off to point of dart. Stitch darts on back of bolero and stitch side and shoulder seams. Press seams open. Stitch the lining in the same way and then place bolero and lining together, wrong sides facing. Baste around edge of bolero and around armholes, matching up seams of lining to those of bolero. Work a line of machine stitching or backstitch ¼in in from all edges and then cover with braid as follows:

Turn under ⅝in at one end of the braid and start pinning it to the right side of the bolero from a side seam. Stretch the braid slightly as you pin so that it lies smoothly around the curves. Join the two ends of braid neatly. Sew the braid on the right side with a small, neat hemming stitch and then hem braid to lining. Use thread the color of the braid.

One front worked in the alternative color combination▼ The bolero▶

Simply work the design from this chart. Each square represents one half cross-stitch.

Normally it is usual to start working a charted design from the center, but in this case it is vitally important to commence working from the point of the dart. This will insure accurate placing of the design so that it will fit into the shaping of the bolero.

Yarn quantities

The numbers in the charts below refer to D.M.C. Tapestry Yarn colors.

Area		Blue/Green Color Combination Yarn Number	Red/Olive Color Combination Yarn Number	Skein Quantities
Background	☐	lime 7504	olive 7485	7
Leaves	◼	blue 7797	red 7600	4
Leaves	◣	green 7909	orange 7946	4
Leaves	⊞	gray 7618	pink 7204	2
Flowers	⊡	blue 7996	blue 7241	3
Flowers and Flower Centers	⊡	mauve 7895	pink 7153	2
Flowers	⊙	pink 7132	orange 7947	2
Flowers	▼	purple 7243	magenta 7157	2
Large Flower Centers	▷	slate blue 7294	dark pink 7136	1
Flower Centers	⊠	blue 7316	mauve 7314	2
Flower Centers	⊠	green 7548	pale green 7351	2
Flower Centers	⊡	dusty pink 7124	salmon pink 7853	1

Collector's Piece

A Danish rose
Cross-stitch is one of the oldest forms of embroidery. For centuries it has been used in traditional European folk and peasant embroideries to decorate national costumes and household articles.
Each country has developed its own particular style to such an extent that it is possible to determine where a particular piece of work or design originated. For instance, modern Danish cross-stitch designs usually depict forms in a very realistic manner. The rounded shapes of flowers, birds and animals are embroidered in delicate, pretty colors in carefully selected tones, which, when worked together, enhance this realistic effect. This delightful rose motif is typical of the Danish style in cross-stitch and can be used in many exciting ways. Here it is shown worked in two ways to create completely contrasting effects. One rose is worked in chunky yarns on coarse canvas, the other in stranded floss on fine linen and mounted in a tiny gold frame.
Worked on linen with 24 threads to 1in over 2 threads each way, the rose will measure about $2\frac{5}{8}$in by $2\frac{1}{2}$in. Worked as a cushion, the same motif measures about $10\frac{1}{4}$in by 10in—the different scale is achieved by working the cross-stitch over 3 threads each way on single-weave canvas with 12 threads to 1in, using 2 strands of knitting worsted throughout.

Needle-point

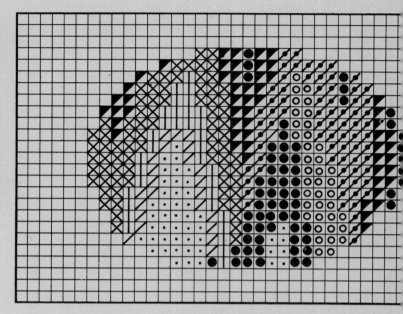

Vibrant pink and red design as a belt buckle

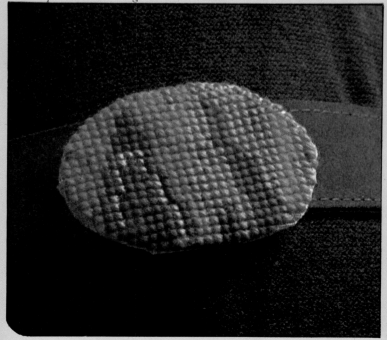

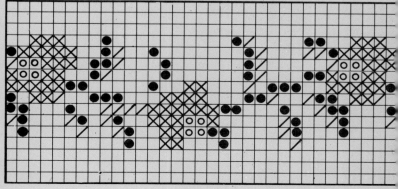

OVAL BUCKLE

Tapestry yarn

- ⊠ 7603 cerise
- ⧄ 7606 orange
- ⊞ 7544 dark red
- ⊡ 7446 brownish red
- ◉ 7153 cyclamen
- ⧄ 7205 pink
- ◎ 7108 oxblood red
- ⧄ 7708 lilac
- ☐ unworked canvas

BUTTERFLY BUCKLE

Six-strand floss

- ◉ 349 dark red
- ◪ 352 orange
- ⊠ 898 dark brown
- ⧄ 436 light brown
- ■ 792 blue
- ⧄ 3326 pink
- ◎ 208 lilac
- ⊡ 335 deep pink
- ☐ background 712 off white

ROSEBUD STRAP

Six-strand floss

- ◉ 907 light green
- ⧄ 841 olive green
- ⊠ 776 light pink
- ◎ 309 cerise
- ☐ background 3346 bright green

Quick-to-make canvas accessories to make you feel special or to work for a friend. Two charming motifs to wear as belt or shoe buckles and two watchstrap designs, one striped and one patterned with rosebuds.

Stitches used

All the designs given in this chapter are worked in cross-stitch (Embroidery Chapter 41) on fine mesh canvas. Color key working charts are given for the two buckles and for the rosebud watchstrap. Work the striped watchstrap by using the illustration as a guide to colors.

Oval buckle

To make the oval buckle measuring about 2¾ inches by 2 inches you will need:
- ☐ Canvas with 10 double threads to 1 inch, 6 inches square
- ☐ D.M.C. Tapestry yarn— one skein each in the following colors: cerise 7603; orange 7606; dark red 7544; brownish red 7446; cyclamen 7153; pink 7205; oxblood red 7108; lilac 7708
- ☐ Small piece strong cardboard
- ☐ Small piece foam plastic ¼ inch thick
- ☐ Small piece lining fabric

☐ Tapestry needle No. 18

To make

Work the design in cross-stitch from the chart and complete the buckle in the same way as instructed for the butterfly buckle.

Butterfly shoe buckle

To make the butterfly buckle, measuring about 2¾ inches by 2⅜ inches, you will need:
- ☐ Double-weave canvas with 14 double threads to 1 inch, 6 inches square
- ☐ Small piece strong cardboard
- ☐ Small piece foam plastic ¼ inch thick
- ☐ Small piece lining fabric
- ☐ Tapestry needle No.24
- ☐ D.M.C. 6-strand floss—one skein each in the following colors: dark red 349; orange 352; dark brown 898; light brown 436; blue 792; pink 3326; lilac 208; deep pink 335; background worked in off white 712

To make

Using four strands of floss in the needle work the design in cross-stitch from the chart. When the work is completed, block the canvas. Cut a piece of cardboard slightly smaller than the area of worked canvas. Glue a piece of foam plastic to the cardboard and trim it to the same shape. Center and stretch the needlepoint over the cardboard and lace firmly in place using strong thread. Cover the back of the buckle neatly with a piece of lining cut to the same shape as the buckle with edges turned in.

Watchstraps

To make the watchstraps you will need:
For rosebud strap:
- ☐ Single-weave canvas with 18 threads to 1 inch
- ☐ D.M.C. 6-strand floss— one skein each in the following colors: light green 907; olive green 841; light pink 776; cerise 309; the background is bright green 3346

For striped strap:
- ☐ Canvas with 10 double threads to 1 inch
- ☐ D.M.C. Tapestry yarn— one skein each in the following colors: dark red 7108; deep pink 7603; and cyclamen 7153

For both straps:
- ☐ Ribbon or lining fabric to make back of strap neat
- ☐ Velcro fastening or buckle

To make

Work from the chart, finish off and sew on buckle or velcro fastening.

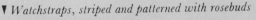

▼ *Butterfly buckle motif for a pretty shoe*

▼ *Watchstraps, striped and patterned with rosebuds*

Chapter 64

Flowered wall panels in cross-stitch

These delightful Art Deco flowers bring a modern look to needlepoint and are fairly simple to design yourself.

By changing the color scheme you can completely change the mood of the panel, using bright, clear colors for summer flowers, as in the summer flowers panel on the opposite page, or rusty yellows and oranges for the autumn ones below.

▼ *This wall panel depicts flowers in the mellow tones of autumn*

This design can be worked in a variety of ways, simply by experimenting with different materials. The most common type of needlepoint is worked on single- or double-weave canvas, but it is also possible to use many needlepoint stitches on softer cotton or jute cloths with Aida weaves.

True Aida cloth is a cotton embroidery fabric, woven in blocks of threads. It has a slightly starched finish which launders out when the embroidery is finally completed. This genuine Aida cloth is altogether too fine for standard needlepoint yarns, but the jute canvas with Aida weave, which comes in only one size, gives six cross-stitches to the inch. This has the effect of producing quick results and means that bold wall panels like these can be finished in a matter of hours.

If, for any reason, you need to use an alternative type of cloth to work on, Binca cloth is similar and just as suitable.

Summer flowers panel

Materials you will need
- [ ] ½yd Aida weave jute canvas (finished size about 15in square)
- [ ] Tapestry needle size 18
- [ ] Hardboard or softboard 15in by 15in
- [ ] 1 skein white, 3 skeins orange, 3 skeins blue, 1 skein brown, 9 skeins pink, 2 skeins yellow, 6 skeins green, 12 skeins turquoise (background)

N.B. You can use either matte embroidery cotton or tapestry yarn. The amounts given above are for tapestry yarn which has 15 yards to the skein, whereas matte embroidery cotton skeins contain about 10 yards. Allowing for an equivalent yardage, in some cases more skeins of matte embroidery cotton will be required. Use one strand throughout.

To work the picture
First find the center of the canvas by working two lines of basting, one from side to side and one from top to bottom as indicated by the arrows (see Needlepoint Chapter 69). Begin to work the design by counting out from the center of the chart, outlining the shapes in backstitch first, then fill in the design with cross-stitch (see Embroidery Chapter 41). Each cross-stitch is worked following the weave of the canvas, which is divided into squares.

To mount the finished work
When the design is completed, block the canvas as described in Needlepoint Chapter 74. Now trim the board edges to the exact finished size of the panel. Center the board over the back of the work and lace the canvas with fine string, picking up the fabric well in from the edge. Take the lacing across the back from side to side and then repeat the process from top to bottom. Pull the lacing firmly so that the work is evenly stretched without puckering. Secure the ends of the string by knotting them several times.

If you want to hang the panel unframed, make the work neat by sewing unbleached muslin or other fabric over the back to conceal the lacing.

Autumn flowers panel

Designing your own picture
To design a flower picture such as the one shown here, work on stiff paper and simply draw around drinking glasses to form the flower shapes. Cut out several flowers in varying sizes and then arrange them, overlapping, until you achieve a pleasing effect. Trace the outline of the design onto the canvas and work in cross-stitch as for the summer flowers.

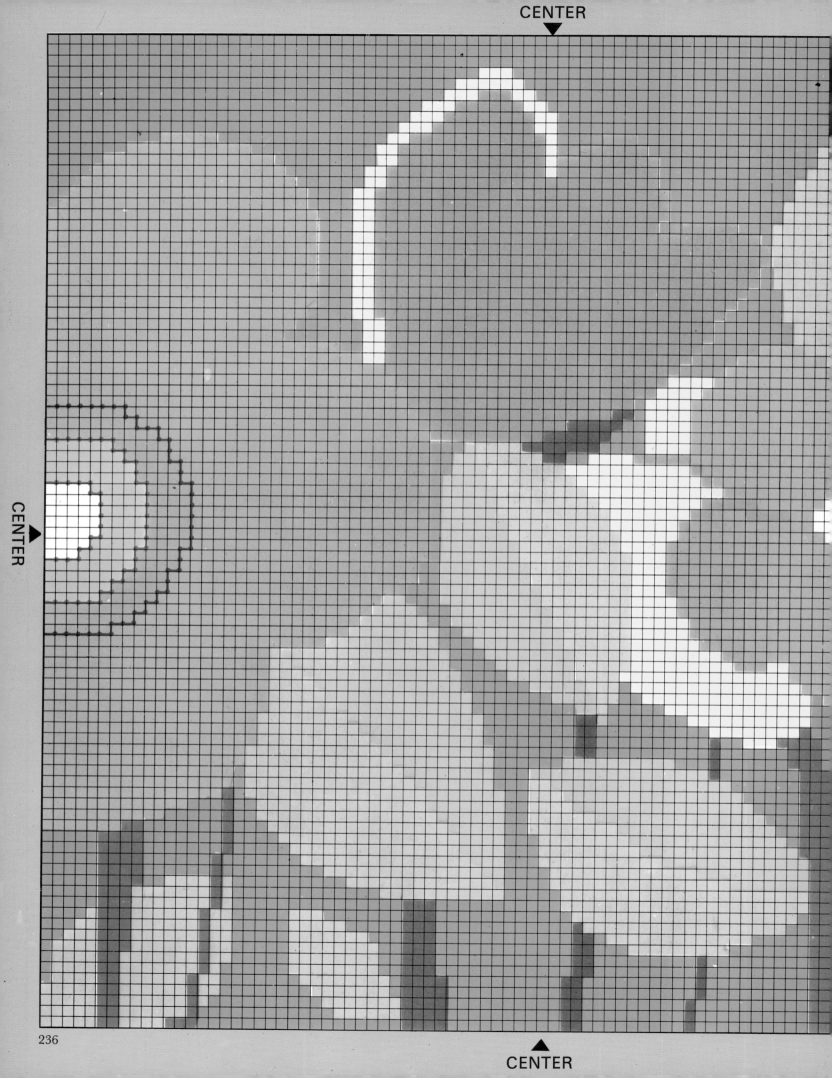

CENTER
►

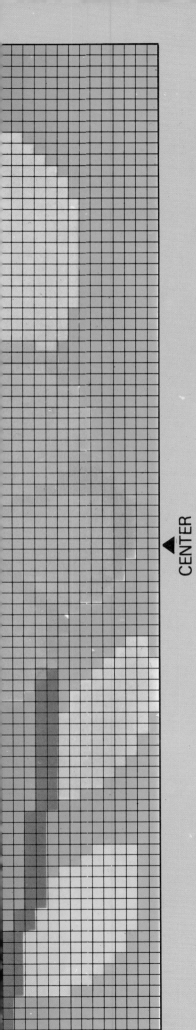

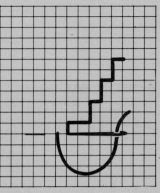

▲ *Backstitch worked in self color to outline shapes*

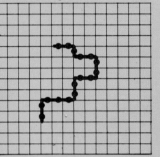

▲ *Backstitch worked in contrasting color indicated on the chart*

Stitch Library

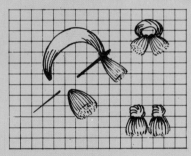

Single or tufted stitch
The stitches are worked between each other in alternate rows and imitate carpet knotting

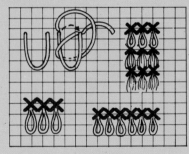

Velvet or astrakhan stitch
All the stitches should be worked before any of the loops are cut

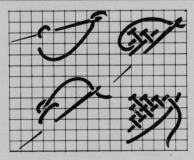

Web stitch
Web stitch gives a woven effect and is useful as a filling for small areas

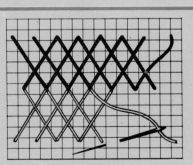

Plaited Algerian stitch
This is worked in the same way as closed herringbone stitch

Chapter 65

A pillow and rug in cross~stitch

This cross-stitched design of pink roses, syringa blossom and burnished autumn leaves looks just as beautiful whether worked on a rug or adapted to a pillow or framed picture. The design chart and color key are on the following pages.

Cross-stitched pillow

You will need:

☐ ⅔yd 36in wide single-thread canvas (14 threads to 1in)
☐ Tapestry or Persian-type yarns (see color key)
☐ ⅔yd 36in wide fabric for backing (e.g. velvet or corduroy)
☐ Tapestry needle size 19
☐ 20in zipper to match backing material
☐ Pillow form 16in deep by 24in wide
☐ Sewing thread
(Finished size of pillow 17½in deep by 24½in wide)

Working the design
Bind the raw edges with 1in wide tape to prevent fraying. Find the center of the canvas and mark it with a pencil or a line of basting stitches. Using cross-stitch worked over two threads of canvas (see Embroidery Chapter 41), work the design from the center outward.

Yarns and color schemes
Although Tapestry and Persian-type yarns are fairly easy to obtain, other types of yarn can be used to give a wider choice of colors and texture.
The background color of the pillow shown here is a very light gray, and the rug border is deep olive green. Although both will blend with most room color schemes, it is easy to adapt a charted design to match different color combinations. Select your choice of colors and indicate them beside the symbols on the color key, covering the original colors to avoid confusion.

Finishing the pillow
When you have finished working the design, stretch the canvas (see Needlepoint Chapter 74) and trim away excess fabric, leaving ⅝in canvas all around for seam allowance. Overcast the edges to prevent fraying. Lay and pin the finished needlepoint on the backing material and cut the pillow back to the same size as the front. With right sides facing, pin and baste the canvas and the back together, along the seam allowance. Working as close to the cross-stitches as possible, machine stitch or backstitch around three sides and each end of the fourth (long) side, leaving 20in unstitched for inserting the zipper. Trim each corner diagonally and overcast the trimmed edges.
Turn the pillow cover to the right side and gently poke out the corners using a blunt pencil. Don't push too hard or the fabric

Pink roses in cross-stitch add welcoming color to a couch

may split.) Still working from the right side, baste the seam allowance of the zipper opening back against the inside of the pillow cover. Keeping the zipper closed, pin and baste the zipper into position along one side of the opening. Open the zipper carefully and pin and baste the other side. Sew the zipper by hand using a half backstitch (similar to backstitch, but a tiny stitch is taken up on the surface and a longer stitch underneath). The zippered edge enables the pillow form to be removed so that the pillow cover can be cleaned (needlepoint should never be washed); however, if the cover is not going to be cleaned, it is possible to close the pillow cover by slip stitching the fourth side.

The cross-stitched rug

You will need:

☐ 1¾yds of 44in wide canvas (10 double threads to 1in)
☐ Tapestry needles size 14
☐ Tapestry yarn or carpet thrums
(5oz of yarn for 1 sq ft of canvas approximately)
(Finished size of rug approx. 41 by 53in.)

The rose, syringa and leaf design in a rug with a classic border

The cross-stitch pillow

The cross-stitch rug

Carpet thrums are the ends cut from the loom when carpet weaving is finished and provide excellent material for rugs in both color and wearing quality.

It is worth remembering, however, that a considerable quantity of one color is required for the border of the rug and the background. It is advisable, therefore, to buy sufficient thrums at one time, since colors are inclined to vary each time they are purchased from different dye lots.

Making the rug
Using both sections of the chart, the center design (used for the pillow) and the border design, work from the center outward in cross-stitch over two double threads (see Embroidery Chapter 41).

Finishing
When you have finished working the design, stretch the canvas and trim away excess fabric, leaving 1½in of canvas all around. Overcast to prevent fraying and turn the 1½in edge under to the wrong side. Pin and baste the turned hem, finishing the rug with hemming stitch all around, using heavy thread.

239

Chart for the cross-stitched pillow

CENTER

CENTER

CENTER

CENTER

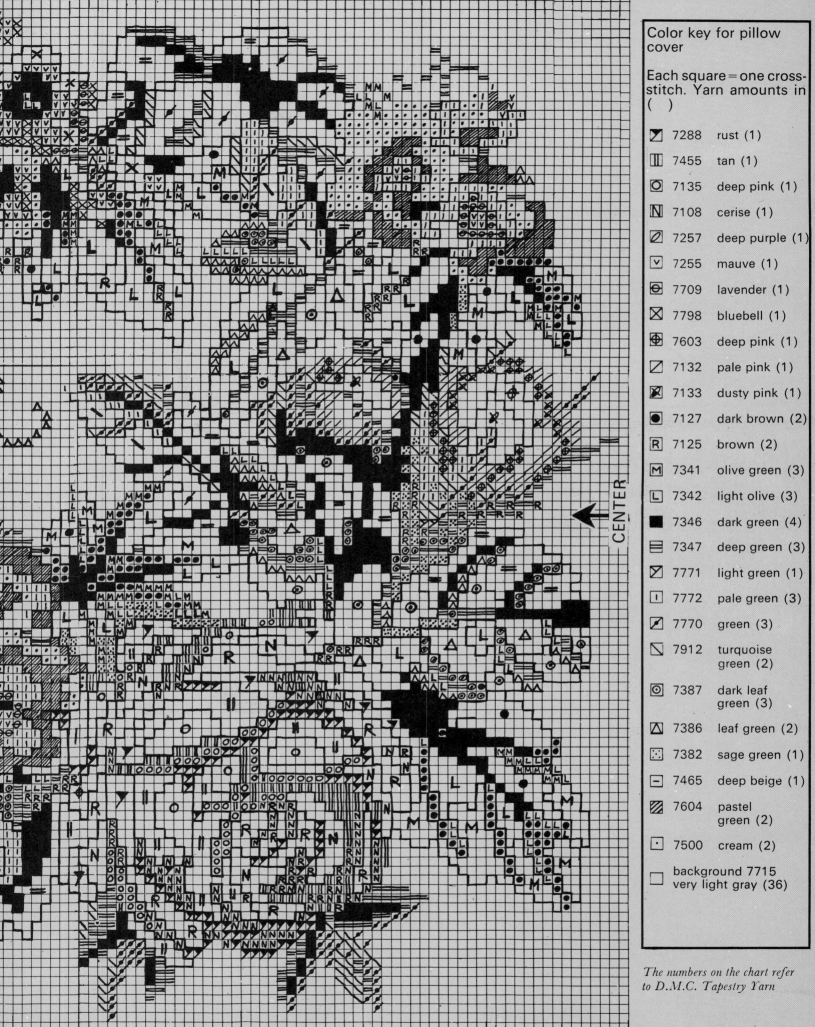

Color key for pillow cover

Each square = one cross-stitch. Yarn amounts in ( )

◣	7288	rust (1)
▥	7455	tan (1)
◎	7135	deep pink (1)
◨	7108	cerise (1)
◪	7257	deep purple (1)
v	7255	mauve (1)
⊕	7709	lavender (1)
⊠	7798	bluebell (1)
⊕	7603	deep pink (1)
◿	7132	pale pink (1)
◩	7133	dusty pink (1)
●	7127	dark brown (2)
R	7125	brown (2)
M	7341	olive green (3)
L	7342	light olive (3)
■	7346	dark green (4)
☰	7347	deep green (3)
◹	7771	light green (1)
ı	7772	pale green (3)
◿	7770	green (3)
◺	7912	turquoise green (2)
◉	7387	dark leaf green (3)
△	7386	leaf green (2)
⬚	7382	sage green (1)
−	7465	deep beige (1)
▨	7604	pastel green (2)
⊡	7500	cream (2)
☐	background 7715 very light gray (36)

CENTER

The numbers on the chart refer to D.M.C. Tapestry Yarn

241

CENTER   **Chart for the cross-stitched rug border**   One quarter of the rug border is shown. Use the pillow top chart for center of rug, extending design with the border.

Diagram shows how to fit the four quarters of the rug border together with the rug center design (used for the pillow)

CENTER ←

Color key for rug border

Each square = one cross-stitch. Yarn amounts appear in ( ).

◩ 7288   rust (6)

⊠ 7852   salmon pink (8)

◩ 7771   light green (12)

L 7342   light olive (24)

G 7463   beige (24)

K 7408   red (4)

− 7465   deep beige (12)

◫ 7132   pale pink (12)

☐ Background to rug edge 7341 olive green (48)

The numbers on the chart refer to D.M.C. Tapestry Yarn

Chapter 66

Panel using a variety of stitches

This dragon design, in a dramatic range of reds and pinks, is shown on a chart so that you can make it in practically any size you wish by choosing a larger or smaller mesh canvas and coarser or finer yarns to correspond.

Work a small dragon to guard your jewels on the lid of a jewel box or a larger one for a wall-hanging. This design would also be impressive on a headboard, pillow cover or rug.

The small dragon is worked completely in 6-strand embroidery floss, while the larger one is worked on heavier canvas using some 6-strand floss together with tapestry yarn and soft embroidery cotton. Using a mixture of yarns will give you experience in variations of texture and show how the planning of different stitches and yarns can add enormously to the finished effect of the work.

Materials you will need
Small dragon (below)
- [ ] Single-weave canvas 12in by 9in with 20 or 22 threads to the in. Finished size measures 7in by 5in.
- [ ] One skein each of D.M.C. 6-strand floss No.352, 351, 350, 349, 321, 894, 891, 309, 326, 603, 600, 605, 3685, 814 and two skeins of 902.
- [ ] Tapestry needle size 22.

Large dragon (right)
- [ ] Single-weave canvas 20in by 18in with 13 threads to the in. Finished size measures 16½in by 11¼in.
- [ ] One skein each of D.M.C. 6-strand floss No.891, 603, 309, 326, 349; D.M.C. Matte Embroidery cotton No.2776, 2351, 2719, 2309, 2326, 2304; D.M.C. Tapestry yarn No.7852, 7850, 7666, 7544, 7208, 7600, 7204; two skeins Matte Embroidery cotton No.2815, three skeins No.2719; twelve skeins Tapestry yarn No.7139.
- [ ] Tapestry needle size 18.

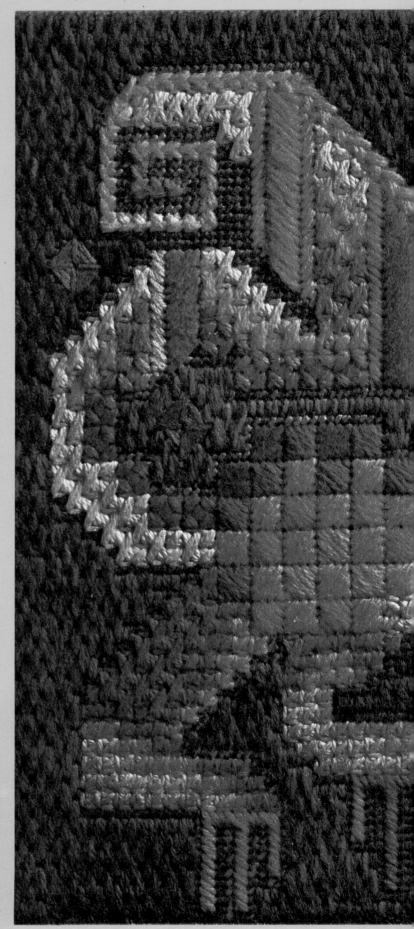

How to use the stitch and design charts

For the small dragon, follow the chart using each square as one stitch. For a larger dragon, one square on the chart represents four squares of canvas. The boldly drawn black lines separate different parts of the dragon's body, described on the stitch chart here and small chart, bottom right. The numbers on the stitch chart refer to Anchor yarns.

Upper table (continuation):

Part of Dragon	Stitch Reference	Symbol	SMALL DRAGON — Stranded Cotton	Stranded Cotton (12 strands)	LARGE DRAGON — Soft Embroidery Cotton (2 strands)	Tapisserie Wool (2 strands)
Tail tip	Long-legged cross stitch		039 (6) 057 043		028 076 043	
Chest	Alternate diagonal rows of: Algerian eye stitch Rice stitch		057 (4) 039 (6) 019 031 011		076 028 031 011	019 065
Bands across front legs	Slanted Gobelin in rows over number of threads indicated by chart		043 (4) 065 057		043 076	065
Rest of legs, front and back	Italian cross stitch		065 (6) 057 066 039 043 013 011 09 031		076 028 043 011 031	065 0895 028 043 013
Claws	Padded satin stitch		011 (6) 013 019 039 057 066		011	013 019 0895
Hips	Cushion stitch squares, alternating direction. Work back stitch (2 strands) between squares		043 (4) 019 039 013 010 011	039 057	043 028 011	019 013 010
Flowers	Make a cross as indicated by heavy lines using straight stitches. Work four blocks of satin stitch over arms of cross		044 (6) 043 011 039 031 057 065 019 072	044	043 011 028 031 076	065 019 0897
Stalk	Long-legged cross stitch		044 (6)		044	
Background	Work 1 row tent stitch round dragon and fill background with alternating tent stitch for small dragon, bricking for large dragon. Use tent stitch between paws and round tail tip. Alternatively speckle by using 1 thread of darker shade with 4 of main		045 (5) 072 (1)		044	045 0897

Lower table:

Part of Dragon	Stitch Reference	Symbol	SMALL DRAGON — Stranded Cotton	Stranded Cotton (12 strands)	LARGE DRAGON — Soft Embroidery Cotton (2 strands)	Tapisserie Wool (2 strands)
Eye	Detached eyelet		031 (3 strands)		031	
Eye surround	1 row long-legged cross stitch		039 (6)	039		
Nose	Work 1 rice stitch		09 (6)			09
Upper and lower jaws	Work in cross stitch see Embroidery Chapter 41		013 (9) 043 019 039 010 09	013 043 039	043 028	013 019 010 09
Ears	Slanted Gobelin. Long-legged cross stitch		065 (4) 069 043 (6) 039		078 043 028	065
Mane	In three shades work short bands in padded satin stitch. Work long bands in long-legged cross stitch		013 (6) 043 039 066	013 043 039		0895
Band down back	Work slanted Gobelin stitch over number of threads indicated by chart see Canvas Work Chapter 68		065 (4) 043 013 011 019	043	011 019	065 013
Top of head and neck	Use upright oblong cross-stitch, filling in odd corners with cross stitch. Work back stitch (3 strands) between the rows		043 (9) 065 039 057 066		043 028 076	065
Tail —textured bands	Upright oblong cross stitch filling corners with cross stitch		031 (9) 057 039 065 069	039	031 076	065 0895
Tail —satin bands	Slanted Gobelin over number of threads indicated by chart		010 (4) 013 039 043 019		078	010 013 019
Blocks at base of tail	Rice stitch		069 (6) 065		078	065

Stitch Library

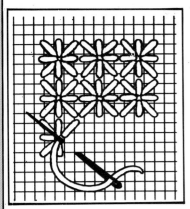

Star stitch

Work clockwise around the star in diagonal rows, until all eight points are completed. (Algerian eye stitch is worked in the same way but sew around the star twice for a more cushioned effect.)

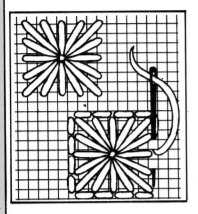

Detached eyelets

Work stitches radiating outward from the central point. Take a backstitch over two threads around the outside of the eyelet. The eyelet shown in the diagram is worked with eight stitches over four threads of single-weave canvas but if a larger one is required work over three or four threads of the canvas for each stitch.

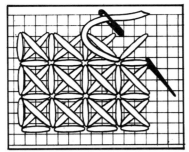

Italian cross-stitch

Work in two stages. In the first stage vertical, diagonal and horizontal stitches are worked over three or four threads repeated along the row from left to right. From right to left work the second stage of cross-stitch over the first diagonal.

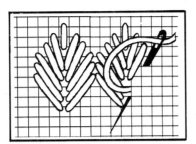

Leaf stitch

Work stitches around the leaf shape bringing the needle inward to the center from the outside edge.

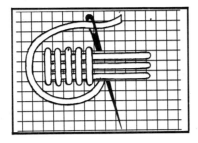

Padded satin stitch

Work satin stitch over a line of horizontal stitches to give a more padded effect.

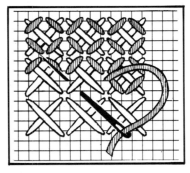

Rice stitch

Rice stitch consists of ordinary cross-stitch with the arms crossed by bars of cross-stitch in the same or different colored thread.

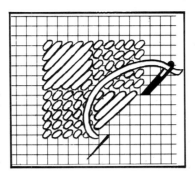

Checker stitch

Work alternate blocks of tent stitch and cushion stitch.

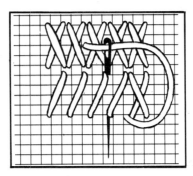

Oblong cross-stitch

Work cross-stitch inserting the needle four holes down, two holes across and so on.

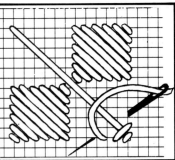

Cushion stitch

Work diagonal stitches into the shape of a square. The diagonal stitch through the center shows the method for padding this gap.

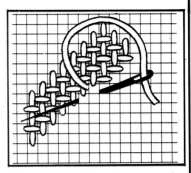

Tile stitch

Work upright cross-stitch so that the upper stitch is alternately vertical and horizontal.

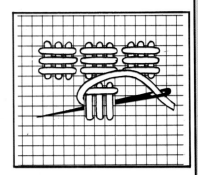

Blocked satin stitch

Cover three vertical satin stitches by three horizontal satin stitches.

Yarn key for dragons

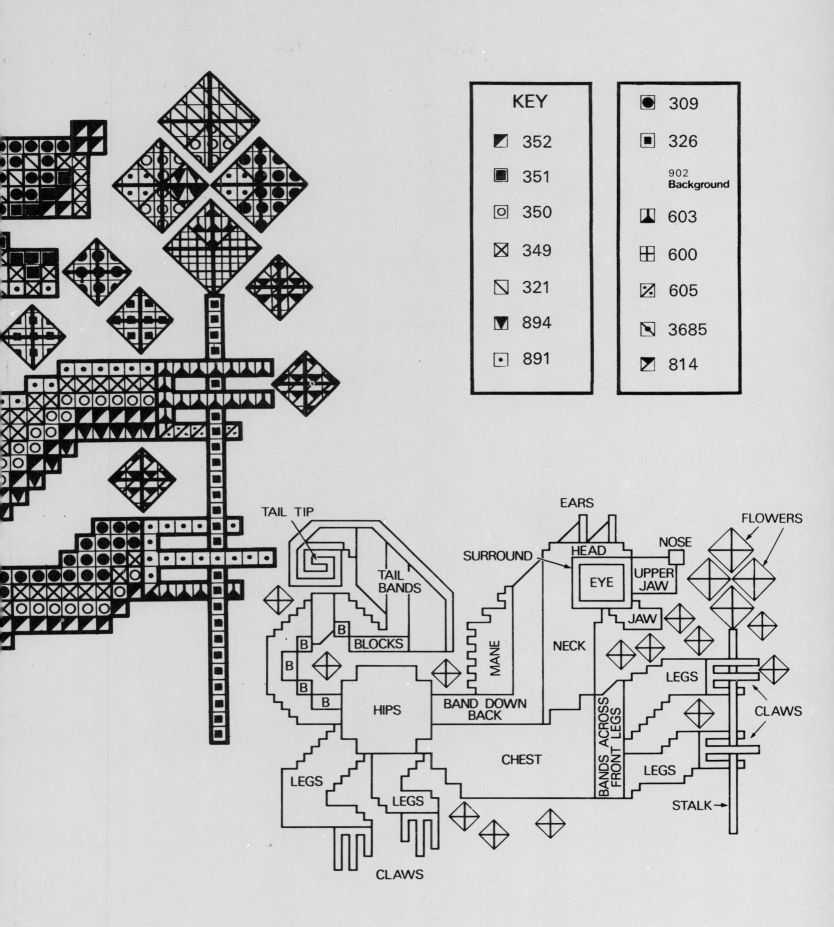

KEY

◩	352
◼	351
⊡	350
⊠	349
◺	321
◤	894
⊡	891

⬤	309
▪	326
	902 **Background**
◣	603
⊞	600
◪	605
◺	3685
◩	814

TAIL TIP

TAIL BANDS

EARS

SURROUND

HEAD

NOSE

EYE

UPPER JAW

JAW

FLOWERS

B
B
B
B
B

BLOCKS

HIPS

BAND DOWN BACK

MANE

NECK

BANDS ACROSS FRONT LEGS

LEGS

CLAWS

CHEST

LEGS

LEGS

LEGS

STALK

CLAWS

Chapter 67

A tote bag in double cross~stitch

Needlepoint is ideal for making all kinds of bags, from elegant evening purses worked in fine silk to casual hold-alls in colorful wool. By following the chart overleaf you can make this richly decorated tote bag, which is worked in tapestry yarn with touches of plastic raffia.

Tote bag

Materials you will need to work both sides of the bag
- ☐ ½yd single-weave canvas 36in wide, 18 threads to 1 inch
- ☐ ½yd lining material, 36in wide
- ☐ Two skeins each of D.M.C. Tapestry yarn in dark blue No. 7319, blue No. 7995, green No. 7344, pink No. 7157, turquoise No. 7912, lime green No. 7435; four skeins pale blue No. 7952; twenty skeins purple No. 7245
- ☐ Two skeins Columbia-Minerva Hi-Straw purple 141
- ☐ Tapestry needle No. 18

To use the pattern
Draw the outline of the bag from the chart onto strong paper and cut out. Baste the pattern onto the canvas, leaving plenty of space around the shape for ⅝ inch seam allowance and blocking. Also make sure that the grain line on the pattern follows the grain of the canvas.
Draw around the outline of the pattern using a felt-tipped pen, or mark with basting stitches. Remove the pattern and repeat the process for the other side of the bag.
Or you could work only one side of the bag in canvas, using a textured fabric such as tweed for the second side, halving the amounts of yarn required.

To work the embroidery
Mark the center of each side with lines of basting (Needlepoint Chapter 69) and plan how to work the design out from the center. Using the chart, work the design on each side of the bag.

To make the bag
When the work is complete block and trim the canvas (Needlepoint Chapter 74) and cut out the two pieces of lining to the shape of the trimmed canvas.
Pin and baste the two sides of the bag together, right sides facing, stitch from A to B (see diagram) using one of the seaming methods given, then stitch the seam of the handle (see diagram).
Snip into the seam allowance on curves, and turn the bag to the right side. Fold back the seam allowance around the upper edge of the bag and handle edges and baste down.
Sew the pieces of lining together in the same way as for the bag, folding the seam allowance around the top and along the handle to the back, and baste. Slip the lining into the bag, matching the

seams to those of the bag. Pin, baste, and slip stitch into place, taking care to bring the lining right up to the edge of the embroidery so that no canvas is visible on the finished bag.

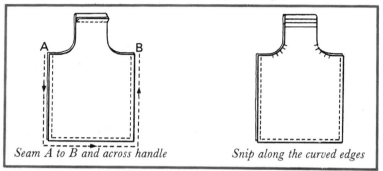

Seam A to B and across handle   *Snip along the curved edges*

Seam methods
For needlepoint items which receive hard wear, a good strong method of seaming is needed.
After blocking the finished work (Needlepoint Chapter 74) trim away excess canvas leaving not less than ⅝ inch seam allowance all around. Place the work with right sides together and pin, matching any patterns carefully, and then baste. Backstitch by hand using either yarn of the background color or matching linen thread. If you prefer to machine stitch the seam, use a strong linen thread matched to the background color. Stitches should be placed as close as possible to the edge of the embroidery.
Overcast the raw edges of canvas to prevent fraying and trim back the corners. Turn the work to the right side and if any canvas shows along the seams, work a slip stitch, picking up one stitch of embroidery from each side of the seam to draw the stitches together over the canvas.

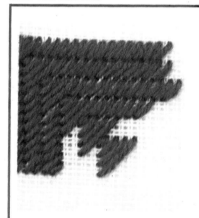

Slanted Gobelin stitch
These blocked rows of slanted Gobelin stitch show the method used for turning a corner (Needlepoint Chapter 68).
Finally, here is one more stitch to add to your needlepoint repertoire.
This stitch produces a damask-like texture which will add richness to your work. It can be used either to highlight areas of a design or as a background stitch.

▼ *Close-up of textured stitches used on the tote bag pictured opposite*

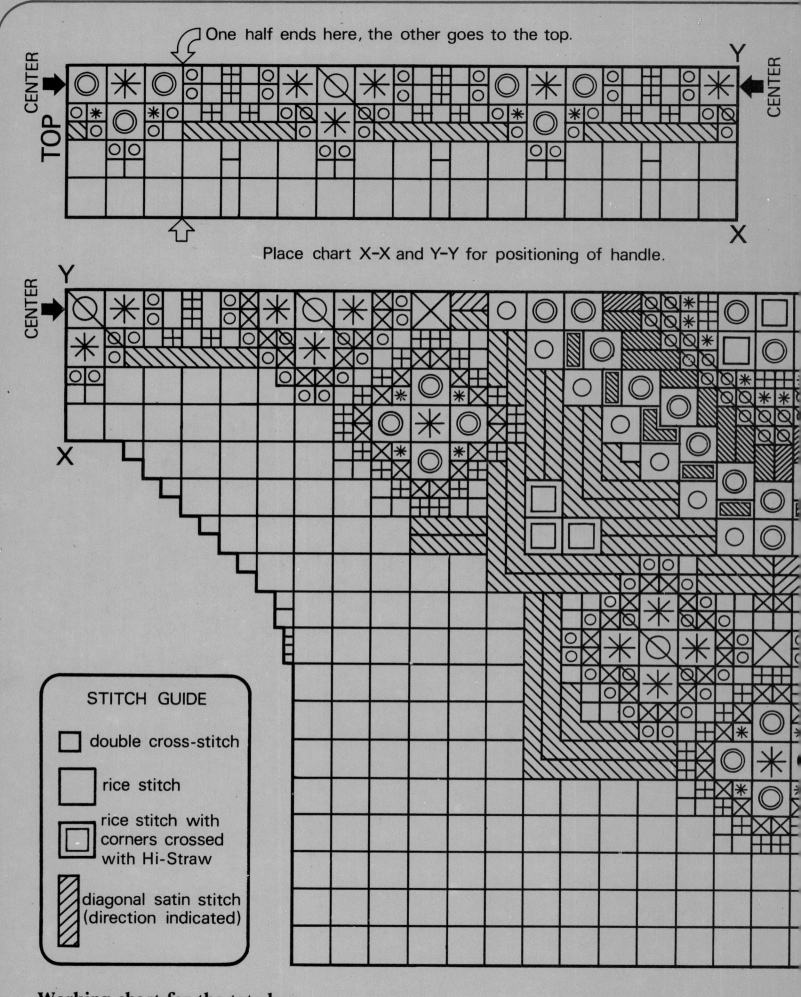

One half ends here, the other goes to the top.

CENTER · CENTER · TOP · Y · X · CENTER

Place chart X–X and Y–Y for positioning of handle.

CENTER · Y · X

STITCH GUIDE

☐ double cross-stitch

☐ rice stitch

⊡ rice stitch with corners crossed with Hi-Straw

▨ diagonal satin stitch (direction indicated)

Working chart for the tote bag

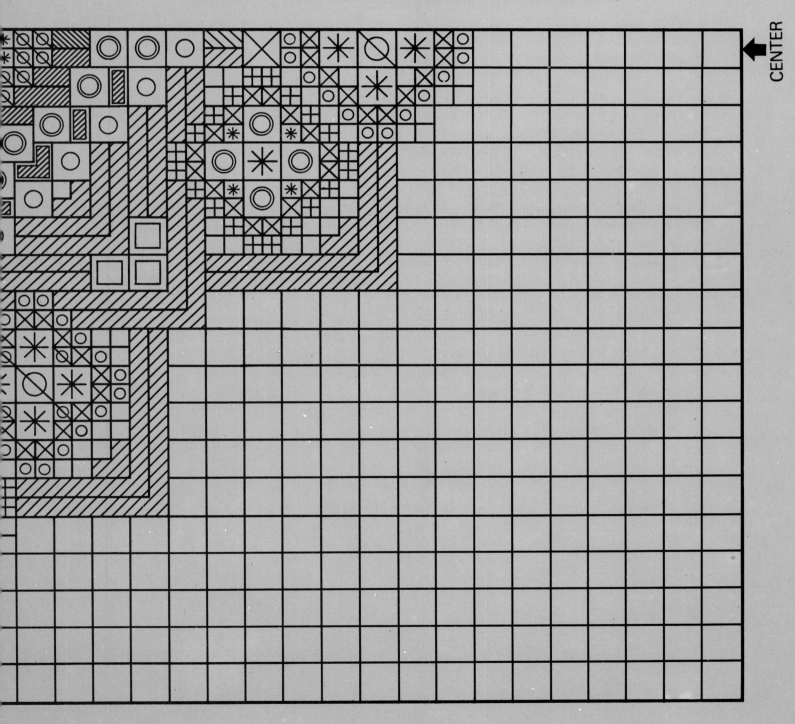

D.M.C. TAPESTRY YARN COLOR CHART

⊡ = pink ——————— 7157

⊠ = dark blue —————— 7319

◎ = blue —————— 7995

⊘ = turquoise —————— 7912

▨ ✳ = green —————— 7344

⊞ = pale blue —————— 7952

▨ = lime —————— 7435

☐ = purple —————— 7245

Hi-Straw color No. 141

Double cross-stitch worked over 2 threads each way.

CENTER

Chapter 68

Introduction to tent stitch

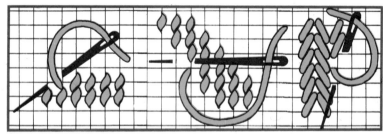

Tent stitch—horizontal, diagonal and reversed

Here are some easy and attractive stitches which can be used as groundings or fillings. They also form lovely patterns on their own when worked in two colors or a subtle contrast worked in two tones of one color.

Tent stitch
This is a basic stitch for petit point and is used for gros point when a particularly durable stitch is required. Work from right to left. Come up in the lower left corner of a stitch. Work back over 1 thread (diagonally). Insert the needle, cross behind 2 threads and come up in the new stitch. When the row is complete, turn the work upside down, then work the next row from right to left again. When working over a large area, use diagonal tent stitch to prevent the canvas from being pulled out of shape. The needle is placed horizontally on the row, as shown in the diagram; on the following row, the needle will be placed vertically. The stitch can also be worked in vertical or horizontal lines in alternate directions; when this method is used, it is called reverse tent stitch.

A bird panel worked in tent stitch

Upright Gobelin Stitch
This is worked with straight up-and-down stitches, usually over four horizontal threads of canvas.

Slanted Gobelin Stitch
This is similar to upright Gobelin, but worked over 2 vertical and 4 horizontal threads.

Bricking
This upright stitch is worked in interlocking rows.
1st row. Work alternate stitches over 4 horizontal threads.
2nd row. Start 2 threads lower and work a row of stitches over 4 threads, between the stitches of the first row.

Slanted bricking
This stitch is also worked in interlocking rows, but over 2 vertical and 4 horizontal threads which gives a smooth, slanted texture.

Parisian stitch
This is a small, close, filling stitch worked in interlocking rows over 1 and then over 3 horizontal threads.

Hungarian stitch
Again, this stitch is worked in interlocking rows, over 2 and then over 4 horizontal threads.

Upright Gobelin Stitch

Slanted bricking

Slanted Gobelin Stitch

Parisian stitch

Bricking

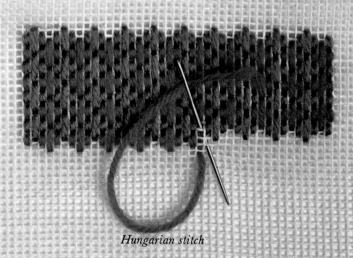

Hungarian stitch

Snowy owls

This magnificent piece of needlepoint is made up of 140,700 stitches—worked entirely in tent stitch on single-weave canvas with 23 threads to the inch. The work took 300 hours to complete and measures 19 inches by 14 inches. The picture was designed and worked by Dr Phyllis Daply, once a surgeon and anaesthetist. Her source of inspiration was a couple of photographs taken by Eric Hosking, the well-known bird photographer on Fetlar, one of the Shetland Islands. Dr Daply patiently interpreted the photographs, and finally presented the masterpiece to Eric Hosking. The realistic appearance achieved relies on a clever

use of shading and color tone. Notice particularly the sensitive treatment used to depict the feathers of the owl to the left of the picture and the smoother texture created by shading on the tree trunk, in contrast to the fluid shading of the many blues in the sea and sky.

If you want to make your own design from a favorite color photograph, the simplest way is to order a big black and white print of the photograph (which is often expensive) enlarged to the size you want your needlepoint to be and then trace off the different tone areas and relate them by numbers to the colors on the smaller color print. Trace these color outlines onto the canvas and number them as a key to the original.

Chapter 69

A pincushion in tent stitch

A pincushion is a good way to begin working from a charted design. Using a chart is less expensive than buying a painted or trammed canvas, which will confine you to the most commercially available designs, while a charted picture gives you the opportunity of picking your own colors and building up your own designs. For instance, you can repeat the apple motif given opposite at random all over a cushion, or turn it into a yellow Golden Delicious or a green Granny Smith.

Using a chart

A chart demands a little concentration when it comes to plotting the outlines, but once these are worked out the rest is easy. Start by finding the center of the chart. In this case you need to find the center of the apple motif, so count the number of squares from top to bottom and from side to side, divide each total by half and mark the center. Then fold the canvas in half both ways and mark its center with a pencil or lines of basting. Start counting and stitching from the center. Each square on the chart corresponds to one thread intersection on the canvas.

If there are large areas of color to be filled in, mark the outline and the smaller areas first, and then fill in the larger areas.

Two pincushions to work: one from the chart opposite, one row by row

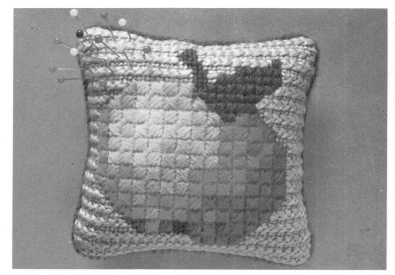

The right stitch for the right texture

Any design loses impact if all areas are worked in the same texture, that is, all rough or all smooth. For the most pleasing effect, it is important to separate areas of the design into smooth, medium and rough textures. (Tent, Gobelin, straight and satin stitches are all smooth. Cross-, rice and star stitches are semi-rough. Double cross-, oblong and tufted stitches are very rough.) Some stitches lend themselves to particular textures and shapes. For instance, slanted bricking (see Needlepoint Chapter 68) has a good texture for walls and brickwork, while fishbone stitch (see Needlepoint Chapter 76) interprets water very well. Tent and Gobelin stitches (see Needlepoint Chapter 68) clarify the line of a design, and for any form of intricate, realistic shading, nothing is as effective as tent stitch.

Strong texture often looks most effective when it is used sparingly. For example, you could work just the mane and tail of a horse in a rough textured stitch, or use different stitches for flower centers and leaves, or the underside of a fish.

Apple pincushion

This plump apple pincushion uses lustrous cushion stitch (see Needlepoint Chapter 66) to interpret the shiny apple, rough reinforced cross-stitch for the gnarled leaf, and precise tent stitch for the neat shape of the stem and eye.

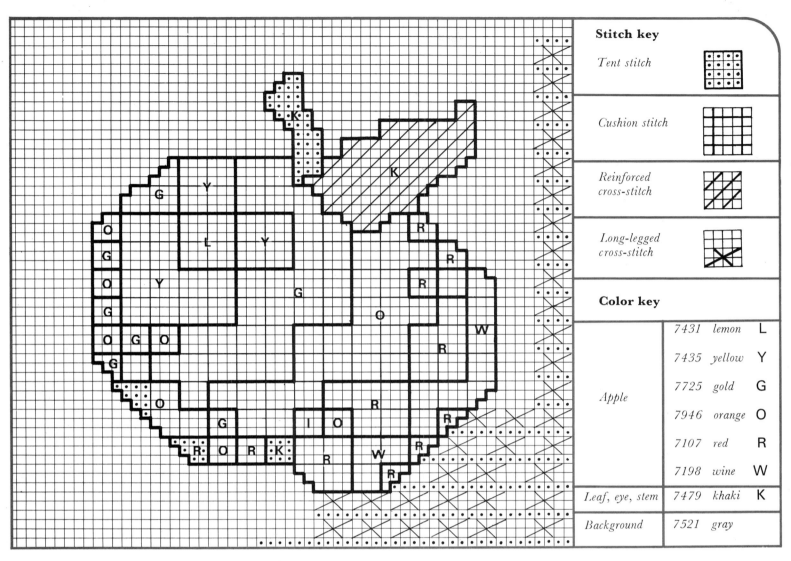

Stitch key

Tent stitch	
Cushion stitch	
Reinforced cross-stitch	
Long-legged cross-stitch	

Color key

	7431	lemon	L
	7435	yellow	Y
	7725	gold	G
Apple	7946	orange	O
	7107	red	R
	7198	wine	W
Leaf, eye, stem	7479	khaki	K
Background	7521	gray	

You will need

☐ Single-weave canvas 10in by 10in, 14 threads to the in. (Finished size about 4in square.)

☐ No.20 tapestry needle and a sharp needle for finishing.

☐ Velvet or other backing material, 6in by 6in.

☐ One skein each of D.M.C. Tapestry yarns 7431, 7435, 7725, 7946, 7107, 7198, 7479; and two skeins of 7521.

☐ 18in of cord for trimming.

☐ Sawdust from the lumberyard for filling.

To work the apple

Prevent the canvas from fraying by binding the edges with masking tape. On the chart, each square represents 1 canvas thread crossing which is to be covered by a single tent stitch.

Apple: Work in cushion stitch in groups of four over 3 threads.

Eye and stem: Work in tent stitch over 1 thread.

Leaf: Work in reinforced cross-stitch (i.e. cross-stitch worked twice over) over 2 threads. This insures that there is a good coverage of the canvas.

Background: Work in alternate rows of long-legged cross-stitch worked over 2 threads, and tent stitch worked over 1 thread.

N.B. To clarify chart, background symbols do not cover entire area.

Stretching the canvas back into shape

When the design is completed, stretch the canvas (see Needlepoint Chapter 74) and trim off excess canvas, leaving ⅝in seam allowances.

Finishing

To back the cushion, cut a square of velvet to the size of the trimmed canvas. Baste the seam allowances to the wrong side to make a neat, accurate square. Pin velvet to canvas, wrong sides together, and whip the velvet firmly into place, sewing into the outer row of needlepoint stitches.

Leave center of one side open for stuffing.

Sawdust is the stuffing which best allows pins to be pushed in easily. Pack it in very tightly—a teaspoon will help. Close the opening with pins and whip tightly when fully stuffed. Brush off any sawdust left lying on the pincushion. Sew cord all around the edge, covering the seam.

Square pincushion

The square pincushion is worked in delightful, bright, rich colors in a simple geometric design using a variety of lovely stitches. Work it outward from a center block of 4 cushion stitches in rows as follows: 2 rows tent stitch, 1 row cross-stitch, 1 row double cross-stitch, 1 row satin stitch, 1 row oblong cross-stitch with bars, 1 row long-legged cross-stitch, 1 row double cross-stitch, 1 row satin stitch, 1 row cross-stitch. For the sides, work 1 row oblong cross-stitch with bars, 1 row long-legged cross-stitch, 1 row double cross-stitch, 1 row long-legged cross-stitch, 1 row oblong cross-stitch with bars. Work long-legged cross-stitching for seams.

Chapter 70

Fashion accessories in tent stitch

Needlepoint has recently been updated by working it in brilliant colors for fashion accessories. The belts and bands given here are worked on double-thread canvas with ten double threads to the inch. Tent stitch is used throughout. All colors refer to tapestry yarn.

▼ *Chart for matching wristband, neckband and fringed girdle*

▼ *Chart for the leather thonged belt on the right*

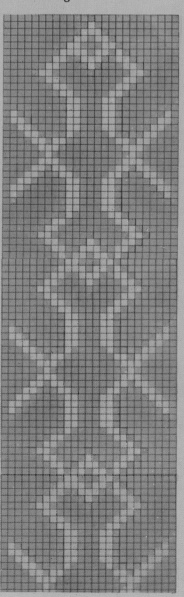

Neckband

Measurements
Finished size—2in wide by neck measurement.

Materials
☐ Canvas 6in by 22in
☐ ½yd ribbon, 2in wide
☐ 24in leather thonging
☐ 4 small skeins of tapestry yarn in red-orange; 2 small skeins each of purple, black, yellow, and lilac which is shown as white on the chart for clarity

Method
Work the design from the chart for the required length. Block and trim the canvas (see Needlepoint Chapter 74).
Turn the raw canvas on the long sides to back of work and catch them down with herringbone stitch. To make the channel through which the thonging slots, turn the raw canvas on the two ends to the back of the work and backstitch them down ⅜ inch from the edge. Line the band with ribbon using slip stitches and working through only one thickness of canvas at the ends so that the thonging channel is left open. Slot the thonging upward through one channel and downward through the other (see illustration).

Fringed girdle

Measurements
Finished size—3¼in wide by the waist measurement, taken loosely, plus 6½in overlap

Materials
☐ Canvas 7in by 36in
☐ Lining 4in by 36in
☐ 8 small skeins of tapestry yarn in red-orange; 6 small skeins in lilac; 3 small skeins each of purple and yellow; 2 small skeins in black
☐ A piece of cardboard measuring 3¼in by 6in
☐ Large snap fasteners

Method
Work the design from the chart for the required length. Block and trim the canvas (see Needlepoint Chapter 74), fold under the raw canvas and herringbone stitch into place. To make the fringe, wind yarn for 3 inches along the cardboard. Carefully sew one end of the loops to the canvas ¼ inch in from the end of the girdle, making sure that every strand is included. Slide the cardboard out and work a row of backstitches to secure the fringe. Complete work by lining the girdle, enclosing the ends of the fringe. Use snaps for fastening, laying one end of the girdle over the other (see illustration on right).

Thonged belt

Measurements
Finished size—2½in wide by the waist measurement, loosely taken.

Materials
☐ Canvas 6½in by 36in
☐ Lining 4in by 36in
☐ 45in leather thonging
☐ 10 eyelets and eyelet tool
☐ 4 small skeins of tapestry yarn in orange, 3 small skeins in red and 7 in lilac

Method
Work the design from the chart for the required length. Block and trim the canvas (see Needlepoint Chapter 74). Fold under the raw canvas and herringbone stitch into place. Line the belt and then insert five eyelets vertically, evenly spaced on each end of the belt. Lace the thonging through and tie.

Wristband

Measurements
Finished size—2in wide by wrist measurement

Materials
☐ Canvas 6in by 10in
☐ ¼yd ribbon, 2in wide
☐ 24in leather thonging
☐ 1 small skein each of the colors given for neckband

Method
Work in the same way and to the same design as for the neckband.

▲ The neckband with leather thonging tie
▼ Wristband to match neckband and girdle

A fringed girdle to wear with a simple dress ►
▼ A belt with leather thonging laces and detail of thonging

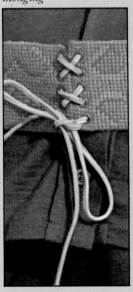

Chapter 71

Director's chair in tent stitch

Directors' style chairs are easy to cover and look marvelous in brilliant embroidery. The stylized flower design in this chapter is simple to copy and looks best in a modern setting.

The modern canvas chair can vary in styling detail. In this chapter you will find two basic methods of making covers and one or the other will adapt to most variations.

Pop-on cover (photographs)

This type of cover simply fits over the original back and seat sections and is easily removed for cleaning purposes.

Materials you will need
- ☐ Canvas with 10 double threads to the inch
- ☐ Tapestry yarns
- ☐ Sateen lining
- ☐ Snap fastener tape for attaching cover
- ☐ Plastic foam 1in thick (optional)

▼ *Detail of the chair design on the opposite page*

To make a pattern

Pin a sheet of strong paper over and around the fabric back and another over the seat of the chair. With a pencil, mark the edges of the shape onto the paper. Remove the paper and even up the shape before cutting out. Once the pieces are cut out, check them against the back and seat to make sure that they fit well.

Pin the pieces onto canvas, following the grain lines of the canvas. Mark the outline onto the canvas with a felt-tipped pen, leaving sufficient canvas all around for seam allowances and blocking.

Completing the embroidery

Plan the flower design as described in Needlepoint Chapter 64, using the chart on the following pages. Work the design in tent stitch or cross-stitch over two sets of double threads each way. When it is completed, block and trim the canvas as described in Needlepoint Chapter 74, leaving $\frac{5}{8}$ inch turnings at the edges.

Padding

For additional comfort, pad between the canvas and the lining with one-inch thick plastic foam.

To make the cover

Cut the lining to the exact size of the stitched and trimmed canvas.

Turn seam allowances to the back and baste. Turn all canvas raw edges to the back of the work and catch in place. Line the shapes with sateen lining. Stitch lengths of snap fastener tape to each end of the needlepoint back and seat sections and then onto the corresponding areas on the actual chair.

Slip cover (drawings)

This type of cover has tube openings at each side of the back section to slip over the back supports, and also at each side of the seat section to slide on rods which are held in place by the structure of the chair. This cover replaces the original back and seat covers on the chair.

Materials you will need
- ☐ Canvas with 10 double threads to the inch
- ☐ Tapestry yarns
- ☐ Dull-finish cotton such as sailcloth for lining back
- ☐ Canvas or burlap (optional) for lining seat

To make the cover

Because the original sections are removed from the chair first, they can be used as a pattern guide. Cut out the pattern and work the embroidery as for the pop-on cover.

Line the back section as for the pop-on cover with sailcloth. The seat of the chair must be reinforced either by backing it with strong canvas or burlap or by using the original seat section.

Once the backing has been stitched to the needlepoint, turn under the ends as on the original sections and sew. Slide into place on the chair frame.

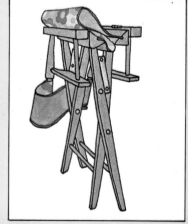

▲ *The director's chair folded*
▼ *The back and seat sections*

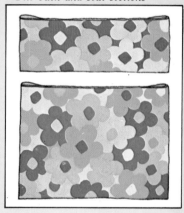

▲ *Slip-on back and seat of chair*
▼ *The director's chair complete*

The working chart for the chair cover

Each square on the chart = 1 stitch

Use one horizontal section of the chart for the chair back and as much as you need of the complete chart for the seat (the chart does not give exactly the same repeats as the photograph).

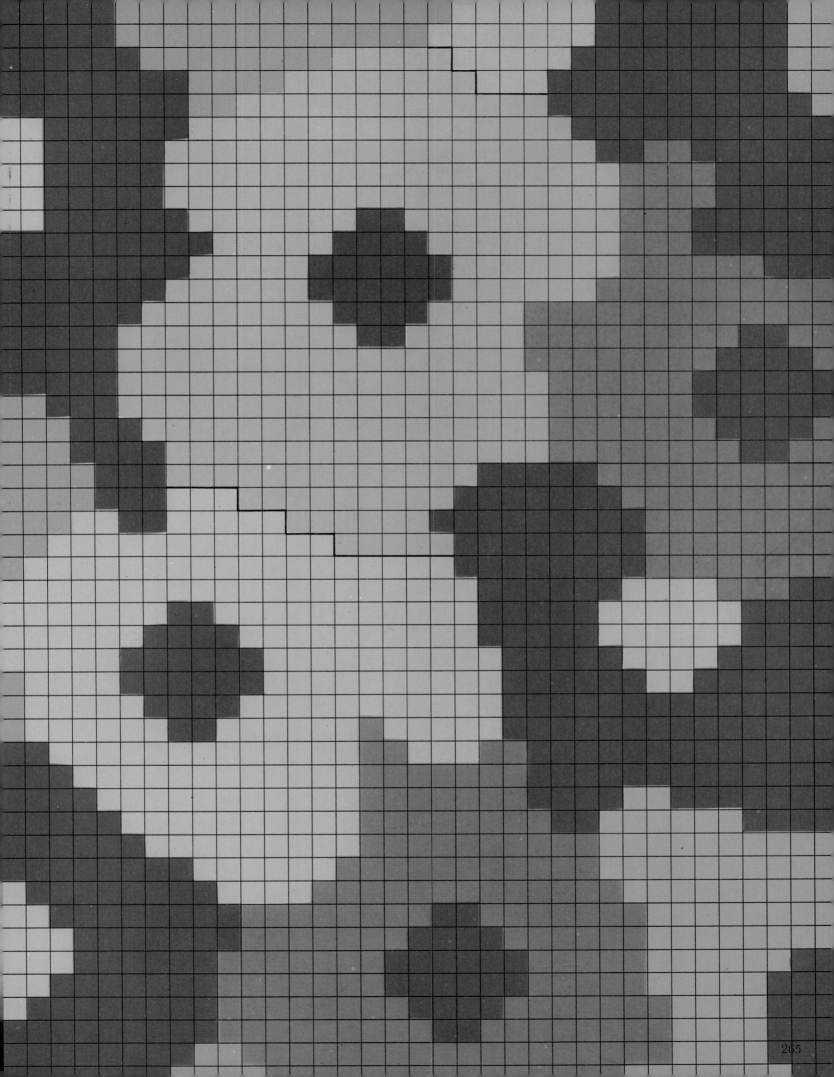

Collector's Piece

The Bradford carpet

This fine carpet, dated late 1600, was formerly the property of the Earl of Bradford at Castle Bromwich in England. The complete carpet measures sixteen feet long by six feet wide, and it was at one time used to adorn a table. It is now displayed under glass in the Victoria and Albert Museum, London, where it covers a complete wall.

The carpet was designed to an exact size so that the lattice work center just covered the table top, with equal edges hanging all around. Because the entire design is worked in fine tent stitch (petit point), the canvas has been distorted from its rectangular shape into a parallelogram. It is therefore 13 inches out of square along a short edge and consequently the figures in the illustration are leaning. Some areas which are left unfinished show the canvas to be linen, with about twenty threads to the inch. The stitching is extremely even and of a refined and delicate coloring. This carpet is a typical example of the Elizabethan tradition, when silk thread was used throughout, giving a soft sheen to the surface.

The design is simple and realistic, as this small section of the border illustrates. The undulating landscape continues entirely around the perimeter of the carpet giving a charming impression of rural life in the 17th century. Against a picturesque background of cottages and flowering trees, the people of the village go busily about their activities. Closer examination of this section reveals a series of scenes portraying hunting, shooting and fishing.

266

A chair cover in tent stitch

Needle-point

Old fashioned flower embroidery designs make a fascinating contrast when they are used with modern furniture. This charming roses pattern, worked in subtle colors from the chart, can be put to a wide variety of uses—chair seats, stool tops, cushions and rugs. The chart shows one complete pattern. Worked on single-mesh canvas with 14 threads to the inch, and working over two threads of canvas each way, one pattern measures approximately 16 inches by 15 inches. The rocking chair illustrated uses two complete patterns.

Yarns and stitches

Crewel wool has been used for the design and the chart is a guide to the colors of yarn used. Work the pattern in tent stitch (see Needlepoint Chapter 68) using four strands of crewel wool.

Yarn quantities

For larger pieces of work, it is possible to work out fairly accurately how much yarn you will need. Cut a skein of crewel wool into 18 inch lengths. Divide these into groups of three or four strands (depending on the stitch you are using). Thread the group of strands into a needle and work the stitch until you reach the end of the length of yarn. Count the number of stitches you have worked and multiply this figure by the number of groups of strands in one skein. This will give you the total number of stitches which can be worked with one skein of yarn. By counting the number of stitches to be worked in that color from the chart you will be able to calculate the amount of yarn required to complete the design.

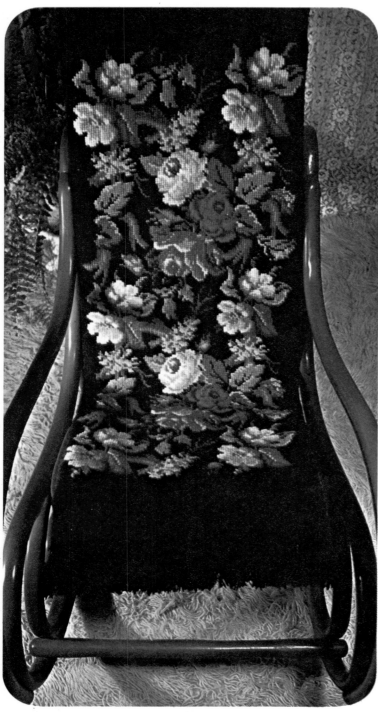

Color and yarn working chart

The colors and quantities in Appletons Crewel Wool given are for working one pattern of the design. The quantities should be doubled for working two patterns and extra background yarn can be calculated according to the instructions given in this chapter. The color key is on the left followed by the Appletons reference range and shade number, and the number of skeins required is indicated in parentheses.

Key	Code and no of skeins
	500/4 (2)
	500/3 (3)
	500/1 (1)
	800/1 (2)
	940/6 (2)
	940/5 (3)
	940/3 (2)
	991 (2)
	550/4 (1)
	550/1 (2)
	310/1 (3)
	340/5 (2)
	340/3 (2)
	430/7 (2)
	430/6 (3)
	430/8 (2)
	240/5 (2)
	900/4 (1)
	994 (2)
	860/4 (2)
	860/6 (2)
	980/5 (2)
	960/1 (2)
	960/7 (1)
	993 4 1oz skeins

Chapter 73

A handbag worked in tent stitch

This chapter gives detailed instructions for making a needlepoint handbag and mounting it onto a metal handbag frame. It also gives some extremely useful hints on the planning of your own designs for handbags.

Designs for needlepoint bags

The traditional floral design worked in tent stitch illustrated in this chapter is always popular, and similar designs can be found either in the form of working charts or painted onto canvas. There are several points to be considered when planning an original design for a bag. The design should fit happily into shape of the bag and should be of neither too large nor too small a scale in relation to the size and shape. For example, one tiny motif in the center of the bag might look insignificant, whereas a very large motif overspilling the size of the bag might look clumsy. Over-all patterns should be designed in a proportionate scale to that of the size of the bag. The placing and planning of a design for the gusset of the bag also requires careful thought. It should neither detract attention away from the main design by being too complex, nor should it appear as a trivial afterthought. If an all-over geometric pattern is used, care must be taken to insure that the lines of the design match accurately on the gusset and the sides of the bag.

To make a needlepoint bag you will need:

☐ Canvas 32 inches by 20 inches
☐ ½yd lining fabric
☐ ½yd burlap
☐ Yarns
☐ Tapestry needle
☐ Crewel needle
☐ Strong sewing thread (for making the bag)
☐ 1½yds piping cord
☐ 1½yds 1 inch wide bias-cut fabric or piece of fine leather for piping
☐ Bag frame measuring 8 inches across top between mounting isles

To cut bag pattern

Draw the pattern for the bag onto 1 inch squared paper. Cut out the pattern and pin it onto the canvas, matching the grain lines of the pattern with the grain of the canvas. Mark the outline of the pattern pieces onto the canvas using a waterproof felt-tipped pen. Leave at least 4 inches between each pattern section to allow for blocking and seam allowances. Mark the center of each side of the bag and the gusset with vertical and horizontal lines of basting stitches. Using the center guide bastings, plan and work the design of your choice on the bag sections.

▼ *The tracing pattern for the bag and gusset*

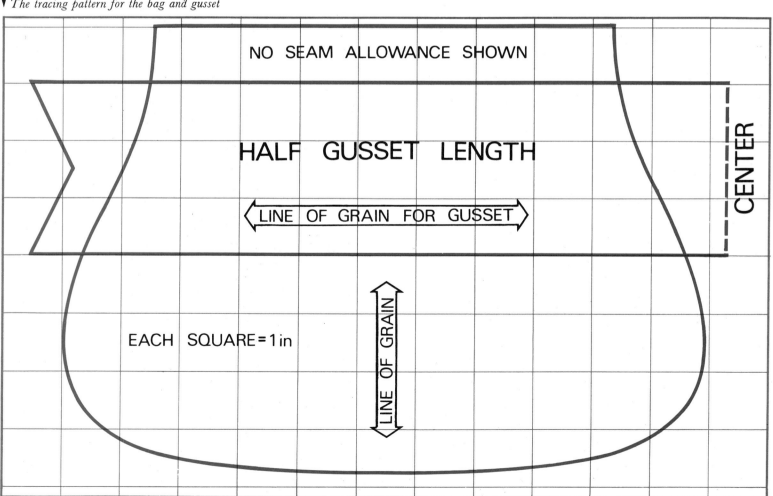

To make the bag

When all stitching has been completed, block the canvas as described in Needlepoint Chapter 74. **Trim the excess** canvas away leaving $\frac{5}{8}$ inch on all edges for seam allowance.

Cut out the burlap interfacing and the lining to match the trimmed bag sections. Pin and baste the burlap sections to each of the needlepoint sections and make up as one.

Make two lengths of piping by covering piping cord with either 1 inch wide bias-cut fabric or strips of leather and pin and baste this around the edge of each side section of the bag.

Match up the center mark on the gusset to one side of the bag, pin and baste the gusset in position, cutting notches on the curves where necessary. Stitch by machine as close to the piping as possible, using the cording foot, or by hand using a strong backstitch starting and finishing at the points of the gusset. Repeat the process for the second side of the bag. Turn and baste the seam allowance around the top of the bag and gusset to the back of the work. Position the bag top on the bag frame, and hold in place with tie tacks through the holes on both sides of the frame at the corners. Stitch firmly in position using sewing silk threaded double in the needle, sliding the needle through the fold along the top of the bag until it is even with a hole in the frame. Bring needle out and make two or three overcasting stitches through the hole and into the wrong side of the canvas.

Sew the lining pieces together and pin into position inside the bag, turning in the edges to fit the inside of the bag frame. Slip stitch firmly into position. If a mirror pocket is desired inside the bag, this should be stitched to the lining before it is sewn together.

▼ *The piping stitched to the bag*

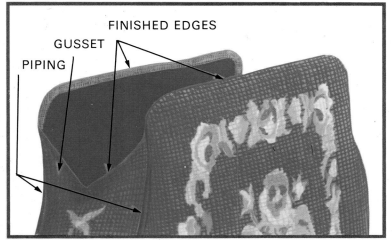

FINISHED EDGES

GUSSET

PIPING

▼ *Stitching the bag to the frame*

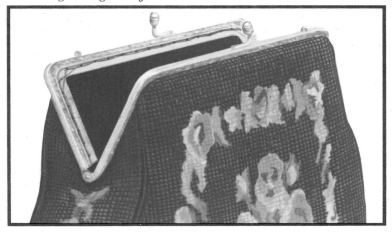

Two views of the completed bag

271

Chapter 74

Needle- point

Stem stitch and mosaic stitch

If you are not yet very experienced at needlepoint, you will find that both a lighter case and glasses case are quick, fun and easy to make. You can try out your favorite stitch to work all-over, rich-textured patterns, or you can use any of the other stitches shown here. Full directions are given for making both items, but you can give each one your own individual look with clever color and pattern combinations.

Stem stitch. Work from the bottom upward over 2 horizontal and 2 vertical threads. The spaces between the rows are filled with backstitches in a yarn of contrasting color.
Mosaic stitch. This is worked in diagonal rows from top left to bottom right of the canvas in groups of 3 stitches; over 1, 2, and 1 threads of canvas.
Mosaic diamond stitch. This is worked in rows from left to right over 1, 3, 5, 3, and 1 threads of canvas.

Instructions for finishing needlepoint

Sometimes needlepoint, which takes quite a time to complete, can be ruined by nonprofessional finishing, so in order not to spoil your careful work follow these instructions.

Blocking or stretching
It is essential to allow for stretching purposes at least two inches of canvas all around the finished size of the work. The excess canvas is trimmed away to the required seam width after blocking. Needlepoint should never be pressed with an iron, as this flattens the textured stitches and ruins the appearance. Most stitches distort the canvas because of their diagonal pull and the best way to restore the canvas to its original shape is as follows:
Dampen the back of the work with cold water. Cover a drawing board, or old work table, with several sheets of white blotting paper. Place the work face down on the board and pin out, using drawing pins at one inch intervals. Pull the work gently into shape, adjusting the drawing pins. Dampen the work again thoroughly and leave for at least 24 hours, away from heat, until it is dry. When the work is completely dry, check for any missed stitches and fill them in.

How to make a seam

There are several seam methods suitable for needlepoint and this one is particularly good for small items which cannot be turned through to the right side after being seamed. The usual seam allowance is ⅝in, but for smaller items, such as a lighter case, ⅜in is sufficient. As canvas frays easily, it is a good idea to overcast the raw edges before finishing. With imaginative use of yarn and stitches, the seams can form a complementary and decorative feature to the piece of work.

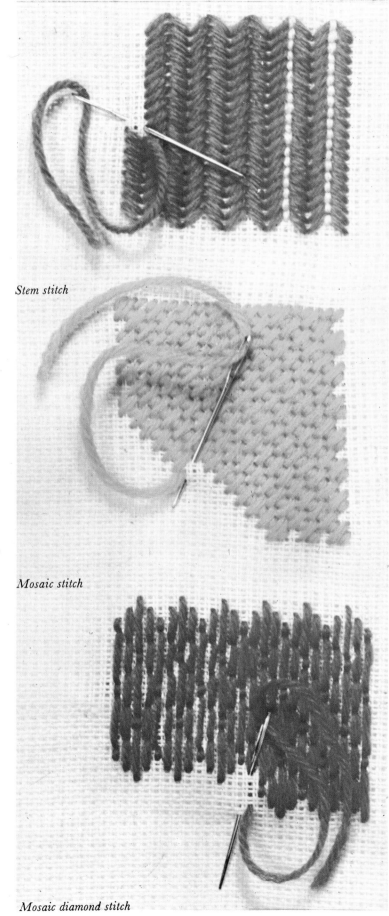

Stem stitch

Mosaic stitch

Mosaic diamond stitch

Method

Trim needlepoint ready to seam and fold all seam allowances to wrong side of the work. Trim and smooth the corners and baste the seam allowance in place. Pin the two seam edges with the wrong sides together, matching up the pattern. Work whip stitch, cross-stitch or oblong cross-stitch along the seam on the right side, picking up opposite threads of the canvas from each side as you work. The seam when completed becomes part of the needlepoint.

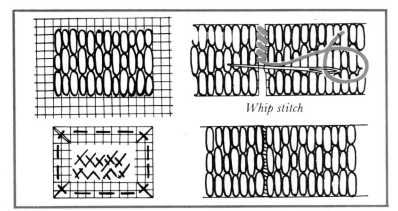

Whip stitch

Linings

The choice of lining is most important since it should not draw attention away from the stitching, either in color or texture. It is best to choose a firm, dull-surface fabric in a plain toning color. Pick the darkest tone used in the design because this will give strength to the design, whereas a light color will draw more attention to the lining than to the needlepoint itself. The lining seams can either be machine stitched or hand sewn with back-stitch.

Glasses case

You will need: ☐ canvas ☐ yarn ☐ 4in length of cord ☐ lining.
Cut the canvas to measure 18½in x 6¾in, and cover an area which measures 14½in x 2¾in with stitches.
Block and trim the canvas, then cut a piece of lining material to the trimmed size.
To prepare the needlepoint for seaming, fold crosswise leaving a 2½in flap, wrong sides facing. Stitch the piece of cord securely to the seam allowance on the right side, one inch down from the opening. Baste edges and seam.
With the right sides of the lining together, turn up 6¾in leaving a 2⅞in flap. Stitch the side seams from the fold to within ⅜in of the opening. Fold the seam allowance around the flap and across the opening to the wrong side of the lining, baste and press. Slip the lining into the case, using a blunt pencil to push it right down into the corners. Pin the lining around the edges of the opening and flap, matching the seams of the lining to the seams of the case, baste them together and slip stitch neatly into place. Remove the basting. Fold over the 2½in flap and tuck it under the cord.

Lighter case

You will need: ☐ canvas ☐ yarn ☐ lining.
For an average size lighter case, cut the canvas to measure 6¾in x 10in and embroider an area measuring 2¾in x 6in. Block the canvas and prepare it for seaming. With the right side of the work facing you, fold it in half and sew the side seams, finishing as described for the glasses case, omitting the flap and cord.

Lighter case

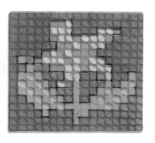

Lighter case

Glasses case

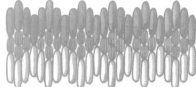

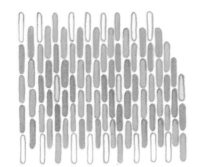

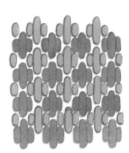

Some ideas for color and stitch combinations

Chapter 75

Stylized panel in a variety of stitches

Once you have built up a repertoire of needlepoint stitches it is fascinating to combine them into a project. This panel incorporates many stitches which are built up into a city-scape of buildings seen by the light of the moon. Norwich stitch is used at the base of the fountain.

Special effects

Each stitch has been chosen for the special effect it creates. Particular examples are the leaf stitch effect on the trees in the square, the paving stones represented in cushion stitch and the blue blocks of satin stitch for a tiled roof (see Needlepoint Chapter 66). Under the arches the areas of shadow are created by using a mixture of pink and gray-pink yarns in the needle.

As well as an imaginative use of stitches, the colors and yarn textures contribute to the atmosphere of the picture. The town hall at the lower right-hand corner and nearly all the houses are in darkness, but a light shines from two windows, one in pink, the other giving a warm red glow. Other windows reflect the moonlight in plastic raffia, and in the square the spray of a fountain sparkles in silver beads. The soft warm tones of the colors are evocative of a hot summer night.

Materials you will need

- 20in by 22in single-weave white canvas with 14 threads to the inch (finished size 11½in by 15¾in)
- Tapestry needle size 18
- Hardboard 11½in by 15¾in
- Fine string
- Embroidery frame
- 5 skeins D.M.C. Matte Embroidery Cotton 2827; 7 skeins 2211
- 1 skein each D.M.C. 6-strand floss 211, 3041, 553
- 1 skein each D.M.C. Tapestry yarn 7987, 7157, 7996, 7259, 7491
- 2 skeins each D.M.C. Tapestry yarn 7318, 6072, 7155, 7292; 3 skeins 7307, 12 skeins 7304
- Small quantities purple wooden beads, small silver beads, dark blue plastic raffia

Working the panel

Work with the canvas in a frame, using the illustration as a chart. Begin by working the left-hand building first, then out and across the other buildings, filling in the background as you progress. If the background areas are left until the buildings are all completed, the worked stitches will have spread the threads of the canvas, thus pulling the remaining canvas threads too close together for easy stitching. Complete the panel by working the outer background on all four edges to the required depth.

Block the work (see Needlepoint Chapter 74) and mount over the piece of hardboard (see Needlepoint Chapter 64). The panel can be hung framed or unframed.

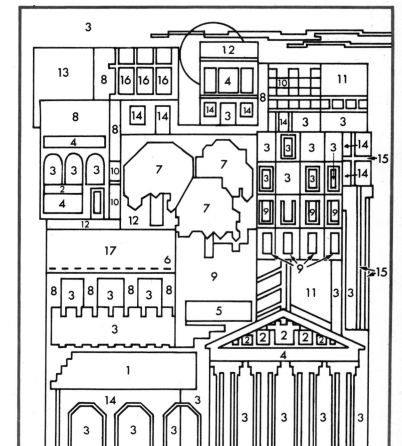

Stitch guide

1. Blocked satin stitch
2. Detached eyelets
3. Tent stitch
4. Rice stitch
5. Norwich stitch
6. French knots
7. Leaf stitch
8. Encroaching Gobelin stitch
9. Cushion stitch
10. Checker stitch
11. Parisian stitch
12. Tile stitch
13. Plaited Algerian stitch
14. Mosaic stitch
15. Satin stitch
16. Double cross-stitch
17. Raised chain band and darning worked on a foundation of encroaching Gobelin stitch

Norwich stitch worked over odd number of threads, in numbered sequence, in directions indicated

Raised chain band edged with darning stitch over a base of encroaching Gobelin stitch

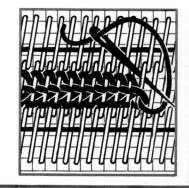

Chapter 76

Introduction to chevron stitches

Here are four more textured stitches for covering large areas of canvas or for working interesting textured backgrounds to designs. Work them in grouped areas of strongly contrasting colors for the brilliant effects shown on the doorstop.

Rep stitch

A stitch worked in vertical rows on double-weave canvas.

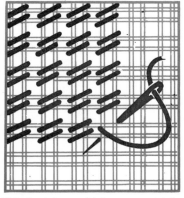

Worked in a thick yarn which completely covers the canvas, the stitch resembles the fabric from which it takes its name.

Basket filling stitch

This is a surface filling stitch usually worked on counted threads, but it makes an ideal

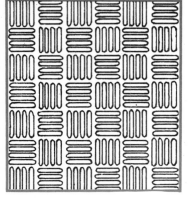

needlepoint stitch, giving a lovely texture for a background. Interesting effects can be achieved by using two tones of one color.

Fishbone stitch

This stitch is worked over three horizontal and three vertical threads of double-thread canvas. Each long stitch is caught down with a short stitch across one double thread of canvas. It is worked in alternate rows from top to bottom and from the bottom upward. The stitch makes a good grounding stitch and can be equally successful when worked on single-weave canvas.

Knitting stitch

This stitch resembles chain stitch but it is worked in a similar way to stem stitch in

vertical rows. It is used only on double-thread canvas. Bring the needle out at the top and insert it two holes down and across to the left. Bring the needle out two holes across and one hole up to the right and continue to the end of the row. The second row is worked in reverse from bottom to top

▲ *Knitting stitch worked on double-thread canvas*

▲ *Fishbone stitch in a single color*

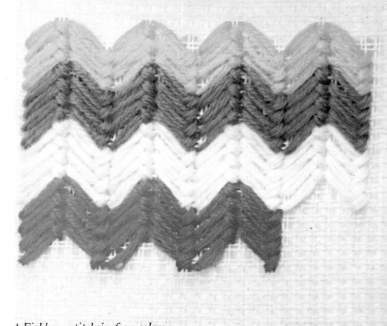

▲ *Fishbone stitch in four colors*

To make a brick doorstop you will need

- ☐ ½yd of double- or single-weave canvas about 24 inches wide
- ☐ A small piece of burlap or felt for backing
- ☐ One brick
- ☐ Yarns
- ☐ Tapestry needle and a crewel needle for sewing up

Making the pattern

Lay the brick on a sheet of paper and draw all around the base. Tip the brick onto a long side, keeping the edge exactly along the longest edge of the line already drawn, and draw around this side. Tip the brick onto a short end and draw again. A pattern will result shaped like the diagram. Cut the shape out. Baste the shape to the canvas, making sure that the edges run exactly in line with the thread of the canvas, and outline it with a felt-tipped pen. Remove the paper pattern and mark the center of the pattern with two lines of basting. Also mark the edges of the top area of the brick so that you can plan the design centrally.

Work the pattern shape with a stitched design. Block and trim away the excess canvas allowing ⅝ inch turnings of raw canvas (see Needlepoint Chapter 74). Slash into the corners to within ¼ inch of the stitching and cut across the outer corners diagonally to within ¼ inch of the point of stitching. Fold all the seam allowances to the back of the work, miter the corners and baste. With the right side of the work facing you, bring A and B together and seam, using the seam method given in Needlepoint Chapter 74. Seam the remaining three corners in the same way. Now cut a piece of burlap or felt for the base of the brick (if using felt, no turnings are required). Fold turnings to the wrong side of fabric, baste and press carefully.

Slip the needlepoint over the brick, pin the piece of burlap or felt to the base and overcast it firmly to the canvas.

Collector's Piece

Florentine from the New World

Popular with embroiderers all over Europe, including England, it was inevitable that the technique of Florentine should have been carried across the Atlantic to the American colonies. The beautiful examples shown here, all from American collections, are dated from before 1800, yet the colors of the yarns are only slightly faded. The group of purses, which are dated between 1750 and 1800, feature the carnation, strawberry and flickering flame patterns. The brilliantly colored purse which is worked with the name of the owner, Hendrick Rutgers, is also worked with the date of its execution— 1761. The Queen Anne type wing chair, dated 1725 and now in the Metropolitan Museum of Art, New York, is a curiosity. The front of the chair, as seen, is worked in Florentine stitch. The back of the chair is rather surprisingly adorned with a magnificent panel, freely worked in crewel wools, showing various aspects of hunting—running deer, pursuing hounds, birds in flight, ducks on a pond, all against an undulating landscape.

Four purses from the Boston Museum of Fine Arts; Hendrick Rutgers purse from the Museum of the City of New York; part of a carnation pole screen from the collection of Ginsberg and Levy; Queen Anne type chair from Metropolitan Museum of Art, New York, a gift from Mrs J. Insley Blair

Chapter 77

Needle-point

Introduction to Florentine

Florentine, also known as Bargello and Hungarian embroidery, is made up of flat stitches worked in a range of different colored threads. Rarely out of fashion, it had a great vogue during the early 18th century when bed hangings, chairs and other household furnishings were worked in Florentine. It was ideal for bed curtains as the wavering designs, creating an illusion of movement, looked handsome whether the curtains were open or closed. Flame stitch, yet another name for this embroidery, aptly describes it.

In its simplest form it is very quick and relaxing work and also adapts to experimentation in both design and color. The samples opposite illustrate this point. Notice the different pattern structures and the way in which the colors alternately blend together and contrast sharply.

Method of working Florentine

The simple, flat stitch is taken over four threads of single-weave canvas and back two (diagrams 1 and 2). The stitches are worked so that only a small amount of thread shows on the back of the canvas (diagram 3). From this beginning lines of zigzag stitching are worked across the canvas and the pattern is repeated above and below the basic line.

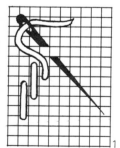 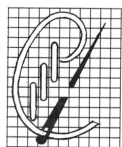 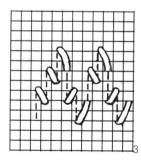

Pattern and color experiments

Try working the samples illustrated opposite by following the design lines from the photographs. Begin with the bright contrast colors and follow the sequence of colors above and below it.

Materials you will need

- [ ] Single-weave canvas 18 threads to 1 inch
- [ ] Tapestry needle size 18
- [ ] D.M.C. Tapestry Yarn in the following colors:
- [ ] Pattern A: 1 skein each in yellow/green range of tones 7445, 7434, 7772, 7364, 7367; 1 skein each in yellow/brown range of tones 7484, 7467, 7468, 7469

- [ ] Pattern B: 1 skein each in red range of tones 7132, 7133, 7151, 7147, 7199; 1 skein pink 7602
- [ ] Pattern C: 1 skein cyclamen 7155; 1 skein each in blue range of tones 7709. 7708, 7243, 7297, 7299
- [ ] Pattern D: 1 skein pink 7602; 1 skein cyclamen 7155; 1 skein each in blue range of tones 7708, 7243, 7299

Suggestions for using these patterns

Any of the samples opposite can be worked on pillows, chair pads, stools or wall hangings. Try combining several for the most decorative effect on a wall hanging or work them on a smaller scale using 6-strand floss on even-weave linen. They could also be used as border patterns on table linen, or decorations on belts.

Florentine pillows

Work Florentine using the samples opposite as a guide. You might experiment using different colors and so vary your design.

Materials you will need

- [ ] 20 inch by 16 inch single-weave canvas with 18 threads to the inch: finished size 16 inches by 12 inches
- [ ] D.M.C. Tapestry Yarn: 3 skeins of each color for patterns B to D and 4 skeins of each for pattern A
- [ ] Lining 18 inches by 14 inches
- [ ] Pillow form
- [ ] 14 inch zipper

Making the pillow

Mark the center of the canvas and the outline of the finished size. Begin at the middle point of the center line from a high point in the pattern and stitch outward. (If you are working pattern A, begin at the center of the green oval.) Continue working on rows across the canvas below this line, until the marked area is filled. When you reach the outline it will be necessary to fill in with half stitches to form a straight line. Stretch the finished work as shown in Needlepoint Chapter 74 and finish pillow as shown in Embroidery Chapter 20.

Two panels in Florentine

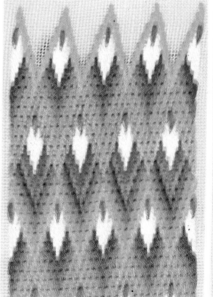 

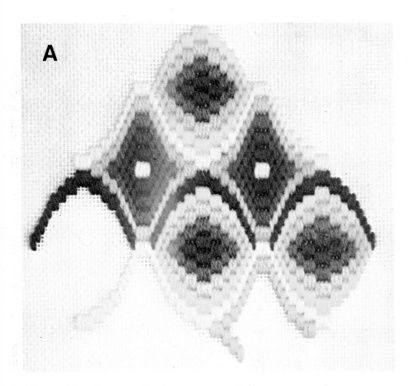

Try working these samples into your own designs

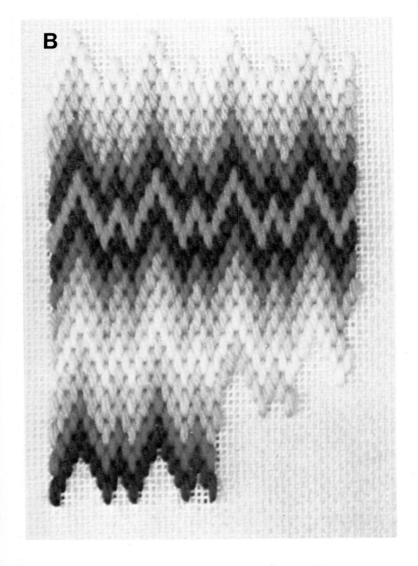

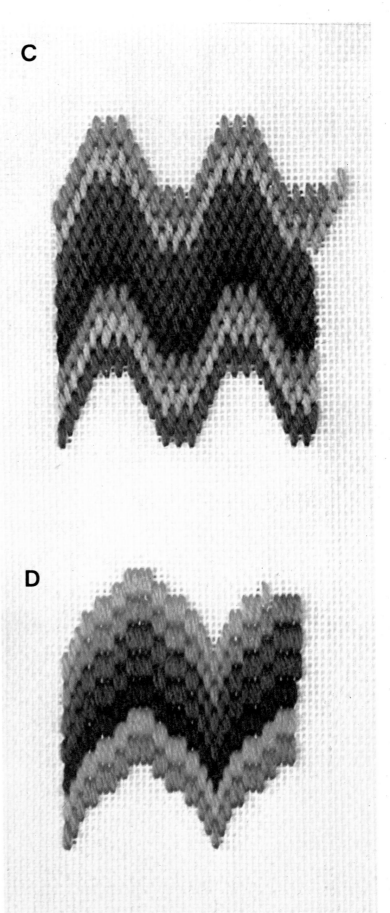

Collector's Piece

Modern Florentine

There has been little change in the basic Florentine designs and techniques since they first became popular several centuries ago. The demands of fashion have influenced the coloring and the threads, while the canvas has a more open mesh. In the 17th century the fabric was a plain-weave linen.

The Florentine couch and cushions shown on the right were designed by Martyn Thomas. They are all worked in zigzag designs, the lines rising and falling into different colors and patterns.

The illustration below demonstrates how effective just one Florentine cushion can look in a modern setting.

Collector's Piece

Cats in needlepoint

Louis J. Gartner, who designed and executed these realistic looking pieces of needlepoint, puts together his designs for needlepoint by "borrowing" the elements, sometimes from magazine and book illustrations.

The leopard cub was taken from a magazine illustration and enlarged to lifesize to fit into a circle fourteen inches in diameter. The original picture was full of small detail which made the designer decide to work the animal itself in petit point against a gros point background. To reproduce the plump roundness of a live animal and the subtlety of the baby fur, he used twelve different "fur" colored yarns plus black and white. The shaded background to the animal was achieved by working colors in slanting stripes so that the tones blended imperceptibly, giving an effect of space behind the cub. The tiger's head was "borrowed", just as it is, from a record album design. The designer began this piece by working the eyes and mouth first, feeling that if he got the expression right from the beginning, the animal would have an identity for the rest of the design. The interesting grass effect in the background was inspired by a piece of *strié* velvet; the velvet was subsequently used for the back of the cushion.

The reclining tiger, originally enlarged from a small magazine illustration, has been simplified into stylized lines with little detail or shading. The design has been worked in petit point using silk thread and the finished piece made into a pincushion, eight inches wide.

Louis J. Gartner is the author of *Needlepoint Design* published by William Morrow & Co. Inc.

INDEX